MORE PRAISE FOR

All Souls

"A guileless and powerful memoir of precarious life and early death in Boston's Irish ghetto ... MacDonald gives new life to this old American story of poor-white pride and prejudice. He also has a knack for quickly grabbing and holding a reader's attention."
—R. Z. SHEPPARD, *Time*

"Harrowing."
—SUSAN ORLEAN, *The New Yorker*

"Peppered with hard-won humor ... the story of a man who understands poverty because he has known it and is blessed with an ability to bear witness in plainspoken prose."
—BRIAN BRAIKER, *Newsweek*

"An incendiary, moving book that startles on every page ... remarkable."
—*KIRKUS REVIEWS*, starred review

"*All Souls* is a memoir filled with desperation and despair, but there is also hope in it ... MacDonald's discovery of his vocation in neighborhood activism is a refreshing change from most memoirs, which so often ... are largely concerned with describing an ascent to celebrityhood."
—JULIAN MOYNAHAN, *The New York Review of Books*

"Michael Patrick MacDonald takes us on a heartbreaking tour of his South Boston family."
—FRANK McCOURT, author of
Angela's Ashes, in *Irish America Magazine*

"*All Souls* hits with the power of a driven fist that crashes through the cynic's intellectual defenses and leaves one speechless."
—*SUNDAY BUSINESS POST* (U.K. and Ireland)

"A brilliantly original memoir of white-working-class life... MacDonald spins stories with a wondrous mix of wild humor and brooding darkness. Though his prose is luminous, he has a purposefulness that goes well beyond that of a raconteur."
—DAVID L. KIRP, *The American Prospect*

"A tough book about a tough place."
—JEFF BAKER, *The Oregonian*

"After reading this harrowing memoir of a Catholic boyhood in a South Boston housing project, 'poverty' will never be a mere category to you again. It will wear the face of a family that loses children to drugs and crime, and that face will be white. Michael Patrick MacDonald has a gift for narrative, an eye for social detail, and a voice of earned authenticity."
—JACK BEATTY, author of *The Rascal King*

"A genuinely good read, a book that defines a multigenerational struggle out of an urban abyss."
—MICHAEL SAUNDERS, *Boston Globe*

"*All Souls* is a rowdy, sometimes raucous venture into the MacDonald family's inner vault. It will leave you weeping and laughing uproariously at the weave of tragic and comic events in this unconventional family. A must-read for the uplift of spirit, and for the courage shared by this grand writer."
—MALACHY MCCOURT, author of *A Monk Swimming*

"[MacDonald] has spent his adult life on a personal crusade to break through [the Southie code of silence], to reach families in pain and, through them, to tell the truth."
—DELIA O'HARA, *Chicago Sun-Times*

"A must read . . . *All Souls* is poised to become one of the most significant Irish American books of the era."
—IRISH EDITION

"The gritty saga of the South Boston MacDonalds should be read by anybody looking for a gripping and full account of poverty in urban America."
—SETH GITELL, *Weekly Standard*

"Michael Patrick MacDonald rips the cover off the myth that poverty and violence happens predominantly in the Black community. His story of growing up poor and white in South Boston reminds me of my own, growing up poor and black in the South Bronx. This is an honest, piercing tale—once you read it, you will never look at our country the same way."
—GEOFFREY CANADA, author of *Fist Stick Knife Gun*

ALL SOULS

All Souls

A FAMILY STORY FROM SOUTHIE

Michael Patrick MacDonald

BEACON PRESS

Boston

Beacon Press
25 Beacon Street
Boston, Massachusetts 02108-2892
www.beacon.org

Beacon Press books are published under the auspices of
the Unitarian Universalist Association of Congregations.

11 10 09 08 07   8 7 6 5 4 3 2 1

Some names have been changed to disguise or protect some identities.

Text design by Charles Nix
Composition by Wilsted & Taylor Publishing Services

Library of Congress Cataloging-in-Publication Data

MacDonald, Michael Patrick.
All souls : a family story from Southie / Michael Patrick MacDonald.
p.   cm.
ISBN 978-0-8070-7213-4 (pbk.)
1. MacDonald, Michael Patrick—Childhood and youth.
2. Irish Americans—Massachusetts—Boston Biography.
3. MacDonald family.   4. Irish American families—Massachusetts—
Boston Biography.   5. South Boston (Boston, Mass.) Biography.
6. Boston (Mass.) Biography.   7. South Boston (Boston, Mass.)—Social life
and customs.   8. South Boston (Boston, Mass.)—Social conditions.
I. Title.
F73.68.S7M33   1999
974.4'6104'092—dc21
[B]   99-30692

FOR THE KIDS, AND MA

Facing page (clockwise from top left): Ma with Davey *(standing)*, Mary,
Joe *(on lap)*, and Johnnie; "Frank the Tank"; Michael on Davey's shoulders,
Joe, Kevin, Johnnie, Kathy, Frankie, and Mary; Kevin; Joe *(left)* and
Davey; Kevin and Sarge

CONTENTS

ALL SOULS'
NIGHT

I WAS BACK IN SOUTHIE, "THE BEST PLACE IN THE
world," as Ma used to say before the kids died. That's what we
call them now, "the kids." Even when we want to say their names,
we sometimes get confused about who's dead and who's alive in my
family. After so many deaths, Ma just started to call my four brothers "the kids" when we talked about going to see them at the cemetery. But I don't go anymore. They're not at the cemetery; I never
could find them there. When I accepted the fact that I couldn't feel
them at the graves, I figured it must be because they were in heaven,
or the spirit world, or whatever you want to call it. The only things
I kept from the funerals were the mass cards that said, "Do not stand
at my grave and weep, I am not there, I do not sleep. I am the stars
that shine through the night," and so on. I figured that was the best
way to look at it. There are seven of us kids still alive, and sometimes
I'm not even sure if that's true.

I came back to Southie in the summer of 1994, after everyone in
my family had either died or moved to the mountains of Colorado.
I'd moved to downtown Boston after Ma left in 1990, and was pulled
one night to wander through Southie. I walked from Columbia

Point Project, where I was born, to the Old Colony Project where I grew up, in the "Lower End," as we called it. On that August night, after four years of staying away, I walked the streets of my old neighborhood, and finally found the kids. In my memory of that night I can see them clear as day. *They're right here,* I thought, and it was an ecstatic feeling. I cried, and felt alive again myself. I passed by the outskirts of Old Colony, and it all came back to me—the kids were joined in my mind by so many others I'd last seen in caskets at Jackie O'Brien's Funeral Parlor. They were all here now, all of my neighbors and friends who had died young from violence, drugs, and from the other deadly things we'd been taught didn't happen in Southie.

We thought we were in the best place in the world in this neighborhood, in the all-Irish housing projects where everyone claimed to be Irish even if his name was Spinnoli. We were proud to be from here, as proud as we were to be Irish. We didn't want to own the problems that took the lives of my brothers and of so many others like them: poverty, crime, drugs—those were black things that happened in the ghettos of Roxbury. Southie was Boston's proud Irish neighborhood.

On this night in Southie, the kids were all here once again—I could feel them. The only problem was no one else in the neighborhood could. My old neighbors were going on with their nightly business—wheeling and dealing on the corners, drinking on the stoops, yelling up to windows, looking for a way to get by, or something to fight for. Just like the old days in this small world within a world. It was like a family reunion to me. That's what we considered each other in Southie—family. There was always this feeling that we were protected, as if the whole neighborhood was watching our backs for threats, watching for all the enemies we could never really define. No "outsiders" could mess with us. So we had no reason to leave, and nothing ever to leave for. It was a good feeling to be back in Southie that night, surrounded by my family and neighbors; and

I remember hating having to cross over the Broadway Bridge again, having to leave the peninsula neighborhood and go back to my apartment in downtown Boston.

Not long after, I got a call at Citizens for Safety, where I'd been working on antiviolence efforts across Boston since 1990. It was a reporter from *U.S. News & World Report* who was working on an article about what they were calling "the white underclass." The reporter had found through demographic studies that Southie showed three census tracts with the highest concentration of poor whites in America. The part of Southie he was referring to was the Lower End, my own neighborhood at the bottom of the steep hills of City Point, which was the more middle-class section with nicer views of the harbor. The magazine's findings were based on rates of joblessness and single-parent female-headed households. Nearly three-fourths of the families in the Lower End had no fathers. Eighty-five percent of Old Colony collected welfare. The reporter wasn't telling me anything new—I was just stunned that someone was taking notice. No one had ever seemed to believe me or to care when I told them about the amount of poverty and social problems where I grew up. Liberals were usually the ones working on social problems, and they never seemed to be able to fit urban poor whites into their world view, which tended to see blacks as the persistent dependent and their own white selves as provider. Whatever race guilt they were holding onto, Southie's poor couldn't do a thing for their consciences. After our violent response to court-ordered busing in the 1970s, Southie was labeled as the white racist oppressor. I saw how that label worked to take the blame away from those able to leave the city and drive back to all-white suburban towns at the end of the day.

Outsiders were also used to the image, put out by our own politicians, that we were a working-class and middle-class community with the lowest rates of social problems anywhere, and that we wanted to keep it that way by not letting blacks in with all their problems. Growing up, I felt alone in thinking this attitude was an injustice to all the Southie people I knew who'd been murdered. Then there were all the suicides that no one wanted to talk about. And all the bank robberies and truck hijackings, and the number of addicts walking down Broadway, and the people limping around or in wheelchairs, victims of violence.

The reporter asked me if I knew anyone in Southie he could talk to. He wanted to see if the socioeconomic conditions in the neighborhood had some of the same results evident in the highly concentrated black ghettos of America. I called some people, but most of them didn't want to talk. We were all used to the media writing about us only when something racial happened, ever since the neighborhood had erupted in antibusing riots during the seventies. Senator Billy Bulger, president of the Massachusetts Senate, had always reminded us of how unfair the media was with its attacks on South Boston. He told us never to trust them again. No news was good news. And his brother, neighborhood drug lord James "Whitey" Bulger, had liked it better that way. Whitey probably figured that all the shootings in the nearby black neighborhood of Roxbury, and all the activists willing to talk over there, would keep the media busy. They wouldn't meddle in Southie as long as we weren't as stupid and disorganized as Roxbury's drug dealers. And by the late eighties, murders in Southie had started to be less visible even to us in the community. Word around town was that Whitey didn't allow bodies to be left on the streets anymore; instead, people went missing, and sometimes were found hog-tied out in the suburbs, or washed up on the shores of Dorchester Bay. The ability of our clean-cut gangsters to keep up appearances complemented our own need to deny the truth. Bad guy stuff seemed to happen less often within the protected turf of South Boston. Maybe a few suicides here and there, or maybe an addict "scumbag," but that was the victim's own problem. Must have come from a bad family— nothing to do with "Our Beautiful World," as the *South Boston Tri-*

bune was used to calling it, above pictures of church bazaars, bake sales, christenings, and weddings.

I agreed to take the reporter on a tour through Southie. We stayed in the car, because I was too nervous to walk around with an "outsider" in a suit. It was bad enough that I was driving his rented sports car. People in Southie usually drove big Chevys, or when they were in with "the boys," as we called our revered gangsters, they'd upgrade to an even bigger Caddy or Lincoln Continental. I wore sunglasses and a scally cap, the traditional local cap once favored by hard-working Irish immigrants and longshoremen, and more recently made popular by tough guys and wannabes. I disguised myself so I wouldn't be identified collaborating with an outsider. Everyone knew I was an activist working to reduce violence and crime. But when they saw me on the news, I was usually organizing things over in Roxbury or Dorchester, the black places that my neighbors thanked God they didn't live in. "That stuff would never happen in Southie," a mother in Old Colony once told me. Her own son had been run over by gangsters for selling cocaine on their turf without paying up.

When I rode around the Lower End with the reporter, I pointed to the landmarks of my childhood: St. Augustine's grammar school, where Ma struggled to keep up with tuition payments so we wouldn't be bused to black neighborhoods; the Boys and Girls Club, where I was on the swim team with my brother Kevin; Darius Court, where I played and watched the busing riots; the liquor store with a giant green shamrock painted on it, where Whitey Bulger ran the Southie drug trade; the sidewalk where my sister had crashed from a project rooftop after a fight over drugs; and St. Augustine's Church, down whose front steps I'd helped carry my brothers' heavy caskets. "I miss this place," I said to him. He looked horrified but kept scribbling notes as I went on about this being the best place in the world. "I always had a sense of security here, a sense of belonging that I've never felt anywhere else," I explained. "There was always a feeling that someone would watch your back. Sure, bad things happened to my family, and to so many of my neighbors and friends, but there was never a sense that we were victims. This place was ours, it was all we ever knew, and it was all ours."

Talking to this stranger, driving through the streets of Southie, and saying these things confused me. I thought about how much I'd hated this place when I'd learned that everything I'd just heard myself say about Southie loyalty and pride was a big myth, one that fit well into the schemes of career politicians and their gangster relatives. I thought about how I'd felt betrayed when my brothers ended up among all the other ghosts in our town who were looked up to when they were alive, and shrugged off when they were dead, as punks only asking for trouble.

I didn't know now if I loved or hated this place. All those beautiful dreams and nightmares of my life were competing in the narrow littered streets of Old Colony Project. Over there, on my old front stoop at 8 Patterson Way, were the eccentric mothers, throwing their arms around and telling wild stories. Standing on the corners were the natural-born comedians making everyone laugh. Then there were the teenagers wearing their flashy clothes, "pimp" gear, as we called it. And little kids running in packs, having the time of their lives in a world that was all theirs. But I also saw the junkies, the depressed and lonely mothers of people who'd died, the wounded, the drug dealers, and a known murderer accepted by everyone as warmly as they accepted anything else in the familiar landscape. "I'm thinking of moving back," I told the reporter.

I moved back to Southie after four years of working with activists and victims of violence, mostly in Roxbury, Dorchester, and Mattapan, Boston's largely black and Latino neighborhoods. In those neighborhoods I made some of the closest friends of my life, among people who too often knew the pain of losing their loved ones to the injustices of the streets. Families that had experienced the same things as many of my Southie neighbors. The only difference was that in the black and Latino neighborhoods, people were saying the words: *poverty, drugs, guns, crime, race, class, corruption.*

Two weeks after I moved back home, every newsstand in town had copies of *U.S. News & World Report* with a picture of me, poster boy for the white underclass, leading the article, and demographic evidence telling just a few of Southie's dirty little secrets. South Boston's Lower End was called the white underclass capital of America, with a report showing all the obvious social problems that usually attend concentrated poverty in urban areas. The two daily papers in Boston wrote stories about the article's findings, with their own interviews of housing project residents, politicians, and a local priest, mostly refuting the findings. A group of women sitting on a stoop in the housing development laughed at the article. "We're not poor," one said. "We shop at Filene's and Jordan Marsh." I remembered how I spent my teenage years, on welfare, making sure that I too had the best clothes from those department stores, whether stolen or bought with an entire check from the summer jobs program. I thought I looked rich, until I saw that all the rich kids in the suburbs were wearing tattered rags.

A local politician said that the article in *U.S. News* was a lie, that it was all about the liberal media attacking South Boston's tight-knit traditional community. A local right-wing community activist called the magazine a "liberal rag." And a *Boston Herald* columnist who'd grown up in one of the census tracts wrote that he was better off not knowing he was poor. But he grew up long before the gangsters started opening up shop in liquor stores on the edge of the housing projects, marketing a lucrative cocaine trade to the children of single women with few extended family support structures or men around.

Our local priest said that it was terrible to stigmatize Southie children with such findings, labeling them "underclass." I didn't like the term either, but I thought at least now some of the liberal foundations might begin to offer real support for social service agencies struggling to keep up with the needs of Southie families in crisis. People from Southie nonprofits had told me that they were constantly denied funding because their population was not diverse, and probably also because the name "Southie" automatically brings "racists" to mind—the same kind of generalizing that makes all black children "gang bangers" in the minds of bigots. One thing growing up in Southie taught me is that the right wing has no monopoly on bigotry. Eventually, I saw, the priest and other local social service agencies started to refer to the article when they looked for funding or other support.

When I first moved back to Southie, I was always looking over my shoulder. I wasn't sure if anyone minded all the stuff I'd been saying to the press. Instead, people I didn't even know started coming up to me, telling me their own stories. It was as if they felt it was safe to come out, and they wanted to take the tape off their mouths. Before this, I would walk through the main streets of Southie and see so many people who had experienced drug- and crime-related catastrophes, but who didn't connect with others who'd suffered in similar ways, the way I'd been doing with people in Roxbury. It seemed that people wanted to talk after years of silence.

I knew we could do it in Southie once I'd seen how a group of families from Charlestown had banded together when their children were murdered, to break that neighborhood's own infamous code of silence. When I was organizing a citywide gun buyback, getting people in Boston to turn in their working firearms to be destroyed, I met Sandy King and Pam Enos. They had founded the Charlestown After Murder Program. Sandy's son Chris had been murdered in 1986 in front of a hundred people who remained silent. Then in 1991, her son Jay was murdered. Pam's son Adam was murdered in 1992 by the same person who'd murdered Jay. The women organized other mothers of the tight-knit one-square-mile Irish American neighborhood, which had experienced up to six public executions a year, to speak out against the gangsters who controlled the town. They assisted in their neighborhood's gun buyback, which brought in the most guns citywide in 1994 and 1995, and they built close bonds with mothers of murdered children in neighborhoods of color. They pressured law enforcement to pay attention to murder in Charlestown, put a media spotlight on "the town," exposed corruption, and organized an annual vigil to bring neighbors out of isolation and fear. When I went to Charlestown's vigil, I saw mothers' faces that looked so much like Southie faces, pictures of murdered children who looked so much like Southie kids, and I looked around at the symbols of a community so much like our own: shamrocks and claddaghs, symbolizing "friendship, loyalty, and love." Their vigil took place at St. Catherine's Church, just outside Charlestown's mostly Irish housing projects. By the time I moved back to Southie, I knew what we could do with all the people who at last seemed ready to tell their painful stories.

"My son P. J. was only fifteen years, four months, and twenty-nine days of age." P. J.'s father stood six-foot-two on the altar, wearing his scally cap and leather jacket. A big guy you could never imagine being beaten down. But he was buckling at the knees now, and trying to read through tears. He was begging for Southie to wake up. For the past ten years, P. J.'s father had been in recovery from heroin addiction. He'd been feeling pretty good, working all hours of the night at a chemical mixing plant to try to get his family out of Old Colony Project. He'd never imagined that the drugs would take his only son before they made it out.

He held himself up, gripping the pulpit at the Gate of Heaven Church. From where I stood on the altar I could see the three hundred or so Southie people who'd come to the vigil to remember their dead kids. They were wide-eyed; they looked as if they didn't know if P. J.'s father would make it through his reading, or if they would. A few in the crowd let out weeping sounds, and I could tell they weren't used to letting go like that. First I'd hear cries and moans that sounded as if they would build into liberated wailings; then I'd hear a gasp, and the sounds of grief were halted, just like that. Some of the mothers who'd buried their own children looked around at anything but P. J.'s father: the crucified Christ, the martyred Saints, their own hands and feet. It was hard to watch a fortress like P. J.'s father cracking.

"On January 19, 1996, our son Paul P. J. Rakauskas, Jr., went into a coma due to a combination of drugs and alcohol. After three days of pain and torture for his loved ones, P. J. died." P. J.'s friends sat in the back pews of the church, away from the adults in the crowd. The teenage boys looked down. I don't know if they cried; their Fightin' Irish baseball caps were pulled low to cast dark shadows on their eyes. There was a time when people would've told the kids to take off their baseball caps in church, but it was too late to teach the symbolic importance of that rule to these kids tonight. Their friends, brothers and sisters, and some parents were dead. And this was not really a mass anyway, it was more like a takeover. It was bringing the streets into the house of God, and finally giving the building some relevance to our lives in Southie. P. J.'s father was on the altar now, not the priest:

> As much as we would like to say drugs and alcohol were the only reasons for his death, we cannot. P. J. was murdered by ambivalence, tolerance, and a general "it doesn't happen here" attitude in Southie.
>
> Ambivalence being the cavalier attitude with which not just a few of us view the use of drugs and alcohol in our neighborhood. Tolerance being the ability to close our eyes to the drug dealers, either because we don't want to get involved, or because "it's so-and-so's son or daughter dealing," and we don't want to be the snitch. Then some of us figure, "They're only selling to each other, so who cares?" And finally, many of us give up. "What can one person do?" we ask.

Some of the young girls were crying. I was glad to see that, because most of us weren't used to crying over our loved ones, no matter how young and tragic their deaths. Growing up in Southie we were supposed to suck it up and get on with our lives. Besides, the deaths were usually the result of things that brought shame: overdose, murder, suicide. "What do you expect from that family?" was what we heard when some kid died, so we just kept our mouths shut. And Whitey Bulger liked it better that way. Our own shame worked to his advantage.

We had come up with a list of "lives lost too soon," and I had spent the night before this trying to fit so many names onto just one page for the service. And we were all asking the same question at tonight's vigil. *How could we have lost more than two hundred young people to violence and drugs over the past decade?* P. J.'s father gave some of the answers in words that cracked through his tears but were clear to all of us, because any one of us could have filled in the blanks.

"We knew our son was wild," he read on. "But we thought it was just youthful abandon, invincibility, and style. We figured he would grow out of it, and indeed he started to. P. J. was in search of a job, was coming home on time, had started to change his attitude, and was becoming a different person. (The fact that he was in love may have had something to do with it.)"

P. J.'s father cracked a smile, and we all relaxed a little bit. The kids in the back pews all looked at P. J.'s girlfriend to see her reaction. She looked frozen.

From what we can gather from the street talk, P. J. was just doing what is considered a "normal teenage thing." Many others with him that night ingested the same pills and alcohol. They survived and our son did not. To the parents of those kids we say hug, kiss, and tell your kids you love them, for they are miracles we sorely wish we had.

Our son was buried on January 26, 1996. With him goes all of our hopes, plans, and dreams of watching our son become a successful man in the world. With him goes the broken hearts of his mother, four sisters, two nieces, two nephews, grandmother, great-grandmother, aunts, uncles, great-aunts, great-uncles, many cousins—and an extremely brokenhearted father.

I stood close behind P. J's father on the altar, and didn't know if I should try to help hold him up. He looked as if he might fall to his knees. I didn't know if I could keep him standing anyway—he was pretty heavy and I wasn't feeling so strong at the moment either. I was thinking about my own brothers. I let him know I was there by moving close to him as he read. Soon more people came to stand next to us: Judy Hartnett, whose daughter had been stabbed seventy-five times and covered in gasoline and set on fire by her own baby's father a few years ago; Cathy Havlin, whose twenty-two-year-old son had been killed a year ago, shot nine times while walking home into the housing project after a scuffle at Aces High tavern; Linda Reid, who just a few months ago had found her seventeen-year-old boy hanging from his belt after complaining that he was fed up with harassment from a local cop. Even though I wasn't sure who would be doing the collapsing and who would be doing the catching, I felt better. Trying to help the others, we had no choice but to be strong and not to focus on our own pain, thank God.

P. J.'s father looked up from the sheet of paper he was reading, stood up straight, cleared his throat, and spoke directly to his neighbors:

When you put your lights out after making sure your children are home, be grateful; when you watch them go out the door for school, be grateful; when you hear the roar of the two-legged bellies—teenagers—plundering your 'fridge at night, be grateful; the next time you argue with your child, be grateful; the list goes on, so please just be grateful.

As far as taking care of our son, all we can do now is watch the grass grow around his headstone, then try to trim it; keep him in our hearts always; and, lastly, all we can do is imagine that we are seeing that wry smile and feeling his tough but gentle touch as we hold his mementos.

My son P. J. was only fifteen years, four months, and twenty-nine days of age.

* * *

They stood in a single file that reached from the altar to the street outside, waiting to say the names of their children who'd died in South Boston. It was All Souls' Night and Gate of Heaven Church was packed with all my old neighbors, mostly from the Lower End even though the church was in City Point. I knew that the 250 names on the list I'd put together were just the ones whose families could get up the strength to deal with it. I knew of many others who'd been murdered or had overdosed or killed themselves, but their families hadn't called me to put their kids' names on the list. Still, I couldn't believe how packed the church was on such a cold and wet night in November.

Ave Maria was sung from the altar, and some of the mothers in the long line wept as they inched closer to the microphone. I knew that for some, this was the first time they were dealing with their loss. I hardly recognized Theresa Dooley when she stepped up to the mike. Her long white hair was simply pulled back into a bun, and her high cheekbones and beautiful blue eyes stood out in her sad face. She couldn't have been more than sixty, but she might have seen centuries. Her eyes stared out at something other than what was in front of her.

"Tommy Dooley and Jonathan Anthony Dooley," she pronounced into the mike.

Tommy Dooley was nineteen when he was beaten to death at Kelly's Cork and Bull. Everyone said the Stokes family did it. They ganged up on him and beat and kicked him over a fight he'd had with his girlfriend, Tisha Stokes. Everyone said his head almost came off him. But no one at the crowded bar saw a thing. No snitches in Southie. A couple years later, Mrs. Dooley's fifteen-year-old son Anthony—"Tone, my baby," she calls him—hung himself. We all knew how much he'd missed his big brother. Mrs. Dooley found him hanging, cut her baby down, and let out screams that many people in Old Harbor Project say they will never forget.

Most people just shake their head and say "poor thing" or something like that when they see Mrs. Dooley walking through the town her kids had once loved, staring at something that's not there. For a few years she wanted justice; she pursued homicide detectives to investigate, but the same people who say "poor thing" wouldn't tell what they knew, what we all knew to be the truth. Plus one of the Stokes brothers had an uncle by marriage who was a Boston homicide detective. She gave up on the courts when homicide detectives told her, "You ain't gonna get anyone to come forward in Southie."

Mrs. Dooley walked off the stage now, her two candles lit. It was someone else's turn to name their dead.

"Help me, you've got to help me!" screamed Marie the gypsy. "My heart is very bad! I'm gonna die! Help me! My son, they killed him! The police won't give me any answers." Marie Pozniac was Ma's friend. She worked at Jolly Donuts and used to give us free donuts, and steal from the register. We all thought she was crazy, long before her son died. Ma said she was a real gypsy, and she looked like one with her kerchiefs and gold earrings. I asked her once about her accent, and she screamed at me that she was "an American, a full-blooded American!" She was known for setting houses on fire to collect insurance, a firebug Ma called her. Ma got a kick out of her, though, with all her gypsy scams.

"My sons, Joseph and Dennis O'Reilly," Nora spoke with a shaky voice. She's the one who told us about the empty apartment before we moved into Old Colony, right across the street from her. Dennis died of AIDS, and Joey was ambushed, shot multiple times in his car.

"My brothers, Timmy and Johnnie Baldwin." Timmy was shot twice in the head, and Johnnie died with three other friends in a drinking and driving accident. They were both close friends of my brothers. Their sister Chucka lit her two candles.

"My stepbrother, Johnnie Grant." They say Johnnie Grant got a "hot shot." That's what they call it when someone intentionally gives you a lethal injection of heroin or coke, or both.

Many walked away from the altar with lit candles and a look of strength and even of pride, feelings they'd lost when their loved one was murdered, or killed himself, or overdosed, or was taken away by whatever unspeakable cause. Some of us brothers and sisters of the dead had a hard time getting into that line with our unlit candles. We understood better than we let on about the brothers and sisters of the dead, the ones who only pretended to be tough until it was time for them to take their own lives, through drink, drugs, crime, or a rope, the ones who crossed over and became the dead themselves, leaving more pain in their wake.

It was my turn now to go up and remember my brothers. I was last in line because I was watching everything, making sure the vigil was going well. I let Dizzo cut in front of me. "Who the fuck was that lady?" he asked, nodding toward Marie. Dizzo thought he knew everyone in Southie—after all, he was ice cream man. I guess Ma had one up on him; leave it to Ma to become friends with the one real gypsy in town. "Hey, how is Ma?" Dizzo asked. I told him how she loved Colorado, but I didn't tell him she'd said she'd never come back to this hellhole of a fucking neighborhood ever again.

Dizzo said his names: "James Dizoglio, John Dizoglio, Stephen Dizoglio, Michael Dizoglio."

It was my turn. I stepped up to the microphone with my four candles, one for each of my dead brothers. I took a deep breath and looked at each candle as if they had the names written on them. I didn't know right then who was alive and who was dead in my family, and the candles didn't give me any clues. I looked up at all the faces of my friends and neighbors who had broken their silence, in a way, by getting up there and saying their loved ones' names through a loudspeaker—in Southie, of all places, the best place in the world. *The kids*, I thought, trying to remember their names. I knew they were right there in the church, but I still couldn't remember who they were. I looked for them, scanning the entire crowd. But there were so many faces. The crowd stared back at me, and for a long time I looked for my family, among the faces of the living and of the dead.

FREEDOMS

M Y OLDEST MEMORIES ARE OF MY MOTHER CRYING.
I don't know how old I was, but I remember looking up from
the floor and seeing her sitting on the old trunk that her father had
carried from Ireland when he was eighteen in search of some good
luck in America. She was only crying a little, and tried to hide it
from me when she saw that I'd noticed. I climbed onto her lap and
asked her why she was sad. She told me then about her baby who'd
died and gone to heaven. She said his name was Patrick Michael, but
that it was all going to be okay now because we had someone watching over us, praying for us every day. She told me that I'd taken
Patrick Michael's place, and that she'd switched the name around,
calling me Michael Patrick, because the Irish always said it was bad
luck to name a child after another who had died.

She showed me the light green knit hat that someone had given
Patrick—she couldn't remember who. He wore that hat home from
the hospital when he was born, and he was baptized in it. It still
smelled like a baby and had yellowing food stains on it. It was all
we had of Patrick. There was no picture ever taken of the three-
week-old baby. Throughout my whole life, whenever I saw her put-

ting out very different emotions for the people around her, I have thought of my mother crying that time when she thought no one would see. And I could never really get mad at her the way most kids did at their parents. I could never judge her or blame her for anything in our lives. After I saw her cry for Patrick Michael, I only wanted to protect her.

I was born in Columbia Point Housing Project, at 104 Monticello Ave., on the South Boston/Dorchester waterfront. Actually, I was born in a hospital across the city. But most children in Columbia Point who were born around the same time I was were delivered in their project apartments, since back in the sixties ambulances wouldn't enter the development without a police escort. Many of these children were born before the ambulance arrived, long after it was called. And many of this generation had birth defects. I was lucky. I was two weeks late, and my mother had planned ahead and arranged through Catholic Charities for the other kids to be placed in foster homes during her stay in the hospital. As soon as they were placed, she called the police to pick her up. She was told she'd have to meet them a mile down the road, outside of Columbia Point. She didn't mind, so off she went. And it's a good thing she had the extra time to make arrangements, because when I was born I was almost thirteen pounds, and had given my mother twenty hours of labor.

I held the record for birth weights in Boston, and Ma always told everyone how the doctors and patients came from all parts of Beth Israel Hospital to see me in the nursery. She said I was twice the size of the other infants, and while they all cried, kicking their legs with eyes sealed closed, I was quiet with two big spooky eyes staring around the room and observing all who had come to observe me from behind the glass window.

I was my mother's ninth child, with two sisters and six brothers before me, including Patrick. And we always did include Patrick in the count. The family had settled into Columbia Point three years before I was born. My mother was still married to Dave MacDonald, but he was nowhere to be seen. According to Grandpa, Ma's father, the marriage of his oldest daughter had fulfilled everything he'd expected of it. On the day of her wedding, Grandpa woke Ma up, and told her to "get up for the market." Soon into the marriage Dave MacDonald beat my mother, fractured her skull on two occasions, and broke her ribs on another. To this day, though, Ma will remind you of that one time she knocked out his teeth with one good kick.

Dave MacDonald was an entertainer like Ma. He played country-western music on the guitar in barrooms throughout Boston. They'd met each other in a Valentine's Day minstrel show at the parish hall. Ma had entered the show and played her Irish accordion while her four younger sisters step danced. Ma always told us that when she first laid eyes on Dave MacDonald, playing Davy Crockett, she immediately remembered that she'd had a terrible dream about him, a nightmare about a bad marriage. Nonetheless, Ma married him at the age of nineteen, and before long they became a musical duo. But the good times were few. He was an alcoholic, and further along in their marriage he would disappear on his wife and kids. A "womanizer," Ma called him. My older brothers and sisters don't remember seeing him around much. Occasionally they'd hear him back in the house, and learned to expect the yelling and things breaking. Ma always said there was "no such thing" as divorcing your husband back then. You lived with whatever you had married, even if it was all turning to hell. When she went to Father Murphy about the cheating and abuse, he told her, "You're a Catholic, make the best of it."

For her, drinking too much was one thing, disappearing and going out with other women was another, and the beatings were bad. But not showing up for your own baby son's funeral? When Ma confronted Dave MacDonald about being down at the local bar while his son's tiny casket was carried through St. Thomas's Church, he said that he'd seen too many buddies go down in Korea to give a shit about one baby dying. That was the official end of the marriage.

Ma had already started to take care of the kids on her own, with financial help from welfare. Ma says that at the time the welfare policy actually encouraged you not to have a man, as you could receive a stipend only if there was no man around. So even when Dave MacDonald had been at home sometimes, Ma started to tell welfare that he wasn't there with them anymore. It was the truth really— he wasn't "there" for his kids like a real father. The family was living with cheap rent in the project—sixty-five dollars a month. The project wasn't a safe place, but it was all we could afford with the sixty-five dollars we got from welfare every two weeks. And with the boxes of surplus cheese, butter, and powdered milk Ma dragged home from the maintenance office, we could survive there.

It was while living in Columbia Point that Ma realized she and her kids were surviving without any help from her husband anyway, money or anything else. She was alone when she had to shove three of her kids into a bush to hide from a shoot-out between two speeding cars. She was alone when she had to confront a drunk mother about her teenage son trying to strangle my sister Mary to death when she was five. She was alone when her kids came home with stories of being chased down and beaten for being white in a mostly black neighborhood. And she was alone when she ran through the project banging on neighbors' doors, frantically trying to breathe life back into the mouth of her baby, already dead in her arms.

Grandpa was the one Ma turned to when she did need a man, and she'd have to be desperate for help because the two of them didn't get along. Grandpa always said, "Didn't I tell you?" or else, "You made your bed, now lie in it." Ma and Grandpa had brought Patrick to the emergency room of Children's Hospital the night before his death. Patrick was having trouble breathing and Ma thought he had a croup. Ma had no health insurance, and Medicaid was a year away. The hospital turned the baby away. Ma says that the hospital had filled its quota of what were called "charity cases," and didn't need to take any more that night. They said it wasn't an emergency case.

The next day Davey, the oldest in the family, found Patrick not moving in the crib, lying still and blue. The coroner said he'd died of pneumonia and should have been in a hospital. Ma later asked a lawyer about suing the hospital for neglect, but the lawyer said there was no case—the hospitals weren't required to admit welfare babies with no insurance.

Ma says that when you lose a baby, it's the worst feeling in the world because a baby depends on its mother for everything, and so ultimately it's always the mother's fault. I suppose that's why she ran around with a dead baby in her arms—a baby that hadn't been allowed into the hospital, in a housing project that ambulances wouldn't come to. It was her baby, her fault, and she was going to do whatever she could do as a mother, which at that point wasn't much.

My family hated Columbia Point Project, and hated living in our apartment even worse after Patrick's death. In the mid-1960s it was one of the higher crime areas in the city, a neighborhood of tall yellow brick buildings with elevators that often didn't work. Even when they were working, Ma says you'd take the stairs up seven flights to avoid being beaten and robbed on the elevator. And rats infested the hallways.

Davey always told me how he used his lunch box as a weapon to and from school, ready to smash anyone in the head who'd attack him or his younger brothers and sisters. Johnnie, the second oldest, tells me he'd be sent down to the Beehive corner store for milk and bread, only to be robbed repeatedly of the money Ma had given him for groceries. When Frankie was five, a gang of teenagers circled him and turned him upside down to shake all the coins bulging from his pockets for penny candy. Mary and Joe, the twins, used to pass one teenage girl in the courtyard who made them pull down their pants in order to get by. Drug dealings and shootings were becoming more common on hot summer evenings, so Ma started to call the kids into the house early in the afternoon.

Besides the usual fights and bullying in the project, the whole family remembers the tension of being part of a white minority in a mostly black development. Ma was always being called "that crazy white bitch" after going after some of the black mothers who'd watched their teenagers chase down and beat my brothers. While most of the project was made up of black families, Monticello Ave. was still about half white. The white teenagers organized gangs to protect their turf from the black gangs, and were admired by the white adults for their ability to "stand their ground," as my mother said. Like us, most of those white teens eventually moved to the all-white housing projects of South Boston. Many are now the parents of today's teens "standing their ground" in the Southie projects, now undergoing integration through what locals are calling "forced housing," after "forced busing."

My older brothers and sisters looked forward to the weekends, when there were free buses out of Columbia Point, to Broadway, the main shopping street in white South Boston. The white families of Columbia Point would all go on excursions to the toy stores and supermarkets there. Many recall seeing my mother getting on the bus, with her long, red country-western hair, leopard coat, fishnet stockings, and eight kids wrapped around her. Everyone talked about her ability to look so good after having all those kids, and even though she had to be both mother and father. Ma wouldn't be seen in public except in spike heels. To keep her figure, she went jogging around Columbus Park, down the road in Southie. She'd walk over to the park in her jeans and spike heels, carrying flat sneakers in a brown paper bag. It was only when she got to the park, where no one could see her, that she changed into the sneakers, putting the spike heels into a bag and throwing them behind some bushes. She might have had to be the man of the house but, as she always said, she wasn't about to start looking like one. Ma liked the praise she got for her looks, and she would remind people, "Imagine, after having nine kids!"

After a day of shopping on Broadway, Ma would sit for a cup of coffee at the Donut Chef and talk to everyone in the room. She was a great talker, and whether you were on a stool right next to her or on the far end of the room, you were part of her audience. While Ma did her storytelling, the kids stood lined up against the wall in descending order, each one hugging a bundle of groceries, watching for the free bus to take them back to Columbia Point. On one snowy day, as my brothers and sisters waited and watched for the free bus, the jukebox began to play the country-western hit that Dave Mac-Donald had written, sung by Doug LaVelle. Ma jumped up and told everyone in the Donut Chef that that very song playing had been written by the kids' father, a no-good bastard if there ever was one. The song was titled "Two Years for Non-Support."

Ma loved the chorus because she could knock twice on the coffee counter, like a judge banging her gavel. "And I gotta go-oh-oh / Because I owe. / Order in the court (*knock knock*) / Two years for non-support." She told everyone in the shop how the song was about her getting her husband locked up. That years ago the kids' father had been sentenced to two years for nonsupport after being brought to court by her, pregnant with their fifth child. She pointed to Frankie in the lineup. He was four now, and was watching Kathy and Kevin, the three-year-old and two-year-old, to keep them in the line. Ma told how Dave MacDonald ended up getting out after two months, broke down the door at Monticello Ave., and tried to strangle her. That's when she kicked him in the mouth and knocked out a couple of his teeth. The next day she had him right back before the judge. Ma says he looked worse from the fight than she did. And when he was allowed to speak before the court he said, "Your honor, she may be a little woman, but she's as strong as any man."

My mother cherished those words and got everyone at the Donut Chef laughing while she made a few of them feel her biceps and showed her leg muscles. My brothers and sisters laughed too. We were on Ma's side when it came to stories about the no-good bastard. We always felt a rush of pride with Ma's favorite line, "I was always a fighter." Grandpa had told her that when she was born she'd had to be brought into the world with forceps, and out she came with two black eyes, clenching the two fists in front of her. She bragged that her life was a battle from the start, and she was proud to show that she could take anything. "Feel that muscle," she'd tell the guys at the Donut Chef.

The free bus came to take them all back to Columbia Point before dark, when it was dangerous to walk even a few blocks. All the other white families from Columbia Point were glad to see Ma and the kids climb onto the bus. They knew she'd be telling stories from one end of the bus to the other, keeping everyone laughing. As the bus approached Columbia Point though, things turned somber, and Ma says that's when the white families would start telling their stories of being attacked and of being scared to be in a black project. If only we could get into Old Colony Project in Southie, they'd say. Many were counting their days on the waiting lists for the white projects. Ma says that a few on the bus would call the blacks that word that we were never allowed to say in our home. Others on the free bus just said they would feel more comfortable around their own, where the kids wouldn't be threatened and attacked for being different.

Before long, we were one of the last white families holding out in Columbia Point. The white neighbors on the free bus were getting few. Many of them had fled to the Southie projects. And my family was beginning to stick out like a sore thumb on those scary walks back to our apartment at nightfall.

At the time, waterfront areas in Boston were still reserved for the ghettos because of the pollution and rodents. But Monticello Ave. is gone now. The streets have been changed around. Today, waterfront properties are some of the most sought-after areas in Boston, and are being developed for people with money. What was once Columbia Point is now a development primarily made up of white urban professionals. The buildings have been renovated, the rats are gone, and the stigma of the past has been erased with a new name—Harbor Point. But one-third of the neighborhood is still occupied by poor black families paying rent according to their income. And a few of the poorer black families say they're feeling they might eventually be squeezed out by the single white tenants who live such separate lives and don't want to pay high rents to live near poor people with kids and the problems that come with all that.

I don't actually remember anything about our days in Columbia Point; I was only a baby when we finally fled. But those stories from my family, repeated like legend, have always been with me. Ma liked to say there was "no time for feeling sorry for yourself," but I knew the blows she received must have hurt. Her fractured skull and broken ribs and the everyday threats made her want more for us than to be living in an unsafe project. I knew that even if he was in heaven praying for us, Ma would have given anything to have Patrick back with us. And I knew she never wanted her kids to be called "charity cases" again.

Ma had only one way out of Columbia Point—to take her parents' offer and move us into their triple-decker in Jamaica Plain, which she did in 1967, less than a year after I was born. The apartment was on a tree-lined street in a neighborhood of working-class Irish families. We'd now have a yard for the first time, much more room, and freedom in more ways than one. My brothers and sisters could go outside whenever they wanted without getting jumped. Plus, it was just us and Ma now. Dave MacDonald was gone from our lives, and this was the greatest freedom of all.

There were only two bedrooms. The six boys slept in one, the two girls in the other, and Ma slept on the couch. We plopped our mattresses onto the hardwood floors and made ourselves at home. The floor of the boys' room was mostly covered by mattresses. The remaining space was reserved for piles of clothes, clean but never folded. We slept side by side, with some lying across the bottoms of the mattresses; usually Kevin preferred this spot. He could fit there best, being the skinny runt we all called him. I always thought it strange at friends' houses to see a high bed, perfectly made, with layers of sheets and blankets for different purposes: one sheet to hug the mattress, another to put over you, a light blanket coming out over the top of a matching quilt. It all seemed like such a big deal to make out of sleeping. I decided my mattress on the floor, covered with a tangled pile of blankets, was better than all that fuss. I felt bad for my mother, though, who had to sleep on the couch and was lucky if she got a blanket at all. Usually she'd cover herself in our winter coats. She said she liked them better than blankets. Even after some religious people came around with loads of army blankets for us, she'd still call out from her bed, asking me to get her a couple of coats to put over her. "Those blankets are scratchy old things I wouldn't give to a dog," she'd complain. The couches Ma slept on were also close to the floor, with their legs ripped off the bottoms. Once one leg broke, the rest of them had to go. In later years, we started to take the legs off our couches immediately after buying them from the Salvation Army. Why wait for the day when one of the wooden legs would crack and throw the couch lopsided while everyone was squeezed together watching Saturday morning cartoons or "Soul Train"?

Neighborhood kids were thrilled at the amount of freedom in our home. Most of them had couches covered in plastic, and had to eat at the dinner table and answer their parents' questions about school and play. We could walk on top of mattresses and couches with our shoes on. Even jump up and down on them, and have pillow fights. We could take curtain rods down from the windows and have sword fights and scream "on guard." We could eat food whenever we wanted and wherever we wanted. We never once sat down at a fixed time at the dinner table. There was no dinner table. Besides, there were just too many of us. Ma would make a big pot of something—usually an invention, mixing the last three days of leftovers into one big mush—and you'd slop some in a bowl, and find a corner of the house where no one would bother you.

Most of the families on Jamaica Street were Irish American, and some parents were actually from Ireland. My mother and her sisters spent a good part of their childhood years on this street, so we were familiar with many families who had been there for a couple of generations. The Sullivans and the Walshes lived across the street, the Rowans next door, Dick and Bridy Burns down the road, and Mrs. Carrol to the left of us. They were all part of a tight-knit Irish community that spanned Boston. The Irish in Boston all feared each other's gossip, and Ma always said that certain news of her would be "all over Ireland." As a kid I imagined that she meant this literally, and couldn't believe that a whole country would care about things like the length of Ma's miniskirts, which seemed to be a preoccupation of my grandparents and the other God-fearing Irish parents in the neighborhood.

My mother continued to play the Irish accordion for money at the local barrooms. The welfare office of course didn't know this, and if they ever found out we'd be in worse shape than we'd ever been in before. We'd be out on the streets. But the welfare check certainly couldn't support all of us, and so Ma made some money for the kids doing what she loved to do: entertaining people. She'd get about thirty dollars for groceries at the end of a night. We'd go to McBride's down past the projects at the bottom of our hill, or else to the Galway House on Centre Street. Kevin would show he wasn't such a runt by carrying her antique accordion, which she'd played since she was sixteen, and which was now held together with glue and electrical tape. It never lost its tuning or its booming volume, though, and she preferred it to any newer accordion. Then she started bringing her guitar to do country-western songs, songs like "Your Cheating Heart" by Hank Williams and "My D-I-V-O-R-C-E" by Tammy Wynette. These songs were often dedicated with a cackle of laughter to her "ex-husband, Dave MacDonald," or "Mac," as we'd all started to call him now that he was a thing of the past.

I'd listen to my mother from a barstool, along with all the old drinkers who were slouched over mouthing the lyrics between long cigarette drags. I'd wait until one of them would notice me and offer to buy me some chips or a pickled egg from the big jar I was staring at. Meanwhile, Kevin would be off scheming about how to get in on a little of the drinking money placed carefully under the noses of all these drunk people. Sometimes he'd put on a sad pauper's face and pass a hat for our mother, as if she weren't already getting paid by the bar. Kevin often got sympathy, being as bony as he was. The drinkers said he looked half starved and would give him a dollar sometimes. But Kevin wasn't collecting for my mother at all. By the age of seven, he was already finding ways to "get over." And since he always shared his spoils with me, I kept my mouth shut. A few times Ma found out and made him hand over the money to her. She was thrilled to get more than the thirty bucks the bar paid. In the end, Kevin didn't mind because it would all be spent to stock our refrigerator anyway, and he was proud to show off that he was "a born provider." Keeping the money from my mother was really just a game to see if he could play the player. Ma always told him that he should've lived during the Depression, that he would've been able to support a whole family back then.

Like my mother, Kevin was outgoing and would use his way with people to make more money. He played the spoons by taping two kitchen spoons together and banging them up and down his legs, arms, and back. He had great rhythm and could keep double-time. He was acrobatic, and could walk on his two hands, his skinny body straight upside-down. The teachers had called Kevin hyperactive, and he bragged about that to friends and strangers alike, as if he'd been given a title of importance. When he wasn't entertaining for money, he was out shining shoes at the bars. He saved up for a shoe-shining box and took special care of it, hiding it in a safe spot every night before he went to bed. He had a sweet look about his face, and people were drawn to him. I spent a lot of time tagging along on Kevin's exploits up and down Centre Street, the main drag in Jamaica Plain. As long as I could keep up with his speedy pace through the store aisles, I'd make out pretty well, getting my fill of candy or toys from Woolworth's. Kevin was generous. Whenever I'd hear the expression "He'd give you the shirt off his back," I'd picture Kevin. I always thought that the expression was made for him alone. He'd literally give you the shirt off his back, and had done so more than once. It might be a shirt swiped from the back of a truck, but that was beside the point.

Every spring we looked forward to the Irish Field Day, way out in the country, in Dedham. It was a day of Irish entertainment, games, rides, and food to raise money for the African Missions, which worked for some starving children far away in Africa—those children we always heard about when we weren't hearing about the poor hungry children of Ireland who would walk miles to school with no shoes at all on their callused feet. It's because of those kids so far away that we were never allowed to complain about our lot, and would get down on our knees to thank Christ for America and those orange blocks of government cheese from the welfare office. The Irish community came from all over Boston to support the African Missions. All our relatives would be there: my aunts, cousins, Nana and Grandpa. Our family usually piled into one of the souped-up cars my brother Joe was working on, with doors, hoods, and a roof that were all different colors. Joe was always fixing up big old cars that he could drive around while proudly smoking a cigar and checking out girls. Joe said he looked like a pimp, but my brother Davey called him Jethro and said that we looked more like the Beverly Hillbillies.

One year we barely made it, breaking down on the dirt roads twice. The backfiring and clouds of exhaust let everyone know that we'd arrived. And we made a scene climbing out of the car windows too, since as usual Joe's doors didn't open. Ma hurried through the crowds to the side of the stage, and hollered up to the emcee, pointing to the accordion over her shoulder to let him know she'd be next to entertain. My grandparents had to run and hide for the shame, but the crowds loved Ma. She made everyone feel they were at a real party back home. Some even dropped their American middle-class airs, to toss each other around, doing set dances on the dirt in front of the stage.

In the meantime, Kevin scouted out the scene for ways to leave with more than he'd come with, and I followed looking for my share. He played a game of darts with his only quarter, and in no time he'd won all kinds of stuffed animals. There was a dart table where you had to aim for the stars scattered across the backboard. What they didn't realize was that Kevin had gone to Woolworth's early that morning to snatch a whole box of those same stars to put on the ends of his darts.

Before long Kevin ended up getting a job at one of the game stands. They were probably sick of him winning and figured it would be cheaper to pay him a day's wages. He ran the games with energy and wit that drew customers from all corners of the field, all the while pocketing quarters when no one was looking. The more customers he drew, the better he made out, and the less likely that anyone would notice a shortage of profits. I watched my brother wheel and deal as I heard my mother's voice from across the field belting out "The Wild Colonial Boy."

"Look, that's Ma!" Kevin was proud of Ma and bragged to everyone around us that our mother was on stage. I was a little worried about it, though. I thought all the Irish would talk badly about Ma, as my grandparents said she was a shame to us all with her accordion, and her long hair and short skirts. "And that was how they captured him, the wild colonial boy." Ma proudly stomped her foot through the last line of the song, and finished like she always did, with a loud "wo-ho!" Then Ma took another musician's guitar away from him and finished up with her all-time favorite by Janis Joplin, putting on her country accent and really belting out "Freedom's just another word for nothing left to lose, and nothin' ain't nothin' honey if it ain't free."

Soon enough Kevin's pockets were full and so were mine. We had plenty of quarters to play more games, as well as prizes and Irish flags to wave all the way home out the windows of Joe's shitbox. Before leaving Kevin led Kathy and Frankie into the woods where he'd hid his spoils and gave them their equal share. When we came back into the field, Kevin saw that there was one table he hadn't gotten to yet: the one that sold raffle tickets for the gallons of booze hidden underneath, behind a tablecloth. He had gifts for everyone and didn't want to forget Ma's cousin Nellie. Nellie had come from Ireland when she was sixteen to live with Nana and Grandpa. All our relatives thought she was too wild, but Ma considered her a sister. We called her our aunt. Kevin knew she loved the drink and that she had no money, raising five kids on her own with no father. Besides, she'd be sure to keep us all laughing on the way home with a few drinks in her. Kevin made us watch the rest of the goods while he slipped under the table when no one was looking. He waited for a signal from Frankie and slipped back out again with a whole case of Irish whiskey. And didn't Nellie go home legless that day from the drink, doing her wild imitations of our relatives and keeping us all in stitches the whole ride home! Kevin once again had provided for everyone, an eight-year-old genius of scams.

Jamaica Street was my only experience living with families who had a father going off to work every day. We were probably the only family on welfare. Looking back I realize our Irish neighbors had some American middle-class pretensions that were at odds with the ways of my mother and us kids. And if we ever did anything considered lower class—like go to the corner store barefoot—in front of someone from Ireland, they might call us "fookin' tinkers." This was the worst you could be, according to Irish immigrants, especially once you'd already made it to the Promised Land.

While we were happy not to be living in the project for once, my family still spent a lot of time visiting the one nearby and hanging out with the other families on welfare. It was a pretty equally mixed project racially, and as a result the tensions weren't as bad as in Columbia Point. This all changed when the Jamaica Plain development shifted toward a black majority and poor whites started to flee. That's when the fights broke out. That's when the chanting started:

Beep beep beep beep,
Walkin' down the street,
Ten times a week.
Ungawa ungawa,
This is black power,
White boy destroyed.
I said it, I meant it,
I really represent it.
Takes a cool cool whitey from a cool cool town,
It takes a cool cool whitey to knock me down.
Don't shake my apples, don't shake my tree,
I'm a J.P. nigga, don't mess with me.

The white kids started to say the same chant, switching "whitey" and "nigga." But for a while, my older brothers and sisters hung out with mixed groups. Especially Mary, who by the mid-seventies had adopted a style that my grandfather criticized in a thick Irish brogue as an "African hairdo." She was dressing too in platform shoes and doing the dances that only the black girls knew. She could do "the robot" like the dancers on "Soul Train." Later, when Mary had two children "out of wedlock" in her late teens before finally marrying the father, my grandfather traced her alleged downfall back to the African hairdo.

There was never much traffic, so we were able to take over Jamaica Street with games of tag, dodgeball, and red rover. All the kids from the other Irish families would join in. Then they'd disappear, called in to dinner. But we stayed outside because we could eat whenever we wanted to. They'd come out again after dinner, but a couple of hours later we were again on our own, as all the other kids on the street had strict curfews, usually before dark.

The kids from the projects could stay out late too, so it was better to hang out with them. Sometimes we'd stay out really late telling ghost stories on the porch. Stories like the one about the hatchet lady, who carried a shopping bag full of little boys' heads. As her bag was very heavy and she was very old, a polite youngster would offer to carry it for her. Before he got to her door with the heavy bag, he'd get curious and ask what was in it. The hatchet lady would let him look into the bag, and while he was bent over, she'd cut his head off with a hatchet, adding another head to her collection. I believed every word of these stories and was horrified when I saw Frankie or Kevin helping an older woman with groceries to her door. But they always got a quarter for their courtesy and still had their heads.

Kids from all over Jamaica Plain started to hang out with us, because they liked our house and could do what they wanted there. My older brothers and sisters set up a clubhouse in the basement, inviting friends over to smoke cigarettes and play spin the bottle. Friends would stay overnight in the cellar, especially when they weren't getting along with their parents, or were running away from home. Most of them started calling my mother "Ma."

On hot summer nights, we'd all sleep on mattresses on the front porch. The house was stifling and we didn't have the air conditioners that others on the street had. Most families in the neighborhood seemed perplexed by our ways. Mrs. Schultz, an older woman from Germany who lived upstairs from us, used to wake us all up to send us inside the house. She was bothered by the idea of having to climb over loads of kids in their underwear, all wrapped in sheets like mummies. She seemed mean, speaking in German and shooing us into the house before we'd had a good night's sleep. Our makeshift way of living seemed normal to us, but it opened us to harsh judgment, like gypsies.

Any time any programs about gypsies were on, Ma would call us all to the TV to watch. She had a great fascination with gypsies, and especially with the tinkers in Ireland. When she'd traveled to Ireland as a teenager, she'd run away from her relatives and hung out with caravans of tinkers, playing the accordion for them. Her aunts wrote back to my grandparents telling them that she was shaming them all over Ireland by joining up with "the tribes." I grew up with a romantic picture of the tinkers from my mother's stories, and always wondered if we had tinker blood in us, blood that my grandparents would never mention.

Looking back, it seems that early on I took over the job of trying to keep things looking whatever way they were supposed to look. I worried both about keeping up with the other families and their ways and about making sure that we looked poor enough for surprise visits by the social workers from welfare.

Ma would get an unexpected call early in the morning saying that the social worker was on her way. She'd wake us all up in a panic about the state of the house. The problem wasn't that the house was a mess, but rather that it looked like we owned too many modern conveniences for our own good. Poor people weren't supposed to have a color TV. We'd all have to get up right away on those days to pull a fast one. I actually loved devising strategies for outwitting the inspectors. In no time flat, we'd be running in all directions, getting rid of anything of any value. Out went the toaster. It didn't work without using a steak knife to pull the bread out, at the risk of electrocution. But a toaster might mean that there's a man living in the house, giving gifts or money to my mother. Welfare wouldn't allow for that; God knows a woman with eight kids shouldn't have a man living in the house! But who needs a man in the home, I always thought, when you have the welfare office? A man would only be abusive, tear at Ma's self worth, and limit her mobility in life. Welfare could do all that *and* pay for the groceries. No man ever did that in our home. But our interrogators seemed to be obsessed with the notion of some phantom man sneaking in during the night and buying us appliances. So out went the blender too. Really poor people have no time for exotic milkshakes. We thought it would be enough to put things in the cabinets under the sink, but the social workers got keen to that hiding place. They were shameless about going through cabinets and drawers. We had to resort to the crawl space under the front porch.

But the new color TV was too big to hide. It was one of those huge wooden-cased televisions with fancy-looking cabinets on either side. So we pulled down a heavy green velvet drape from one of the windows and threw it over the television, turning it into a lovely table to serve the social worker a cup of tea on. We had to look as if we had *some* television-watching in a house with so many kids, so we pulled out the contraption we'd been using before we finally entered the modern age of Technicolor. It was two sets actually, one sitting on top of the other. One had only sound, and the other had a black-and-white picture that would get scrambled from time to time. You'd have to get someone to hold a butter knife to the place where the antenna used to be, in order to keep the picture straight. Usually that someone was me; everyone raved that I had some kind of magic power to set that TV straight. Ma said that I was the seventh son, and therefore had special powers that the others didn't have. I was so proud of myself that I would sit for hours holding the butter knife to the back of the TV, forming a human antenna while my family watched its shows: cartoons, "Soul Train," or stories about gypsies and gangsters. For a while this was all we had, and I often felt helpless when "The Brady Bunch" would proudly advertise "in color" at the beginning of the show, knowing there was no way that that butter knife would help on that score.

By the time the social worker arrived, everyone would've left for school except me, as I wasn't yet school age. I got to walk through the house with her and my mother, proud that we looked like we owned nothing at all. Just a few mattresses and an awkward-looking table with an ugly green velvet tablecloth that reached well beyond the floor. And of course while the social worker had her tea on top of our well-draped color television, I sat holding the butter knife to the back of the other TV contraption, reaching my head around to the front to watch morning cartoons. I used to guess at what colors the characters on the set would be if I were watching the TV that the social worker was sitting at. And I couldn't wait for her to leave so I could find out if I was right.

The interrogation lasted about an hour, and it usually focused on men. The social worker would take time out to ask if we had heard from "the father." Ma always said she had no idea where he was. Of course she knew exactly where Mac lived, but didn't want to let on, reminded as she was of the days of abuse with no groceries at all.

There had been times when "the father" had tried to come back. I'd always heard the story of the time he came over drunk, smashed the front door window, and started beating on my mother once he got inside. I was less than two years old, standing in a crib. Ma had stored her accordion on a shelf near the crib, and she always loved telling me how I picked it up and smashed it over Mac's head. She said he was knocked for a loop, and quieted down after that. Of course I don't remember any of it, but I was proud of the way Ma told the story of me putting up a fight.

But Ma didn't tell the social worker any of that. There were a few things Ma didn't mention. She never told the social worker that there were men living in our house from time to time. She never had a problem meeting men as she was very beautiful and played it up with her long red hair, spike heels, fishnet stockings, and penciled-on beauty mark on her right cheekbone. Whenever we passed construction sites in town, all the workers would stop everything and come running to the fence to gawk and catcall. Ma ignored them, strutting through the streets singing her country-western songs and holding my hand. She could have got us a father with a job on the construction site, but she didn't, and I thought it was just as well because I was horrified to see them looking at Ma that way, like animals in a cage.

The trouble was, Ma was drawn to men who would end up living off us, rather than providing for us. Ma was always trying to save someone from the gutter, and that's literally where she met some of her boyfriends. They were usually Irish or Irish American and often alcoholic and jobless. But before long she'd have them sober and scrubbed up, with hair slicked back, a clean collared shirt, and shiny shoes from the thrift shop on their feet. Off they'd go to get a day's pay from Casey and Hayes Moving Company or some other job. But by then she'd be fed up with them and would send them off into the world to fend for themselves. Just when they were primed to bring some money into the home as an able-bodied working father figure. Within weeks we'd all wake up to some new scruffy soul off the street, lying on our legless couch watching the color TV that the social worker didn't know we had. The men were always startled to see eight kids climbing out of the woodwork bright and early to inspect their new dad. We just gathered around and stared. And they stared back.

But these were not stories for the social worker's docket. Before long Ma would offer to play the social worker a few tunes on the accordion. Of course she knew that would help to hurry our visitor off to the next inspection in her caseload, since most social workers had no hint of fun in them. So off each one went with Ma's threats of jigs and reels. Finally I could get on with my day, eating toast, blending shakes, and watching TV programs in full color.

I was five, the youngest at the time, and my mother and I were often alone in the house. Kevin was eight and had gone off to school with the rest of them. I was close to my mother and was called a mama's boy by all my brothers. I spent my mornings watching cartoons cross-legged on the floor, while Ma talked on the phone, sitting on the legless couch behind me. She talked for hours to her cousin Nellie. The two of them were born hell-raisers. They'd laugh hysterically, talking about their relatives or other people in the Irish circles. They had a nickname for everyone. Their Aunt Hannah was called "the neuro," short for neurotic, and Grandpa was "Murphy." Their boyfriends had nicknames too. In later years Ma's boyfriend Coley, the father of my two little brothers, came to be called "the little man" because he was short, and the African American father of Nellie's youngest daughter was called "Blackie."

After rambunctious conversations with Nellie, my mother took on deeper discussions with me. She'd try to engage me in spiritual topics like God and nature. I knew she really did think that I had some kind of insight, being the seventh son to her. One day, while I was glued to the TV, she decided to tell me that I was "different" from the other kids for another reason. I ignored her and kept watching cartoons. She told me that I had a different father from the other kids. I turned and looked at her for a moment, then looked back at the TV. I'm not sure what the word "father" meant to me, and I remember thinking, *Why's she bothering me with this stuff?* She said his name was George Fox, that she liked him because he was handsome, had a good job, and was much more intelligent and decent than the other kids' father, Mac. I was suddenly relieved that I had nothing to do with that monster Mac, and I couldn't wait to tell the other kids that I was special because I had a special father, and that he had a job. But I acted as if it all meant nothing to me, shrugging my shoulders and staring at the TV. All the while, though, I was thinking about how I might use my new special status in the world. I had a good father. Then I wondered where he was and what he looked like and why he wasn't there if he was so decent.

I never asked these questions. I chose to work with the good news I'd received, and to elaborate on the fantasy that I had a great father. I soon told all my friends in the neighborhood, as well as their Irish parents, who told me in quick murmurs to hush up about it, that there was no such thing as one family having two fathers. My best friend Tony's parents asked me to leave the house so their kids wouldn't hear of such nonsense. I knew something was wrong then. But I kept bragging. I bragged to all of my brothers and sisters when I was mad at them or couldn't get my way. Soon everyone knew, but what my friends said they all knew was that I was illegitimate, a bastard. The bastard part I didn't take very kindly to, but "illegitimate" I had to have Kevin look up in the dictionary. Kevin said the dictionary also called me a bastard, *and,* he added, "unlawfully begotten." I didn't know for sure what begotten meant, but I didn't want to go any further with it, especially if it was unlawful. I never again spoke of having a father at all. In fact, when people asked, I said I didn't have one. This too raised a few eyebrows, especially when I started school, but at least I wasn't called a bastard. The teachers just looked a little confused at first, and then changed the subject quickly. I was thrilled to hear at church that God was my father, and I started to imagine that probably something like the Immaculate Conception had created me, no sex at all, no unlawful filth, and no bastard was I.

I wasn't technically the seventh son after all, since that would probably require one consistent father. And God knows we never had one of them. But my mother kept up her spiritual conversations with me. I used to draw pictures while I was home and the others were off at school. One day I asked Ma what I should draw. Looking up at our velvet glow-in-the-dark picture of the Last Supper, she said to draw a picture of God. What I gave to her vaguely resembled a face, but the features were made up of the elements of nature: the earth, the sun, the moon and stars, trees, birds, and other animals. She jumped to her feet and said she couldn't believe the thinking of a five-year-old. She carried the picture around all day and in every conversation she had, she talked about my drawing and said that I must be some kind of genius. This gave me the biggest rush of pride that I'd ever known. She said she knew there was something different about me and that it must have something to do with my replacing Patrick Michael. She thought he must be very close to me, kind of like a guardian angel. She said that she'd had me to replace him in a way, and that when she was pregnant with me, she'd had a vision of exactly what I'd look like, and that a voice had told her I was a "child of light." I thought then that God might truly be my real father, and the praise I got for deep thinking made me want to do more of it.

On Sundays, Ma sent us all off to St. Thomas's Church at the bottom of our hill. She'd give us pennies for the poor box, which I thought must be called that because we were so poor we only gave pennies. I figured that this must be another way of keeping the social workers from thinking we had too much. Maybe they'd be watching from behind us in the pews to make sure we could only afford to give a few pennies. Actually, we usually ended up giving nothing at all, because Bob's Spa was on the way to St. Thomas's, and it had the greatest penny candy counter in Jamaica Plain. Most of the time we spent all our money there. When the poor box came around at mass, I'd feel so guilty with penny candy in my mouth that I'd motion my hand as if I was dropping a coin into the basket. When my invisible coin didn't make the clinking sound that the other churchgoers' coins made, the collector would look at me as if I was going straight to hell. Some of the families around us would look at us too, and knew exactly what we'd been up to, but I kept giving my invisible penny anyway and stared right back at them.

The other kids had their parents with them, and I wondered why Ma never came to church with us. When I asked her, she told me it was because she was divorced from Mac, and anyone who was divorced wasn't allowed to receive Holy Communion. I thought the church was wrong for wanting my mother to stay with Mac, broken ribs and all. I often thought that my mother should come to church with us, and walk right up to receive the Host. But I knew that the other kids' parents would whisper and stare, and news of it would be "all over Ireland." I later found out that my mother had her own spiritual life, away from St. Thomas's. While we were all off eating candy at mass, she was finding her own secluded spots down by the park, where she could be alone in nature and pray. She considered herself Catholic. She prayed through the Saints, and mostly through the Blessed Mother. But there was no point in going to mass if you couldn't receive Our Lord. Naturally my mother's beliefs shaped my own. Even as a kid I always felt torn between the Catholic Church and its rules for who's in and who's out with Jesus, and a deeper relationship with God that might be found anywhere.

We went to summer camp every year. The camps were run by Morgan Memorial and the Salvation Army, and were for city kids, who all seemed to have the same stories about bright orange blocks of cheese, social workers, and no fathers. The charitable organizations that ran the camp figured what we all needed was some fresh air, away from the city. Most of the kids in camp were black and would try to jump us, thinking we were like the white people they saw on TV programs like "The Brady Bunch." Kevin would spend the first day proving himself all over camp, beating up anyone who looked at him wrong, and taking the canteen money that the kids' mothers had given them. The grown men who ran the camp used to put us through all kinds of punishment when we broke the rules, like speaking out before being spoken to by an adult. We'd have to do fifty pushups or leg lifts, or when we were really bad, we'd have to go into a quiet dark cabin deeper in the woods. At first, Kevin would get all of these punishments. But he could do way more pushups and leg lifts than they imposed, and looked very much at ease at the end of them, offering to do more. He also loved the dark cabin, and would move right in, finding the light circuitry and making his own pad to settle into. In the end, they all loved him and put him in charge of doling out punishments for the others. Kevin ran the country paths like he did the city streets, and I was terrified the summer he took off from camp and found his way back to Ma's doorstep. I was left to fend for myself, and had to keep promising the black kids that he'd be back any minute now to knock their heads off if they touched me or tried to get their canteen money back from me.

One summer we all came home from camp to find the house rearranged and very tidy. There was a stranger sitting on the couch.

He was scrubbed and sober, but Ma hadn't gotten rid of him yet. At first we thought we'd walked into the wrong house, and he thought we must have too. Ma came out and introduced us to the man she'd married while we were away. His name was Bob King, and she'd met him downtown while he was bumming spare change in the Boston Common. He seemed decent enough. We got used to him, and he got used to us. He was our new father.

It didn't last long. His cleanliness didn't amount to much. He never went looking for work, and before long he was back on the booze. By November Ma started noticing money missing from her pocketbook. Then the stash of Christmas money she'd been saving for our toys disappeared. One day while I was watching morning cartoons, I heard a loud crash in the kitchen. When I ran in, Bob King was on the floor bleeding. Ma had smashed his head with the wine bottle he was drinking from, knocking him off his seat. I started shaking, and she told me to go grab the Kotex pads from the bathroom so he could sop up the blood. She sat him back on his seat and tore into him about stealing her Christmas money. When she was through, she sent him on his way, and off he went down Jamaica Street holding the Kotex pad to his head. That was the end of Bob King, except that Ma liked the name Helen King and has kept it to this day.

I started attending college with Ma when I was five years old. She was going to Suffolk University on financial aid from the government, but didn't have a babysitter. I would sit in the university library with comic books. The librarian kept an eye on me. She was a black woman who said she had four kids herself, and had gone back to school and had been able to get off of welfare. I felt safe with her, and had never been anywhere so quiet in my life. I loved finding something to whisper about to her, so that I could show that I knew just how to behave in a library. So I kept whispering that I had to go to the toilet—every ten minutes. She finally realized that I didn't have to go to the bathroom at all, and would divert my attention by bringing me gifts of books, paper, and Magic Markers. I loved my days at Suffolk University, and was sad to stop going.

My Aunt Theresa had agreed to take me in while my mother was at college. Theresa had two kids—Sean and Kathleen—who were home days. It was hard to get used to being away from my mother. I had an overwhelming fear that while I was away my family would be plotting to leave me for good. I learned to love being at Theresa's, but my fears never really went away. I knew my family would be leaving me someday, and sometimes I'd cry about the day it would happen. They'd leave because of some fault of mine, which I couldn't put my finger on. Whatever it was, I figured it must be the same reason my real father wasn't around.

But there was more freedom than fear for me in those days. It seemed the traumas were in the past, coming out only in Ma's stories that made people laugh, or else wonder at her strength. *I wouldn't trade my family for all the fathers in the world*, I thought. I was learning from Ma's example to ignore what other people thought. Ma had told me that when she was fifteen, she'd thrown open all the windows and screamed "Fuck the neighbors," working her parents into a panic. Every night I was surrounded by a huge family. I'd play Kevin on the new pool table that became yet another draped table when the social worker came over. I'd sneak downstairs to hide and watch the older kids smoking cigarettes without Ma knowing. And I'd sit with Davey and Johnnie, who were good artists, to draw more pictures that made Ma proud. Ma was looking happy too, working toward her college degree, and bragging to the neighbors, "Imagine, with all those kids." Those were happy times, until Davey ran away from home.

Davey was the oldest in the family. He excelled in school, so it was no surprise when after taking the exam he was accepted in the ninth grade to the prestigious Boston Latin School. As the oldest, though, he had borne the brunt of his father's abuses, getting beatings when Mac came home drunk. Sensitive and deep thinking, he carried the weight of all the havoc he'd seen at home. It had been Davey who discovered baby Patrick dead in the crib. And one day on his way to Boston Latin, Davey dumped his heavy stack of books into a trash can and ran away.

For months I watched my mother on the telephone talking to police to find out if her boy had been found, fearing he'd turn up dead. One morning Ma hung up the phone in tears. They'd found Davey. He'd gone to California and was stealing to get by. He'd been arrested after breaking into a house, and was being held by the police out there. The authorities agreed to release him to be sent back to his mother in Boston. When he got home, he continued to get into trouble and wasn't easy to have around. Ma figured what he needed was a change of environment, fresh air, and hard work on a farm in Ireland. She sent him off to her cousin Danny Murphy in Kerry, and Grandpa gave Danny Murphy a little money to look after Davey for the summer.

When Davey came home from Ireland, he seemed different, shaking and edgy. He started to fight a lot with Ma. One morning I awoke to my mother's screams. She was lying face up on the floor, crying and pleading, with a look of pain. Davey was on top of her, beating her up, and all of the other kids were trying to drag him off. Very soon afterward Davey went to Massachusetts Mental Institution for observation.

At first the doctors said Davey would be out after the weekend. In fact, he didn't get out for another three years. They later told Ma that he was in bad shape, that he'd had a nervous breakdown. The doctors at Mass Mental convinced Ma and Grandpa that what Davey needed was shock treatment, to eliminate his aggressive and potentially criminal tendencies. At age fourteen Davey received shock treatment, and he was never the same again.

I went with Ma every day to Mass Mental. She again had no one to babysit me, and I never wanted to leave her side anyway. The first time I went was terrifying. We walked into the big brick institution on Fenwood Road in Mission Hill, and immediately I was overtaken by an unnatural smell that I would forevermore associate as "institution smell." Hospital, juvenile corrections facility, prison, or morgue—all would smell the same to me from here on. It wasn't a putrid smell. It was almost hygienic but nonetheless sickening. It smelled like *This is not where you want to be, and you'll never go out the way you came in; that's one thing we'll make sure of.* The steel elevator doors slammed behind us, and up we went to the ward. I looked up at the others on the elevator and started my newly invented game of trying to figure out which ones were the inmates and which ones the attendants. I was usually wrong. I'd have my answer once the patient became fixated on me and went out of control with laughter, sadness, or rage. I seemed to trigger emotions for the patients, and Ma said it was because I was a kid and that they were being brought back to whatever happened to them in their own childhoods. I thought it was because I was the seventh son and had special powers that only they could read. Most responded to me with a sad fondness, and often one would seem to be pleading with me from across the elevator.

We got off, and the hygienic institutional smell was now mixed with the stink of piss; the heat blasted from radiators under barred windows that were locked down; and a layer of cigarette smoke hovered just above my head. I held onto my mother's hand as howls, shrieks, and fits of laughter echoed down empty corridors. This was like the haunted house at the carnival, but it was far worse because all of the lights were on, we could see the spring sun shining brightly outside, and there was no doubt that the suffering in this place was real.

We walked into the TV room where the air was blue with cigarette smoke, blowing in all directions. Everyone we saw there had a favorite body motion that they would repeat over and over again while muttering some monologue. We saw Davey, who let out a big happy "Ma!" when we walked into the room. One or two of the people in the room continued their movements oblivious to our presence, but most of them acknowledged us with only a short pause. Then they all went back to whatever the hell it was that they were doing: pacing, rocking, jerking, and chain-smoking. It was almost as if they were disappointed when they realized it was only us, and that things would be just the same as they ever were, with or without me and Ma.

It was always a relief to see Amen. He was a baldheaded black boy who jumped up and down, clapping like a Hare Krishna, overjoyed by Davey's excitement to see Ma. He'd memorized all my family's names, and after doing his happy dance, he always greeted us with, "And how is John MacDonald?" We'd say, "John MacDonald's fine, Amen." "And how is Joseph MacDonald?" "He's good, Amen." "And Mary MacDonald, how's she?" He'd ask about every one of us, all the way down the line to Michael MacDonald, even though I was right there in front of him. When he was finished, off he'd go, back to his daily business of clapping. I looked forward to seeing Amen every time we entered Mass Mental. Even if only for a moment, he took my mind off the heavy doors slamming behind us.

We soon became family to many of the inmates. Ma, her social self even in Mass Mental, was intrigued by the minds of the mentally ill. She would point to her own head and tell me that she liked to see what made people tick. So I always thought that was what patients were doing when they rocked, paced, jerked, and smoked: they were ticking. We brought Davey a carton of cigarettes every other day. He didn't smoke that many in two days, but when all the patients saw his smokes, of course they all wanted one. We got to know Anna, who didn't tick much. She just looked at me helplessly with tears running down her face, crouched forward with arms folded. I knew she wanted something from me, and there was nothing I could do to heal her or to save her from this place. I felt like telling her I wasn't really the seventh son, that I would've had to have been the seventh son in a row from the same father, and I didn't even have a father. I started stealing a few cigarettes from Davey's carton so that at least I had something to offer when the patients' pleading eyes overcame me with guilt. I would give them a smoke and they'd be delighted with me.

One morning we got to visit with Davey in our own private room, away from the TV and the ticking. An attendant who was so nice I thought he was a patient invited us in, telling us the room would be more "homey." It had bare walls, painted a glaring institutional green. That combined with the smell of piss and ammonia made for anything but homey. There was no kidding ourselves—we were all exactly where none of us wanted to be, no homey about it. This was the haunted house, with the fluorescent lights and radiators on full blast, and the sun shining outside on a beautiful spring day. But it was nice of him anyway.

Davey and Ma talked. I stared out of the room's doorway at an elderly woman lying in what looked like a crib, with iron bars going up the side of her bed. She rattled the bars and lifted her head, gasping in terror, as if it might be her last breath and she didn't want it to be. There was something she still had to do before leaving us all. Like the rest of them, she looked at me like she was begging something of me. I reached in my pocket for a smoke to give to her, but was too scared to go near her. I felt helpless and wanted to cry, but I couldn't because who knows what that would set off in this place.

I turned away from the old woman, looked outside beyond the barred windows, and saw birds gathered in a tree, chirping away. But I couldn't hear a thing they were chirping. Just then "Joan the Hooker" ran into our room. She was wearing her blonde curly wig that day, and was decked out in a red miniskirt and white platform shoes. She screamed "rape" and started to barricade herself—and us—into the homey room. She blocked the doorway with couches and bureaus that seemed to have no other purpose than for times like this. Joan had been through this before: "Black Willey" was after her again. He started to bang down the door and push through the barricade of furniture, which was buttressed by Joan and Ma. Davey roared with laughter, but I was so nervous I shit my pants.

Ma started to talk to Willey from behind the furniture. It worked. She got him to calm down, sit on the couch, and talk to us, while Joan sat on Ma's other side and cried. Willey told Joan that he was sorry, that he was in love with her, that's all. He apologized to me too.

Once everything seemed calm, the attendants finally showed up out of nowhere and tackled Willey to the ground. Willey fought them off and started to get the best of them, saying he would beat their white boy asses black and blue. Some of the other inmates took a break from the ticking and gathered around to cheer Willey on. It took six attendants to restrain Willey and take him off to "the quiet room." We knew then that we wouldn't see or hear from Willey for a good long time. Joan screamed as they took him away, Davey laughed and told Willey to keep fighting, and I could still feel my legs shaking as I looked out the window again, thinking visiting hour was almost over.

At least I could leave every day. Davey couldn't, whether we wanted him to or not. The doctors said he was a danger to himself and to others. His imprisonment was made painfully clear to me one day when it was time for us to go, and he begged Ma not to leave him. "This is the fucking nuthouse," he said, and he was starting not to feel so good, with all the medication they were forcing on him. There was no more laughing at the nuts. He didn't belong in here. "These people are fucking nuts, and the fucking attendants are even nuttier." He'd stopped swallowing his medication and was able to blow the pills up his nose, to hide them when they made patients drink a cup of water and show their tonsils to make sure the pills went down. Then he'd spit them out when no one was looking. He wanted to come home with us. He wasn't crazy and didn't want to get crazy from this hellhole. The attendants made us leave when they saw Davey getting worked up. As we went toward the steel elevator doors, Davey bellowed "Ma" and tackled my mother from behind, knocking her to the ground. About four attendants were on top of the two of them, pulling Davey off Ma. I hated every one of them and started pounding on their heads. One of them restrained me, and the rest dragged Davey down the long corridor toward the quiet room.

When we went to the offices downstairs, the doctors assured us that no one was going to hurt Davey, that what he was going through was a normal phase that many patients go through after deciding that they're different from the rest and don't belong there. They insisted that Davey was a danger to himself and to others. They'd diagnosed him as schizophrenic.

The next time we went to visit Davey, he was locked in the quiet room. We looked through the small glass window in the heavy door. The room had no other windows at all, and everything was padded—walls, ceiling, floor. And there was Davey restrained in the middle of the floor, pleading something we couldn't hear through the thick glass. Ma pushed me away from the door, saying I shouldn't see this. Sometimes Ma got this voice, and you could tell that she wanted to cry but she wouldn't. That's what she sounded like now. We found out that we wouldn't be able to meet with Davey for a few days. So we gave out his carton of cigarettes and left. All the way home, Ma tried to reassure me, and probably herself, that Davey was okay, that the doctors were just getting him to calm down, and that he would be out of the quiet room and Mass Mental in no time. I thought that maybe all he needed was a cigarette, and he couldn't even have one, and that not being able to smoke would make him worse.

I'd come to hate Mass Mental. It didn't seem right. I knew the inmates weren't bad people; and whatever was wrong with them, it seemed as if they'd been put away so that the outside world wouldn't have to deal with their pain. I knew Davey'd been through bad things, growing up with a father like Mac and finding his baby brother dead. And to me, it seemed he was being punished for having gone through bad things. Ma said that Davey felt things more than others—the bad things in the world—because he was so smart, and I thought she was right.

Even at the age of six, I had to wonder what good it might do anyone to be at Mass Mental on a beautiful spring day, so cut off from anything that's good about the world. I knew it wasn't good for Davey, no matter what the psychiatrists said. For my family, freedom had become the rule above all others. But now I knew, having felt the locked-up pain of the people in Mass Mental, that for Davey, those days were gone.

CHAPTER 3

GHETTO
HEAVEN

IN THE SUMMER OF 1973, MY GRANDFATHER DECIDED TO sell the house on Jamaica Street. He was having problems with us as tenants. Joe had car parts on the back porch, the cellar was looking like a teen clubhouse with mattresses and couches thrown about and glow-in-the-dark paint on the walls, and we were always using some pancake griddle invention of Joe's that Grandpa said was a fire hazard. He took everything he didn't like out to the backyard and stomped on it, making a statement obvious to all of us. We were out. Ma didn't know what we'd do. We had no place to go that we could afford, and she was sure we'd end up once again in a place like Columbia Point.

One day after a trip to the beach in South Boston, Ma walked through the Old Colony Housing Project in Southie and talked to some old friends who'd moved there from Columbia Point. She spotted an empty apartment at 8 Patterson Way and went right into the office of Dapper O'Neil, a local city counselor, who has since acquired a reputation in Boston as a bigot, often making public statements about blacks and whites staying separate. But he also has a strong record for constituent services, for doing anything he can for families in trouble, regardless of their race. Dapper saw that Ma was in an emergency situation with eight kids and no money and nowhere to live, and pulled a few strings for us to get the apartment at 8 Patterson Way.

Ma was thrilled, as if she'd died and gone to heaven by getting a place in the all-white South Boston housing projects. She yelled up to all the neighbors on Jamaica Street that we'd struck a great bit of luck, six rooms for eighty dollars a month, heat, light, and gas included, and it's all white—we wouldn't have to go back to the black projects! I didn't know why the white thing was so important. While I'd become familiar with the nightmarish stories from Columbia Point, my own experience had been that we got along much better with the black kids in Jamaica Plain, who seemed to have more in common with us than the other kids with Irish parents.

We drove into Old Colony in one of Joe's shitboxes, with a few mattresses tied to the top of the roof, and each of us carrying a garbage bag full of clothes and canned goods. We rolled slowly through the maze of red bricks, checking out the neighborhood, with its groups of young mothers sitting on the stoops, rocking their baby carriages back and forth. Kids splashed in wading pools on the hot summer day, while gangs of teenage boys huddled on street corners, shirtless and with rolled-up bellbottoms, no socks, and expensive sneakers. An occasional man would stroll down the street, more than one with a bottle in a brown paper bag. I knew what was in the bag because that was how my Aunt Nellie kept her booze hidden when she wanted to drink outside.

They all stopped whatever they were doing to watch us coming down the street. Tough-looking teenagers approached the car, standing apart from the crowd as if to challenge anyone willing to take them on. My mother just kept smiling and waving at all our new neighbors. She pointed to all the shamrock graffiti and IRA and IRISH POWER spray painted everywhere, and said it looked just like Belfast and that we were in the best place in the world. She walked up to people and talked to them, trying to get in on their conversations. The other mothers couldn't help answering her questions, but they remained standoffish, not wanting anyone to think they'd be welcoming outsiders into the private world of Old Colony. Neighbors watched our every move from windowsills and doorsteps, and I was scared.

I'd seen tough-looking people before. But these were white, like us. There were a couple of young people in wheelchairs, people with deformities, and one teenager with recent stab wounds in his stomach. While we carried bags and mattresses up to our third-floor apartment, larger groups of teenagers began to gather. A group of girls about Mary's age stared her down and muttered something about her being a "nigger lover" (Mary still had her Afro). She stepped up to them and told them to speak up and say it to her face. They all kept quiet. The local boys laughed and tried to instigate a fight. My mother just kept smiling and waving at everyone in the midst of the tense atmosphere. Calling "Hey, how ya doin'?" up to people in windows, as if she'd known them her whole life long. She figured that they were all Irish, all in the same boat as she and her kids, and besides, she had to make this work. She carried up her accordion and warned everyone that she'd be playing a few tunes tonight on the front steps.

We went into the apartment and started to paint the walls with the paint the maintenance office had left for us. It was the same color that all of the walls already were: that glaring green that I'd seen at Mass Mental. We brought out the rollers and brushes, and I got busy painting the bathroom as soon as possible, before my mother could take on the job and do her usual scheme of painting every inch of the bathroom the same color, including the ceilings, floor, toilet, sink, and bathtub. She always did this, and within weeks we'd have big white spots on our tub and sink, where the paint had started to chip and peel. I painted the four walls and left signs up for nobody to touch the wet paint, and for nobody to paint the toilet.

Ma came out of one of the rooms carrying a pointy brown bug with a coat of armor and antennas waving in all directions. Ma said it was a cockroach, that we'd had them in Columbia Point, and that I'd better get used to them because the place was loaded with them. She wanted to get to know some of the neighbors and she figured that the cockroach might be a good conversation piece to bond over. She knocked on the neighboring apartment door and asked the woman who answered if the bug she was holding in her palm was really a cockroach. The woman looked disgusted and wouldn't open her door more than a crack, saying she wouldn't know what it was, or what a cockroach looked like, that she'd never seen one in her life. Then she slammed the door. Ma came back laughing, saying the woman was a phony bitch, "And how could someone live in the project and not know what a cockroach looked like?" I was worried that the neighbors would start blaming us for bringing all the cockroaches into Old Colony, for loads of them had started staggering out of the walls and cabinets, dazed by the smell of paint. Ma said that the new paint would chase them out of our house for a couple of weeks, loading up the woman next door with them. "And that'll show her what a cockroach is!"

The kid on the first floor was friendly and offered to carry some bags up for us. He was my age, and my mother dragged him upstairs to show me my new friend. We both went downstairs and sat on the front stoop of 8 Patterson, and he laid out the rules of the neighborhood. He told me I'd have to get in a few fistfights before I became part of the neighborhood, that I'd better not be thinking about bringing niggers or spics over from Jamaica Plain, and to never ever rat on anyone to the cops. Danny was a good kid and was trying to look out for me. I wondered if I'd have to fight the teenage boys whose teeth were already knocked out, and who were now staring up at our windows. He assured me that they wouldn't bother me. They'd be waiting to jump my older brothers. "They'd never mess with anyone smaller than them." Those were the rules.

Just then, Danny's mother came out of her apartment screaming and calling him a "cocksucker" because there was no Pepsi in the house, and why hadn't he gone out to the store earlier, when she told him to. She was carrying a butcher knife. "I'll cut the fucking dick right off of ya," she shouted loud enough for the whole street to hear. He ran from the front stoop, disappearing down one of the tunnels that cut through the maze of brick buildings, and soon returned with a bottle of Pepsi. When he came outside again, he had his four-year-old brother with him, and his mother screamed for the two of them to go fuck themselves and slammed her door.

Danny forced a chuckle and shrugged his shoulders, and asked me if I wanted to go to the park with him and his little brother, Robbie. I went upstairs to tell Ma where I was going, and found her on her hands and knees painting the toilet and sink, including the pipes that carried water into them. I gave up on explaining why we couldn't paint certain parts of the bathroom, and went off with Danny and Robbie. He showed me Carson Beach, and drew a line in the sand right about where we weren't supposed to cross over into "Niggerville." Just across that line was the black beach, and Columbia Point Housing Project about fifty yards away. He told me all about Columbia Point, and how there were all these blacks living there with no teeth, bottles of booze in paper bags, and guns and knives. I didn't dare tell him that I was born there. When we went home, we bought a can of tonic to share and put it in a brown paper bag, laughing and pretending it was booze, just like the blacks, and the guys in Old Colony, and my own Aunt Nellie.

We hung out in front of J.J.'s Liquors drinking our fake booze until a group of kids our age came walking by. They said hi to Danny, but one of them bumped into me with his shoulder, backed up, and threw his two arms up in the air saying, "I offer you out." I had no idea what this meant, but it sounded too polite to be coming from a kid with a black eye and a scowl on his face. Danny told me this meant the kid wanted to fight me. I put up my two fists the way my brother Frankie'd taught me, one for defense and one for offense, and stood in the boxer pose with one foot forward. He kicked me in the balls and when I was bent over he pulled my T-shirt over my head and started beating me with anything he could pick up: sticks, rocks, and the beer cans that littered the street. The other kids formed a circle around us, and Danny and Robbie were the only ones cheering me on. Some adults came out of the liquor store to take sides as well. When they saw a cop car pull up, the adults chased us all back into the project across the street, calling us little bastards. We ran in all different directions.

My older brothers were pissed off that I'd lost a fight, and Frankie started to schedule daily boxing lessons for me. I'd have to meet him every day after school to start punching the bag. Frankie told me I'd soon be able to beat the hell out of Brian Noonan, the kid in front of the liquor store. There came a time when I believed I could beat him, and wanted to prove it in a street fight, but by then I didn't know how to "offer out" someone I had, by then, nothing against. Brian and I had become friends, the day after our fight, which was nothing more than my initiation into Southie's housing projects.

My brothers and sisters had their own initiations to face. One day, Mary and her friends from Jamaica Plain were taking me to the park. We began to pass through one of the tunnels that cut through the courtyards of Old Colony, and we saw a gang of girls lined up against both sides of the tunnel wall. When Mary and the two girls from J.P. passed them, the Old Colony girls jumped them from behind. Mary grabbed two of the girls by the hair and banged their heads against the brick wall. Then, holding on only to another girl's hair, Mary flung her body against the wall. This was the leader of the group, Sally Duggan, a neighbor. After this, word spread not to mess with Mary, and she became accepted among the tough crowd.

But we still had a hard time from the boys in the neighborhood. Within the first week of moving into Old Colony, a bottle came through the open window of one of our bedrooms and smashed against the wall. When we looked out we saw a group running through the back courtyard laughing and slapping each other five. Later in the day, the same group was outside in front of our building, leaning against cars and pointing up to our windows. They were drinking beer, and in the sweltering heat they'd taken their shirts off and tucked them into the back pockets of their rolled-up dungarees. Johnnie, Joe, and Frank decided to go downstairs to face them. They walked slowly out of our building with their own shirts off. My brothers were built—they'd been bodybuilding—and each of them carried a machete at his side. They walked right up to the crowd of scrawny toughs and asked which one had something to say. Ma was up in the third-floor window and pointed out which one had thrown the bottle, and he tore down the street yelling back at my brothers, threatening them with names of gangsters that meant nothing to us yet. My brothers came back upstairs once it was clear that no one else had anything more to say to them.

The next day, a neighbor tipped us off that the boys from Old Colony had called their friend Freddy Callaghan, a known street thug and a murderer, about us. We'd heard that he'd recently walked into a bar in Andrew Square and shot up the place in retaliation for his own brother's murder, which had never been solved. Freddy Callaghan was planning to come over that night, a neighbor told us, to give us a lesson in real Southie street justice. Freddy was known to carry a gun, and someone said he'd definitely shoot all our windows out. Ma went to his older brother, who said there was nothing he could do about him. Freddy was gone in the head, he said.

Ma went into nearby D Street Housing Project that day with her new boyfriend, Coley, and bought a double-barreled shotgun from an apartment there. Things were heating up around our place in Old Colony, and Ma walked right up the steps to our building, shotgun in plain view, so all the sightseers would know that she and her kids weren't to be fucked with. At sundown she called a taxi to get "the three little kids"—me, Kevin, and Kathy—out of town. We'd have to spend the night at Grandpa and Nana's in West Roxbury, where they'd moved from Jamaica Plain. Davey, who was now making weekend visits home from Mass Mental, would come with us. A crowd had gathered outside 8 Patterson Way by the time the taxi pulled up. The three of us little kids and Davey walked out of the building while Ma sat up in the window, keeping us covered with the shotgun. As we drove through Old Colony, we noticed that some of the local toughs were following our taxi, taking shortcuts from courtyard to courtyard. Davey yelled for us all to hit the floor, and we did.

Our grandparents were confused by our arrival out of the blue. My aunts Leena and Sally were still single and living at home with Nana and Grandpa, and one of them called Ma to find out what was going on. Ma told them, and they all began pacing the floors and looking out the window to see if the "gangsters from Southie" had followed us there. Davey kept retelling the story, expanding each time, until my aunts' shrieking questions made us feel as if we'd all die tonight for sure.

Things calmed down a bit as the evening wore on. We'd called Ma and she'd said that Freddy Callaghan had come and gone, after circling our building a few times. We all finally got to sleep. At about three in the morning, we awoke to the screams of Sally and Nana. They were crying, saying that we'd been followed, that there was someone banging at the front door downstairs. Grandpa, with his oversized underwear and chicken legs, jumped out of bed and grabbed a long pipe that was by his bedside, ready to march downstairs and defend his family. Leena, Sally, and Nana begged him not to go, pulling on his undershirt to hold him back. Davey jumped out of bed, grabbed a curtain rod, and urged Grandpa onward. They went downstairs, Sally still crying and calling us little bastards for bringing those gangsters over here to kill us all. I thought for sure I'd never see Grandpa or Davey ever again, but after a few minutes we heard friendly voices talking in the kitchen, and the sound of Nana boiling tea and setting the table. When we went downstairs we saw Joe Malone, a friend of the family's from Ireland, nursing a bloody wound on his head with a towel soaked in hot water, and telling Grandpa and Davey about the terrible car accident he'd been in, that he'd been out drinking and hit a damn construction truck that was parked in front of him on his way home. Instead of going to a hospital, he'd come to be taken care of at Nana's. They all laughed at what a good thing it was that Grandpa had recognized him through all the blood on his face. "He'd have had the head knocked off of him otherwise," Davey said.

We went back to Old Colony in the morning, and found Coley asleep at the windowsill with the shotgun as his pillow. When we said his name, he was startled and pretended he'd been awake all along. He aimed out the window with one eye closed still awaiting a gunfight with Freddy Callaghan, muttering in his Connemara Gaelic what sounded like fighting words.

From here on in, the whole neighborhood was friendly to us. Being the youngest in a family with a rep for being crazy, I'd never have to fight again in Old Colony, or in any of the areas immediately surrounding the project.

One day not long after we moved there, my friend Danny and I left Old Colony to walk Southie's main streets. Our first challenge was not to pass through anyone else's territories in the Lower End, which I'd quickly learned was the more run-down section of South Boston, with its three huge housing projects—Old Colony, D Street, and Old Harbor—and mazes of three-deckers lining alleyways and small lanes watched over by mothers in lawn chairs and tough-looking teenagers milling about on the corners. When I looked down the side streets of connected houses and concrete, I saw more groups of teenagers and kids hanging out in front of corner stores, keeping guard, popping up their heads to inspect us and to make sure that we knew better than to come down their street.

At the top of Dorchester Street we came to Broadway, grocery stores, toy stores, donut shops, liquor stores, and barrooms crowding every block. Danny told me that if we walked up the hill to the right we'd be on East Broadway, heading toward City Point and the rich people in Southie, and that if we went left we'd be going down West Broadway where things were a little more normal. He said we'd be better off sticking to West Broadway, which passed through the Lower End.

We saw people we knew from Old Colony strolling down West Broadway, a parade mostly of young women with baby carriages. I started to notice that Southie people had a similar look about their faces. There was a toughness to everything but the eyes. Everyone had those humorous sparkly eyes that I knew were Irish, having seen them in Jamaica Plain and at the Irish Field Day in Dedham and in the countenances of my own relatives. But these Irish eyes were set in faces that looked as if they'd spent much of their time defying whatever shit had come their way. It was a proud look, though, and only the eyes betrayed the hearts behind the hard-as-a-rock faces they'd learned to project. When folks from Southie smiled or laughed, they looked like completely different people. Groups of teenagers from different territories of the Lower End passed each other without saying a word. They were on neutral ground on West Broadway. There was also what Danny called "the wall," a long red-brick partition alongside Southie Savings Bank, lined with dozing winos who sometimes stirred to fight each other. The wall was the perfect place to watch the coming and going on Broadway, but few people ever wanted to sit there, for fear of being seen with the winos.

A young balding man with an unsteady head made a beeline for us with his hand stretched out. He didn't look at me directly; his head was wobbling too much. He peered at me out of the corners of his eyes and asked, "Gotta quarter?" I dodged him, ducking under his hand, and he spun around repeating, "Gotta quarter?" and chasing after me. When he spotted someone else in his path, he immediately switched to them for a donation. Danny caught up with me laughing, and told me I'd met "Bobby Got-a-Quarter." Everyone in Southie knew Bobby and was used to him. While most adults automatically paid the obligatory toll, the kids walking down Broadway played with him. They knew he especially liked girls, so they would send him after one of the young girls with his hand stretched out. But he was part of the neighborhood, and I noticed that no one really bothered him.

At the bottom of West Broadway was D Street Project. Danny said we could only walk around the border of it, because we were from Old Colony, and the kids in D Street wouldn't allow us even to pass through. I was curious then, and wanted to see what the people looked like and if D Street was anything like Old Colony. A few people came walking out of D Street and Danny pointed out to me that they were dirtier than Old Colony people, that's why they were called "D Street dirtballs." People in Old Colony usually sported designer labels—sometimes stolen, as I'd learned, off the backs of trucks or from the department stores in town. But the D Street kids looked hopeless. Danny told me that the people who ended up in D Street were "white niggers." I'd never heard the term before; and I ran it around in my head over and over again, trying to picture what it might mean, and wondering whether white niggers were friendly with the black niggers over in Columbia Point, where we were also never to cross through.

I didn't hear the term "white nigger" again until I passed through City Point and found out that I was one myself. City Point was on the other end of Southie from us, with houses that usually had some distance from each other—if only about five feet—and where most kids had a father. What looked rich to us actually meant working class. The fathers mostly had jobs with the city or the Mass Bay Transit Authority, or in construction. One day Danny tried to take me to see Castle Island, a peninsula that juts out from the South Boston neighborhood, and that has a colonial fort that looks like a castle. To get to Castle Island we had to pass through "the Heights," or Dorchester Heights, where a sign said something about George Washington taking control of the hill and forcing the British to evacuate Boston. I was more impressed by all the trees, and the nicely painted houses that lined the streets leading to the bay. Further along, in "the Point," I noticed the people looked different. They still had the Irish faces, and many had a tough look. But they wore turtlenecks and chino pants, pressed and cuffed just right. Some had Irish knit sweaters, but these were draped over their shoulders the way rich people did. They also wore lots of green, I guess to prove that they were still Irish. I found out in City Point that we were "project rats" and "white niggers." The Point kids chased us back down the hills to the Lower End, "where you belong!" they yelled from the Heights, standing ground at the invisible line they too didn't dare cross.

I spent hours in our apartment in Old Colony trying to grasp this hierarchy of niggers that I'd discovered. I wanted to know exactly where I fit into the scheme. Of course, no one considered himself a nigger. It was always something you called someone who could be considered anything less than you. I soon found out that there were a few black families living in Old Colony. They'd lived there for years and everyone said that they were okay, that they weren't niggers but just black. It felt good to all of us to not be as bad as the hopeless people in D Street or, God forbid, the ones in Columbia Point, who were both black and niggers. But now I was jealous of the kids in Old Harbor Project down the road, which seemed like a step up from Old Colony, having many families left over from when housing projects were for war veterans, and where some of the kids had fathers. Of course, we were all niggers if we went to City Point, so forget going there again to see the beautiful beaches and Castle Island. I wondered if the Point kids might be niggers to people who'd really made it, like out in tidy West Roxbury or the suburbs that everyone talked about moving to when they won the lottery.

In Old Colony, we had all the right gear, but we didn't match as well as the Point kids. We weren't able to get *everything* in green; we had to take what we could get from Skoochie. She was the local klepto, who went into town daily to steal what she could from Filene's and Jordan Marsh. She went door-to-door in the project, with huge shopping bags filled with designer labels. I thought Skoochie looked important, earning a hard living for her kids and never taking a day of rest. She walked more proud and straight-shouldered than the other young mothers, and was always dressed to kill: tight Gloria Vanderbilt jeans tucked into spike boots and a red leather jacket with a fur collar. But she had the face of a rat. She became friendly with Ma, and started to come by weekly, as we had so many kids to clothe. She'd lay everything out on the couches and tables, and show the Ralph Lauren label and the attached price tag. The standard price for hot goods was always one-third the ticket price, but my mother usually got her down to about one-fourth. Skoochie sold us everything, from sneakers to fur coats for my sisters. Joe and Frankie would light up when they saw the leather coats she had. Kevin got excited too, calling the brown leather coats with the wide pointy collars "pimpin'."

People in Southie had a unique "Southie look" that crossed all turf lines, the only difference being that the kids "up the Point" were a little more polished, and the kids in D Street were just plain dirty, their clothes not as new. In the summer, we rolled up our bell-bottoms to about midcalf, and flipped our collars up. Hospital pants and shirts were popular—and sometimes a surgical mask around the neck!—and everyone had a "Southie cut," the trademark hairstyle that proved you were from the neighborhood. I had to get a Southie cut once I noticed everyone had something to say about the bushy mess of curls I'd inherited from Nana's people in the hills of Donegal. The Southie cut consisted of hair severely parted down the middle in a perfectly straight line, cut very short, and blow-dried back to form wings. People walked with a stiff neck to keep all their hairs in place. The toughest guys in Southie looked as if they'd spent hours getting their hair just right for a day of milling about on the corner.

All the boys had homemade tattoos, done with a sewing needle and green ink. Some had a shamrock outline and "Irish Power" on their arm. On some afternoons you'd see teenagers sitting on curbs tattooing a cross onto each other's middle fingers, and a dot onto their wrists. The "Southie dot" identified you as okay within the neighborhood but would get you into trouble if you ever ventured into downtown Boston, where everyone said there were loads of blacks looking for fights, and liberals who branded Southie kids as thieves, punks, or racists. Most people in my neighborhood didn't have any reason to go downtown anyway, except to steal bikes from college students or to shoplift, none of which ever was to be done within the neighborhood. Those were the rules. And if you ever ended up in jail, your Southie dot would make you a target among the black inmates. But everyone went ahead and did the Southie dot anyway, to prove their loyalty to the neighborhood, regardless of the consequences in the outside world.

If South Boston was its own world, Old Colony was a world within a world. Aside from the strolls up Broadway, we mostly spent our entire day in the project, especially in the summer when school was out. There was plenty of excitement. Every stoop had its own group of mothers and babies sitting all day, next to wading pools and a hose that spilled water onto the sidewalk and into the gutter. The water in the gutter was called polio water, because it stank so bad from mixing with mud and garbage, and if you ever stepped into it you were branded for a whole day as the one with polio on your sneaker. Skoochie and a few other shoplifters went door-to-door, with people excitedly calling them from windowsills to come up and show them the hot goods. Dizzo came down our street with his ice cream truck about five times a day, blasting the warbling recorded melody to "Three Blind Mice." Dizzo knew everyone in the neighborhood and got out of his truck to share all the latest news with the women up in their windows or on the stoops, while kids poured out of the woodwork to buy their third or fourth ice cream for the day. If the little kids couldn't get the ice cream money from their mothers, there was always some neighbor who had an extra quarter, and Dizzo was known to give a free ice cream if you looked really desperate or put on a "left out" face at the truck's window.

Like us, most of the kids in Old Colony had no set time to go into their apartment to eat. So around what would have been suppertime, someone would pull out the illegal firemen's wrench and open a hydrant, spilling more water into the gutter, making floods of polio water at the bottom of the street. The news traveled all over the project in minutes, with kids calling up to their friends' windows that the hydrant was open. We lined up at the mouth of the hydrant to jump into the blast of water and were pushed across the pavement on our backs all the way to the other side of the street. If we touched the polio lakes forming on the downslopes of the pavement, we could wash it right off with the rush of hydrant water. When cars came down the street, we all stopped what we were doing and played innocent. There'd be some stop and go, as the driver inched toward the water stream and we pretended to be ready to blast him. When the driver felt it was safe and that we were just faking, that's when one of us would put two hands at the bottom of the gush of water, sending a spray through the windows of the car. Usually the driver would get out and chase us, unless he wasn't from the neighborhood, in which case he'd rather speed off than get into trouble in Old Colony. Most people from the neighborhood knew better, and simply kept their windows closed, getting a free car wash. Unlike outsiders, they thought nothing of showing us kids that they didn't trust us, rolling up all windows before going forward.

The hydrant provided about a half hour of entertainment until the cops came to chase everyone away and to shut the hydrant off. Usually someone's mother would yell from the window to warn us that the cops were coming. Everyone ran in all directions. When the coast was clear, after there'd been about two minutes of silence on the street and the police officers had paced in circles around the hydrant to make their presence known, everyone came running out again, one kid carrying the firemen's wrench to turn the hydrant back on. This went on for hours, between the cops chasing us away and shutting off the hydrant, and us turning it back on again. If they ever got hold of the wrench we used, that would be the end of it all, until we found someone else with connections at the fire department to steal a wrench.

There was always something to do in Old Colony, and it seemed a much bigger place than the six or so blocks it actually was. In fact, it seemed bigger than the whole outside world, bigger than Broadway, the beach, downtown, and Jamaica Plain all put together. When you walked into the maze of red bricks and tunnels after being on the outside, it was like walking into another world. We had our own beaches—plastic wading pools and lawn chairs on the cement in front of the buildings. And we had our own friendships and fights. At the edge of the project, Old Colony even had its own corner stores that would cash welfare checks, and liquor stores for anyone who needed a drink. The liquor stores even delivered to some of the older people who didn't come out of their houses much. We had a church on the corner that would fill on Sundays, mostly with second graders preparing for First Communion and elderly women. Carson Beach was right down the street, but most people didn't bother with that. Many of the teenagers and young women lay their beach chairs out on the roofs of the project, and you could smell the tanning oil and hear groups like Earth, Wind, and Fire blasting from radios all tuned to the same station. Old Colony was all ours, and we never wanted to leave.

The kids in the neighborhood created every bit of fun that we had. Mothers never had to find something for us to do. Sometimes we'd get bored, but that's when we'd go up to the rooftops and throw splashes of pebbles down onto the heads of outsiders passing by the outskirts of the project. We'd duck then, and they wouldn't dare come after us, unless a car window broke and we'd have to run before the cops came.

On summer nights, after the hydrants were abandoned, it was time to set the dumpsters on fire. We knew that this would bring the big red fire trucks out from Engine 6. As the trucks came roaring down Patterson Way, sirens and lights and all, you could feel the excitement like electricity. Kids appeared from hallways and tunnels, chasing after the fire trucks. The firemen clambered out to extinguish the dumpster fire, with flames that reached as high as the second-floor windows, while we climbed on top of their trucks, hanging from the ladders and ringing the bells.

There was usually one fireman still left to mind the truck, and he'd help us up and place us in the rear ladder seat that had a steering wheel of its own. Engine 6 had gotten used to us. It seemed they were in on our fun. I figured they'd be bored to tears if it weren't for us kids inviting them into our private world. Many a time the firemen actually stayed on Patterson Way a good half hour after putting out the dumpster, talking to us kids and answering our questions about being a fireman. We didn't know too many guys with jobs, let alone a fun job with all the effects: the lights, the sirens, the fire, and gushers of water. We even liked the black firemen, who must have been aware of their unusual status in being welcomed into Old Colony. They were the most friendly to us, and always seemed happy to see us. We got to know most of the firemen, and we knew we'd see them again soon, same time, same place, unless there was a real fire going on somewhere else.

The teenagers in the neighborhood made their own fun too. The firemen thought they were punks, though. Sometimes the older kids brought Engine 6 down Patterson Way by tying someone they didn't like to the firebox in his underwear and pulling the alarm. This was occasionally a lesson to outsiders not to hang out in Old Colony. The firemen would come out and untie the poor captive from the firebox, but afterward they usually weren't in the same mood as when the little kids brought them out with an innocent dumpster fire.

By about ten o'clock we'd all go into our apartments, and on the hottest nights we wondered what fights would break out that we could watch from our windowsills. Ma always said that the heat brought out the craziness in the neighborhood, just like it brought out the craziness in the hordes of cockroaches that would take over our kitchen in the middle of the night. Mothers hung out on stoops gossiping and chain-smoking and watching every move on the street. If a car came down Patterson Way, everyone would stop talking to watch the car drive past. It seemed as if we were all hoping for some action, all the time.

Groups of teenagers would gather around the same spot in the middle of the street, leaning against parked cars on both sides of Patterson Way. They usually told war stories of fights they'd been in, or had seen. They gave blow-by-blow reenactments, throwing heroic punches and kicks, and acting out in slow motion how the victim reacted to the blows. They would stop what they were doing to talk to someone in a car that pulled up, popping their whole upper body through the open window for a few seconds. Then they'd pop out again, and the car would speed off. Other times a local would walk up to them and be escorted into a dark hallway, again for just a few seconds. Then they would be off in a flash as well. I knew the teenagers were selling pot but I never said a word about it, just kept my mouth shut. In Southie the worst thing you could be was a snitch. Those were the rules. Kevin was only eleven, but he sat by the teenagers who were running the show, and it wasn't long at all before he became the one popping his upper body into a car window or taking someone's mother into a dark hallway.

One night as I sat in the window watching and waiting for something to explode, I saw a giant cockroach appear out of the corner of my eye. I thought it was a rat it was so big, and I completely forgot about the tension building outside on one of the hottest nights of the year. It was about four inches long and more than an inch thick. I'd never before seen a cockroach the size of that one, and I yelled as loud as I could. The mothers all looked up from the stoop, Kevin and his friends in the street barreled upstairs, and my mother and sisters came out of their rooms. This was great, I thought. My whole family and a good portion of the neighborhood were sticking together to gang up on the giant cockroach. Kevin laughed when he saw what it was, but he led everyone else on a chase through the house after it. The mothers didn't budge from the stoop, but they wanted to know what was going on and waited for updates from our window. Just when Kevin had cornered the roach, and it knew its moments were numbered, it suddenly discovered it had a means of escape. It spread its huge wings and attempted to fly, but could only make long leaps. You could hear it landing with a small thump from wall to ceiling. We threw shoes and it finally leapt into the bathtub and down the drain. Ma turned on the water, as the gang of neighborhood kids looked on, crowded into our small bathroom. One of the teenagers said it was a "water bug" brand of cockroach and that we'd see plenty more of them this summer, especially on muggy nights. "Did you fuckin' kill it yet or what?" one of the mothers yelled up with a laugh. We weren't sure, so I kept the water running down the drain all night. The episode had broken that night's tension on Patterson Way. It was good to be part of the neighborhood.

On some days I sat for hours in the window, watching the comings and goings on Patterson Way. In no time at all my own family had become part of the moving picture of the street.

There was Joe with his head in the engine of someone's car, with a line of neighbors ready to barter with him. Joe was the neighborhood mechanic, always out front fixing cars for everyone in the project, and he could fix anything for less than they would charge at the garages. Sometimes customers would offer him a "nickel bag" of pot if they didn't have the cash.

Across the street I'd see Kathy, all dolled up in her bellbottoms and tube top, one of the best-looking girls in the neighborhood, smoking her cigarettes with some of the tougher twelve-year-olds. She was known to be able to beat up any boy her age, even the roughnecks she dated.

Frankie would come and go. He'd stop to hang out with Joe under the hood of a car before heading off to the local gym to box. He never sat still for long, though. He worked out constantly, boxing, running, or lifting weights in the house.

Then there was Kevin; he'd follow Frankie off to go running or to work out. He was good at almost any sport, but he was always pulled back to the distractions of the street, the wheeling and dealing on Patterson Way. The neighborhood started calling him "Mini Mac" because he was so much smaller than the rest of us.

Even Davey, on his weekend visits home from Mass Mental, had become a character in the brick landscape. He paced up and down the street, with a peculiar high bounce to every step. Some would imitate his bouncy walk, but no one bothered him. Little kids in the neighborhood would call him over to do his famous imitations of the Burger King from the commercials. He'd break away from his intense thinking and walk over to them with a smile. After he did his imitations, back he'd go into his own world, pacing up and down Patterson Way.

Mary's new boyfriend, who we called Jimmy the Greek, would come down the street to pick her up in his long white Lincoln Continental. We'd all stop what we were doing when we heard his horn blast a trumpet charge to announce his arrival. The teenagers all admired his "pimpin' wheels." "What in the hell kind of a horn is that?" Ma would say. Mary said it was a Greek horn. Ma didn't like Jimmy and she just called him "the Greek." She thought he was too old for Mary, since she was sixteen and he was twenty-three. But Mary'd rather date an outsider than the limited pool of project guys who were usually at the center of girl fights.

I noticed that even our new dog, Sarge, having faced his own initiations, now roamed Old Colony forming his own alliances with certain packs of dogs. He'd go to the door to be let out for the day, and in the streets he'd only acknowledge you briefly, as if appearing too attached to us, his family, might make him less of a dog's dog.

Ma was part of the picture outside too, but only momentarily, clacking by in her spike heels and talking to everyone in their windows on her way up to Broadway for a day of grocery shopping and telling stories in the coffee shops. Ma never sat on the stoops, though; she was too worried about her figure. She couldn't get over the amount of sitting the mothers did. "And they're still in their nightgowns no less," she said. "By Christ, that's how they get the wide and flat-as-a-pancake asses." Ma didn't want one of them.

I was in the second grade at the John Boyle O'Reilly public school. When I came home from school every day, there was Coley sitting on the floor watching cartoons. I'd join him. You couldn't distract him when he was watching cartoons. He wouldn't hear a word you said. He'd just laugh away, and wait with anticipation for Bugs Bunny's next move. Sometimes he'd duck his head, or throw a punch at the air, according to whatever was going on in the story. We all liked Coley. He was Ma's best boyfriend. He'd gone sober in those days, and he was always keeping us laughing. Being from Connemara in Ireland, his first language was Gaelic. And he sat there chewing on seaweed while he watched TV. He said they all ate it where he came from. He fixed the house up, building new cabinets, shelves, and even a wooden-box couch that I thought looked like a coffin. He cooked dinner every night for us, before watching his other favorite program, boxing. He was a boxer himself, and he'd throw blocks and punches while he watched the matches too. He actually thought he was in the ring, and you couldn't break his concentration. He never tried to act like he was our father, and he never told us what to do. He was like one of the kids, and I think he knew Ma was the boss.

The second grade was when I started to lie about where I lived. The kids at the O'Reilly were mostly from the housing projects, but we all said we lived in a house. The funny thing was that we all knew who was lying. Sometimes we'd accuse each other of being on welfare and eating "wellie cheese." And we'd tell jokes about each other, about what someone couldn't afford, the "You're so poor" jokes. "You're so poor you can't afford to wipe your ass!" Whatever that meant. Then there were the "Your mother's so poor" jokes, which were always enough to start a brawl.

Ma used to give me a dollar food stamp to buy candy on the way home. I'd stop by the store extra early in the morning to buy something for a nickel so that I'd have the ninety-five cents to show on the way home, when I was with the other kids from school. I didn't want to pull out the food stamp in front of them, even though I'd seen their own mothers shopping with food stamps. Ma was generous with money and sometimes she'd give me two or three dollars in food stamps. But then I'd have to go to two or three stores to buy something for a nickel at each and collect the change. The stores were nice enough about letting kids buy candy or gum, which I don't think was actually allowed by the government. I didn't want to push it, though, by changing three different food stamps in one visit to the same store. Kathy and Kevin would sell theirs on the street for a little less than they were worth, so they could buy some smokes, which was definitely not allowed with food stamps. And one time I brought food stamps to the movie theater on Broadway. I thought no one would see me with them when I tried to buy popcorn, but the popcorn lady got everyone in the lobby laughing as she told the story to whoever came by the counter. "That's the best one yet," she howled. "These people think they can use food stamps for anything they want!" I had to hide from her the rest of the night. A few days later I saw her using food stamps herself at the supermarket, and she got a pack of cigarettes with them.

We all were on food stamps, but most of the jokes around town were about black people on welfare. The same thing with living in the projects and eating wellie cheese—those were black things. So was shoplifting and selling hot goods, although we justified that as long as we didn't steal from businesses within the neighborhood, or from other neighborhood folks. One time when a Southie kid stole another Southie kid's bike, it was called "niggerish." He should've gone into town to get one from a rich college student if he was going to do it at all. But he was new to the neighborhood and hadn't learned the rules yet.

The Boston Housing Authority came through the apartment on a regular basis, to make sure the house was kept up. The house was looking great since Coley had moved in with us, building furniture and cleaning rugs. But whenever the inspectors were coming over with their pens and notebooks, Ma had to get rid of Coley for the day. Our apartment passed inspections, but the project itself wasn't looking too good. The ancient mailboxes in the hallway were falling apart. Everyone had to greet the mailman on welfare check day, so as not to risk having it stolen from a flimsy mailbox. The trash incinerators had the steel shutters broken off, with open flames coming out of the stack. You had to throw your trash from a distance in order to avoid being set on fire. The front doors to the buildings were hanging off their hinges. And when a hallway window broke, it would stay broken through the winter.

Long after the BHA inspectors were gone, when it got dark, the roaches would come out in droves. They didn't like the light, so if you ever got up in the middle of the night, you'd see them scatter all over the place as soon as you flicked the switch. They'd be covering the kitchen floor, carrying food and hovering around the slightest drop of liquid. They loved tonic, especially Sprite. I'd figured this out one morning after I'd left half a glass of Sprite out overnight and had woken up to find about twenty dead cockroaches floating around in the cup. That's when I realized that they had wings too, just like the huge water bug roaches that came out in the summer. But they never used them until they started to drown in the Sprite. They all floated in the cup with their useless wings spread out. I stared at them for a good long time, wondering if they didn't know how to use their wings, or if they just didn't know they had them, until it was too late to save themselves.

We were keeping the house as clean as we could, and the roaches were still taking over. So at night I started to leave all the lights on so I wouldn't have to deal with them if I woke up to go to the bathroom. I also put glasses of Sprite in all the corners of the house, to kill as many as I could. I'd count them in the morning, and one night I got about a hundred. It became fun. We weren't the only ones with the problem. I started to notice that most of the other apartments in Old Colony were also lit up all night long. What did we care. We weren't paying electric bills—that came with the rent. We weren't paying heat bills either, and the project didn't mind blasting the heat into our apartments nine months out of the year. Most people in Old Colony had to leave their windows open all winter long. You couldn't really control the levels on any of the radiators, and the heat would kill you if you ever closed the windows.

I was always shocked to go to my cousins' house in the suburbs, where they'd shut off any light that wasn't being used and turn the heat way down at night. I was used to project heat and would freeze if I ever slept anywhere else. *There's no place like Old Colony,* I thought. All the rules we were learning didn't make any sense anywhere else. Not the rules about heat and light, not the rules about what to wear, not the rules about money. In the suburbs the kids were wearing cheap Wrangler corduroys and scruffy sneakers. Our designer clothes had to be spotless so that no one would call us "project rats" or accuse us of being on welfare. There'd been a few times when Ma had brought home sneakers that cost $1.49 at Kmart, thinking we'd wear them—but no way! Everyone in the neighborhood called the cheap sneakers "bobos." We made Ma get the very best from Skoo-chie's shopping bag of designer goods. She was always generous with whatever money she had. When we'd go to the store with our cousins, we'd ask Ma for a few dollars, whether in food stamps or real money. She'd give me a fiver sometimes. My cousins would each get about a quarter from their mother and father. *And they're the rich ones living in the suburbs with a father and all,* I thought.

* * *

Even though Ma would give us whatever money we wanted, I started to get in on some of the scams local kids would come up with. It wasn't big stuff. We didn't get a lot of money; it was more for something to do. I'd go out to the main intersection outside the project, along with Kevin and my friend Danny, to hit up the commuters going back to the suburbs from their jobs in downtown. We took a tin can from the trash, covered the sides with white lined paper from a notebook, and wrote SOUTH BOSTON YOUTH HOCKEY on it. On the top of the can was a plastic lid with a slit cut into it for dropping money in. We'd approach the drivers, and I couldn't believe how nearly all of them would give us money while they were stopped at the red light.

During rush hour, we'd make about ten bucks each. We started doing it every day, and the only time we were chased away was by one of the drivers who was a local from City Point, who said that he was a coach for South Boston Youth Hockey himself and had never seen us before in his life. Kevin told him we had to save up to buy the hockey sticks and pads and helmets before we could join, and he got out of his car and said he'd better not see us out there again. That's when we changed our labels to OLD COLONY BASKET-BALL. Kids in the project were more likely to play basketball anyway. It was cheap; all you needed was a ball and a hoop. No one at the intersection would know if we were really in a league or not, and certainly no one in Old Colony would care to investigate it. In Old Colony we stuck together.

It was on one of those days at the intersection in the spring of 1974 that we saw the headlights blinking and heard the honking and loudspeakers screaming something about the communists trying to take over South Boston. Everyone came running out of the project to line the streets. At first it was scary, like the end of the world was being announced. But then it seemed more like a parade. It was even

along the same route as the St. Paddy's Day parade. One neighbor
said it was what they called a motorcade. The cars in the motor-
cade never seemed to stop coming. It went on for a good half hour.
Irish flags waved out of car windows and one sign on a car read
WELCOME TO MOSCOW AMERICA. Many more had RESIST or
NEVER written on them. My favorite one was HELL NO SOUTHIE
WON'T GO. That was a good one, I said. I started clapping with
everyone else. But then I had to ask someone, "Where are we not
going?" One of the mothers said, "They're trying to send you to
Roxbury with the niggers. To get a beatin'," she added. Someone else
told her not to say that word to the kids, that they were blacks, not
niggers. "Well it's no time to fight over that one," someone else said.
"It's time now to stick together." When I asked who was trying to
send us, someone told me about Judge Garrity; that a bunch of rich
people from the suburbs wanted to tell us where we had to send our
kids to school; that they wanted us to mix with the blacks, but that
their own kids wouldn't have to mix with no one, because there
were no blacks in the suburbs.

Everyone waved to Dapper O'Neil when he rode by in the motorcade. They loved him. But they got really excited when they saw
Louise Day Hicks, their favorite committee woman. I'd never heard
of her before. She looked nice enough, though, like someone's
grandmother, a tubby older woman with a flowery old-fashioned
dress like Nana wore and a small church hat perched on top of her
round Irish face. People said she was from Southie, but she didn't
have a face that looked like she'd been through much. Her father
was a judge and she lived in a big beachfront house in City Point,
but she was okay with us. "She's the only one sticking up for us,"
someone said. So I liked her too. Someone on a bullhorn started
shouting about the rights of the people, and about not letting the
government force this and force that on us. I knew he was right, and
I felt myself getting angry along with him. And I also knew that
these adults were going to put up a fight for *me*. God, we couldn't

have been living in a better neighborhood! *Everyone's sticking together*, I thought. *Everyone's going to fight for us kids.* We all cheered as the motorcade made its way toward City Point.

When the motorcade had passed, everyone lingered on street corners in the project talking about "forced busing." It was going to begin in the fall, they said. They all seemed to know it was going to happen, but win or lose, everyone believed in going down fighting. I saw neighbors talking, people I knew had grudges against each other before. In the following days, I even saw people who were from different parts of Southie getting over their differences to talk about the busing. Mothers from City Point talking on Broadway to mothers from the projects. I couldn't believe it. The whole feeling in the neighborhood was changing. Before long, we kids could cross any turf line. We were united. Some said it was the communists who were making this happen. Still others said it was rich lawyers, judges, and politicians from the suburbs, and that it had nothing to do with the blacks, that they didn't want to come to Southie any more than we wanted to go to Roxbury. In the end it didn't really matter who we were united against, as long as we kept up our Southie loyalty.

Some of the neighbors raged against "the niggers" more than ever before. But others were starting to talk about how this wasn't about race. That it was about poor people being told that they have to do things that rich people don't have to do. Our mothers couldn't get over people thinking that we had something in our schools that blacks in Roxbury didn't have. "Our kids have just as little," they said. "Neither side has a pot to piss in and now they want us to fight over who can piss in what alley." I couldn't believe that there were people who were now willing to admit they were poor. I'd never heard that one before in Southie, especially not in the project. We weren't poor; that was a black thing, being poor. But the ones who talked about us being poor were few and far between, and it wasn't long before the talk became all "niggers this" and "niggers that."

Toward the end of the school year, we could feel that our lives were about to change. Like most of the mothers in Old Colony and in South Boston, Ma was trying to get us out of the public schools so we wouldn't have to be bused. The first year of busing, Phase One, would only include kids at the high school levels, matching up Roxbury with South Boston. Then the next year, Phase Two, would bring busing to the whole city. But parents were in a race to get their kids into Catholic schools before the seats filled up. The teachers at the John Boyle O'Reilly were talking to each other about how strange it was that the officials had picked the poorest all-black neighborhood and the poorest all-white neighborhood for "their social experiment." Even the second graders at the O'Reilly talked about getting ready for the bloodbath. Ma got us into St. Augustine's School down the road. The priests were letting people pay according to their incomes, and some of the poorer mothers would now have to work St. Augustine's bingo nights for their cheap tuition. I'd been getting to like the O'Reilly School, but I was glad that I'd be able to stay in the neighborhood, away from the bloodbath.

One day that June, we had to stay in our classroom a couple of hours extra. It was getting warm outside and we all wanted to go home and play and get ready for the motorcades, which had become a weekly protest in the neighborhood. But we weren't allowed to leave. We saw the police and state troopers starting to assemble on the streets outside. The teachers told us that they were afraid there would be riots today and that we couldn't go home until it was safe. Racial fights were breaking out around the city after a white woman had been covered in gasoline and set on fire in Roxbury. A police officer came to all of the homerooms to make it clear that we weren't allowed to leave the school. I was scared and just wanted to be with my family. After a while they let us go, and when I got back to Old Colony, with the police cruisers still speeding up and down streets, all the talk in the neighborhood was about the coming race war.

* * *

Along with the craziness and the cockroaches, the summer of 1974 brought with it great anticipation for the fight of our lives. Motorcades and marches became arenas for our daily play. We still set dumpster fires, and a couple times we were able to light up a stolen car, stripped and abandoned in Old Colony, before the BHA finally removed it. But organized protests brought more thrills than anything we'd ever known. Most of the marches and rallies were peaceful, though the threat of violence filled the air. You could hear it in the throats of politicians like Ray Flynn and Dapper O'Neil, who led the cheering crowds. And you could see it in the watery swelled-up eyes of mothers, not sure whether they would cry or lash out. I knew these women were doing everything in their power to do neither, to hide their pain. But what mattered most was seeing how much they cared about us kids, and to tell the truth I wouldn't have minded if they'd brought out the Molotov cocktails from the beginning.

My whole family kept up with the wheres and whens of the motorcades and rallies. In Southie, news spread best through word of mouth—besides we didn't want the other side to sabotage our plans by knowing them ahead of time. Ma started to volunteer for Jimmy Kelly and his South Boston Information Center, which controlled much of the information in the neighborhood. Southie couldn't rely on what Jimmy Kelly called "the liberal media establishment," and whatever that meant I knew I too wanted nothing to do with it. It was us against them, and my family was now part of the "us," as the neighborhood closed off more and more to the outside world.

CHAPTER 4

FIGHT THE
POWER

'Twas on a dreary Thursday morn'
As the buses rolled along.
They came up to our peaceful town
With orders from The Law:
Desegregate and integrate
Or you will pay the price
Of loss of pride, humility,
And even your children's lives.

But Southie's spirit was so strong,
They made us a barrack town.
They took their horses, dogs, and guns
and set them on the crowd.
The TPF, their sticks did crack
On the young and old alike.
But united still, our spirits high,
We'll fight for freedom's right.

—HELEN KING

MA'S TUNES ON THE ACCORDION STARTED TO BE ALL about the busing. She played them at rallies, sit-ins, and fundraisers for the struggle, all over Southie. The songs sounded like a lot of the Irish rebel songs we grew up with. They had the same tunes, but the words had changed: "So come on Southie, head on high / They'll never take our pride...." The Black and Tans, the murderous regiments who'd wreaked havoc on Ireland on behalf of the English Crown, became the TPF (Tactical Police Force), the special force that was turning our town into a police state. The Queen of England was gone from Ma's songs too, her place taken by Judge Garrity, the federal judge who'd mandated busing, "the law of the land": "Judge Garrity and traitors too / We've just begun to fight." Garrity had an Irish name, which made it all the worse, as the Irish hated nothing more than a traitor. That's why we hated Ted Kennedy; he'd sided with the busing too, and was seen as the biggest traitor of all, being from the most important Irish family in America.

The English themselves weren't completely absent from our struggle, though. They ran the *Boston Globe* and were behind the whole thing. My friends and I started stealing stacks of the *Globe* left outside supermarkets in the early mornings. We could sell them for a dime to people on their way to work, who'd have been paying a quarter if it weren't for us. That's when I found out the *Globe* was the enemy. We tried to sell it in Southie, but too many people said they wouldn't read that liberal piece of trash if it was free, that it was to blame for the busing, with all its attacks on South Boston. I heard a few people say it was a communist paper. "Not only are they communists, they're the rich English, keeping up their hate for the Irish and Southie," Coley told me. He showed me the names of the *Globe*'s owners and editors: "Winship, Taylor. All WASPs," he said, "White Anglo Saxon Protestants, forever gettin' back at the Irish for chasing them out of Boston."

Boy, was I confused now that the English were involved. We'd always hated the English for what they did to the Irish. But whatever that was, listening to Ma's Irish songs, I'd thought it was in the past and across a great big ocean. Now it was right here in Southie. I was glad to be doing my part anyway, stealing the *Boston Globe* and making a couple bucks on their loss. The rich English liberal communist bastards!

That September, Ma let us skip the first week of school. The whole neighborhood was boycotting school. City Councilor Louise Day Hicks and her bodyguard with the bullhorn, Jimmy Kelly, were telling people to keep their kids home. It was supposed to be just the high school kids boycotting, but we all wanted to show our loyalty to the neighborhood. I was meant to be starting the third grade at St. Augustine's School. Ma had enrolled Kevin and Kathy in the sixth and seventh grades there as well. Frankie was going to Southie High, and Mary and Joe were being sent to mostly black Roxbury, so they really had something to boycott. But on the first day, Kevin and Kathy begged Ma not to send them. "C'mon Ma, please?" I piped in. It was still warm outside and we wanted to join the crowds that were just then lining the streets to watch the busloads of black kids come into Southie. The excitement built as police helicopters hovered just above our third-floor windows, police in riot gear stood guard on the rooftops of Old Colony, and the national news camped out on every corner. Ma said okay, and we ran up to Darius Court, along the busing route, where in simpler times we'd watched the neighborhood St. Paddy's Day parade.

The whole neighborhood was out. Even the mothers from the stoop made it to Darius Court, nightgowns and all. Mrs. Coyne, up on the rooftop in her housedress, got arrested before the buses even started rolling through the neighborhood. Everyone knew she was a little soft, and I thought the excitement that day must have been a bit too much for her. She ran up to the roof and called the police "nigger lovers" and "traders," and started dancing and singing James Brown songs. "Say it loud, I'm black and I'm proud!" She nearly fell off the roof before one cop grabbed her from behind and restrained

MICHAEL PATRICK MACDONALD

her. Everyone was laughing at that one: big fat Mrs. Coyne rolling around on the rooftop kicking and screaming, with a cop in full riot gear on top of her. Little disturbances like that broke out here and there, but most people were too intent on seeing the buses roll to do anything that might get them carted away.

I looked up the road and saw a squadron of police motorcycles speeding down Dorchester Street, right along the curb, as if they would run over anyone who wasn't on the sidewalk. The buses were coming. Police sirens wailed as hundreds of cops on motorcycles aimed at the crowds of mothers and kids, to clear the way for the law of the land. "Bacon . . . I smell bacon!" a few people yelled, sniffing at the cops. I knew that meant the cops were pigs. As the motorcycles came closer I fought to get back onto the sidewalk, but it was too crowded. I ran further into the road to avoid one motorcycle, when two more came at me from the middle of the street. I had to run across to the other side of the road, where the crowd quickly cleared a space for me on the sidewalk. All the adults welcomed me, patting me on the shoulder. "Are you all right?" "Those pricks would even kill a kid." "Pigs!" someone else shouted. I thought I'd lost Kevin and Kathy, but just then I saw them sitting on top of a mailbox up the street for a good view of the buses. They waved to me, laughing because they'd seen me almost get run over.

The road was cleared, and the buses rolled slowly. We saw a line of yellow buses like there was no end to them. I couldn't see any black faces though, and I was looking for them. Some people around me started to cry when they finally got a glimpse of the buses through the crowd. One woman made the sign of the cross and a few others copied her. "I never thought I'd see the day come," said an old woman next to me. She lived downstairs from us, but I had never seen her leave her apartment before. I'd always thought she was crippled or something, sitting there in her window every day, waiting for Bobby, the delivery man who came daily with a package from J. J.'s Liquors. She was trembling now, and so was everyone else. I could feel it myself. It was a feeling of loss, of being beaten down, of humiliation. In minutes, though, it had turned to anger, rage, and hate, just like in those Irish rebel songs I'd heard all my life. Like "The Ballad of James Connolly": "God's curse on you England / You cruel hearted monster / Your deeds they would shame all the devils in Hell." Except we'd changed it to "God's curse on you Garrity."

Smash! A burst of flying glass and all that rage exploded. We'd all been waiting for it, and so had the police in riot gear. It felt like a gunshot, but it was a brick. It went right through a bus window. Then all hell broke loose. I saw a milk crate fly from the other side of the street right for my face. More bricks, sticks, and bottles smashed against the buses, as police pulled out their billy clubs and charged with their riot shields in a line formation through the crowds. Teenagers were chased into the project and beaten to the cement wherever they were caught.

I raced away about a block from the fray, to a spot where everyone was chanting "Here We Go Southie, Here We Go," like a battle cry. That's when I realized we were at war. I started chanting too, at first just moving my lips because I didn't know if a kid's voice would ruin the strong chant. But then I belted it out, just as a few other kids I didn't know joined the chorus. The kids in the crowd all looked at each other as if we were family. *This is great,* I thought. I'd never had such an easy time as this, making friends in Southie. The buses kept passing by, speeding now, and all I could see in the windows were black hands with their middle fingers up at us, still no faces though.

The buses got through the crowd surrounded by the police motorcycles. I saw Frankie running up toward Southie High along with everyone else. "What are you doing out here!" he yelled. "Get your ass home!" He said there was another riot with the cops up at the high school, and off he ran with the others. Not far behind were Kevin and his friends. He shouted the same thing at me: "Get your ass home!" I just wanted to find Ma now and make sure she wasn't beaten or arrested or anything, so I ran home. The project was empty—everyone had followed the buses up the St. Paddy's parade route. Ma wasn't home, but the TV was on, with live coverage of the riots at Southie High. Every channel I turned to showed the same thing. I kept flipping the dial, looking for my family, and catching glimpses of what seemed to be all the people I knew hurling stones or being beaten by the police, or both. *This is big,* I thought. It was scary and thrilling at the same time, and I remembered the day we'd moved into this neighborhood, when Ma said it looked just like Belfast, and that we were in the best place in the world. I kept changing the channels, looking for my family, and I didn't know anymore whether I was scared or thrilled, or if there was any difference between the two anyhow.

The buses kept rolling, and the hate kept building. It was a losing battle, but we returned to Darius Court every day after school to see if the rage would explode again. Sometimes it did and sometimes it didn't. But the bus route became a meeting place for the neighborhood. Some of my neighbors carried big signs with RESIST or NEVER or my favorite, HELL NO WE WON'T GO. There was always someone in the crowd keeping everyone laughing with wisecracks aimed at the stiff-looking state troopers who lined the bus route, facing the crowds to form a barrier. They never moved or showed any expression. We all wanted to get them to react to something. But we wanted a reaction somewhere between the stiff inhuman stance and the beatings. When my friends and I tried to get through to them by asking questions about their horses and could we pet them, they told us to screw. And it wasn't long before some kids started trying to break the horses' legs with hockey sticks when riots broke out. One day the staties got distracted by a burning effigy of Judge Garrity that came flying off a rooftop in the project. That's when I saw Kevin make his way out of Darius Court to throw a rock at the buses. A trooper chased him, but Kevin was too fast. His photo did end up in the *Boston Globe* the next day, though, his scrawny shirtless body whipping a rock with all his might. It looked like the pictures we'd always seen of kids in war-torn countries throwing petrol bombs at some powerful enemy. But Kevin's rock hit a yellow bus with black kids in it.

I threw a rock once. I had to. You were a pussy if you didn't. I didn't have a good aim, though, and it landed on the street before it even made it to the bus. I stared at my rock and was partly relieved. I didn't really want it to smash a bus window. I only wanted the others to see me throwing it. On that day there were so many rocks flying that you didn't know whose rock landed where, but everyone claimed the ones that did the most damage. Even though I missed, a cop came out of nowhere and treated me just like they treated the kids with good aim. He took me by the neck and threw me to the dirt. I sat there for a few minutes to make sure that everyone had seen that one. I was only eight, but I was part of it all, part of something bigger than I'd ever imagined, part of something that was on the national news every night.

Every day I felt the pride of rebellion. The helicopters above my bedroom window woke me each morning for school, and my friends and I would plan to pass by the TPF on the corners so we could walk around them and give them hateful looks. Ma and the nuns at St. Augustine's told me it was wrong to hate the blacks for any of this. But I had to hate someone, and the police were always fracturing some poor neighbor's skull or taking teenagers over to the beach at night to beat them senseless, so I hated them with all my might. SWAT teams had been called into the neighborhood. I'd always liked the television show "S.W.A.T.," but they were the enemy now. We gave the SWAT sharpshooters standing guard over us on the rooftops the finger; then we'd run. Evenings we had to be off the streets early or else the cops would try to run us down with their motorbikes. No more hanging out on corners in Old Colony. A line of motorbikes straight across the street and sidewalks would appear out of nowhere and force everyone to disappear into hallways and tunnels. One time I had to jump into a bush because they were coming from both ends of the street. I was all cut up, and I really hated them then.

It felt good, the hate I had for the authorities. My whole family hated them, especially Frankie, Kathy, and Kevin, who got the most involved in the riots. I would've loved to throw Molotov cocktails myself, along with some of the adults, but I was only a kid and the cops would probably catch me and beat me at the beach. So I just fantasized about killing them all. They were the enemy, the giant oppressor, like Goliath. And the people of South Boston were like David. Except that David won in the end, and we knew we were going to lose this one. But that made us even more like the Irish, who were always fighting in the songs even if they had to lose and die a glorious death.

One Friday in early October we took part in what Louise Day Hicks called National Boycott Day. Everyone boycotted school again. We'd all heard about the kids who'd gone to school during boycotts and who were threatened over the phone with getting their things cut off. Kevin told Ma we'd better not risk castration, and we got to stay home and watch the rally and march down Broadway. The rally was a good one. When the thousands of people sang the national anthem, with their right hands over their chests, I cried. It was as if we were singing about an America that we wanted but didn't have, especially the part about the land of the free. Louise Day Hicks really squealed that part out from the bandstand microphone, and we all knew what she was getting at.

When the rally was over, the crowds marched to Judge Garrity's home in the Boston suburb of Wellesley. We weren't allowed to go because Ma thought people would surely be arrested. I wanted to go because I'd heard that where the Judge lived everyone was rich and white and I wanted to see what they looked like. But I couldn't, so I just watched the march on its way down Broadway.

The signs at the marches were starting to change. Instead of RE-STORE OUR ALIENATED RIGHTS and WELCOME TO MOSCOW AMERICA, more and more now I saw BUS THE NIGGERS BACK TO AFRICA, and one even said KKK. I was confused about that one.

The people in my neighborhood were always going on about being Irish, with shamrocks painted on the brick walls and tattooed to their arms. And I had always heard stories from Grandpa about a time when the Ku Klux Klan burned Irish Catholics out of their homes in America. I thought someone should beat up the guy with the KKK sign, but no one seemed to mind that much. I told my friend Danny about the Ku Klux Klan burning out the Irish families, and that the guy with the KKK sign was in the wrong town. He laughed. He said he'd never heard that one before. "Shut up," he said. "They just hate the niggers. What, d'ya wanna be a nigger?" *Jesus no,* I thought to myself.

With National Boycott Day, everything got more scary. In the afternoon, after all the speeches, chants, and the tearful national anthem, crowds gathered at Darius Court once again to taunt the police and to throw rocks at the buses. The TPF chased one man into the Rabbit Inn tavern across the street, and a crowd of people at the bar protected him from the cops. Everyone knew the Rabbit Inn was no place to mess with. That's where the Mullen gang hung out—the toughest bar in Southie. The next night, after dark, we were all called out of our apartments in Old Colony. The mothers on the stoop were yelling up to windows that the TPF was beating people at the Rabbit Inn to get back at them for the night before. Ma wasn't home, so I ran to Darius Court with all of the neighbors, some of them carrying baseball bats, hockey sticks, and big rocks. When I got there, the dark streets were packed with mobs rushing the police. I saw Kevin running through a maze of people carrying a boulder with both hands. He was excited and told me that the TPF had beat the shit out of everyone at the Rabbit Inn, with their police badges covered. Just then I saw people covered in blood being taken from the bar into the converging ambulances.

The mothers in Old Colony showed their Southie loyalty that night. They went up against the entire police force that was filling the streets. I kept getting knocked around by bigger people running in all directions. Someone said the TPF had split open an eleven-year-old's head. I pushed through the crowd to get a look at the kid, and was relieved to see through all the blood that he wasn't Kevin. I wondered if I'd better get home, in case people started getting killed. As the sirens screeched, I saw the blue lights flashing onto the face of Mary Beth Duggan, a four-year-old from the project sitting on her big brother's shoulders and smiling at all the excitement. I figured if she could stay out then so could I.

Someone propped up his stereo speakers in a project window, blasting a favorite at the time: "Fight the Power" by the Isley Brothers. We always did that in Old Colony, blare our speakers out of our windows for the whole neighborhood to hear. It was obvious this guy was doing it for good background music to the crashes and thumps of battle.

Everyone sang along to "Fight the Power." The teenagers in Southie still listened only to black music. The sad Irish songs were for the older people, and I never heard anyone listening to rock and roll in Old Colony. One time an outsider walked through Old Colony wearing a dungaree vest with a big red tongue and THE ROLLING STONES printed on the back. He was from the suburbs and was visiting his cousins in Old Colony. He got a bottle thrown at his head and was called a pussy. Rock and roll was for rich suburban people with long hair and dirty clothes. Mary had a similar tongue painted on her bedroom wall, but that was for Rufus and Chaka Khan; it was okay to like them. Of course no one called it black music—we couldn't see what color anyone was from the radio—but I knew the Isley Brothers were black because I'd seen them on "Soul Train." But that didn't bother anyone in the crowd; what mattered was that the Isley Brothers were singing about everything we were watching in our streets right now, the battle between us and the law: "And when I rolled with the punches I got knocked on the ground / By all this bullshit goin' down."

The mob started pushing and swaying toward the cop cars, blocking them from going down the street. Mrs. Coyne was out there again, and was the first to put a bat through a police windshield. Then everyone surrounded the cops and smashed all of their windows. I started to see things fly through the air: pipes, bricks, bats, and even a hubcap.

Just then I saw my mother pushing through the crowd, yelling at me to run home. "They're beating kids!" she screamed. She kept getting knocked from side to side. She grabbed me by the collar and said she couldn't find Kevin and Kathy; she had a crying voice on her. I didn't want to go home without her, but she made me, while she went looking through the crowds, dodging everything flying through the air. Later on Ma dragged Kevin and Kathy home and gave into us for running up to Darius Court to join the riot. Frankie was still up there, Ma couldn't find him, and we were mad that the three of us couldn't do everything that the older kids could. Ma couldn't yell at us for long; Kevin drowned her out by blasting the television news reports. And soon we were all glued to the set once again, watching for those we knew in the crowd getting dragged into paddy wagons at Darius Court.

On Monday Ma made me, Kevin, and Kathy go back to St. Augustine's. There were no buses coming that day because the NAACP had taken the black students to some kind of meeting at the University of Massachusetts. The black leaders were asking for federal troops to be brought into South Boston, and wanted to see what the black teenagers thought about all that. We didn't want the troops; it was bad enough with the state troopers, SWAT teams, and the TPF, who Ma called "the Gestapo."

We walked to school past Darius Court and up Dorchester Street. The streets were completely empty, still littered with all the things that had flown through the air on Saturday night. Fewer teenagers were finding a reason to go to school anymore, unless they wanted to get in fights. And on this Monday morning everyone had heard on the radio that the buses weren't coming that day, so many in Old Colony stayed home. The silence on Dorchester Street was spooky.

I was walking with my head down, looking at all the garbage in the street, when Kevin came up from behind and pushed me. I went flying and when I looked up I saw that I'd been headed straight for a bloody pig's head on top of a post. I let out a yell that should have woken up the neighborhood. I looked up the street, and it looked like something from a horror movie. More signposts with pigs' heads on top of them, some with apples in their mouths. Blood was on the street, scrawled into letters that said KILL THE PIGS or FUCK THE POLICE. We touched the pig's head—we'd never seen real pigs before. I pushed an eyeball and it squished, and then it fell out of the socket onto my shoe. I yelled again. The whole thing seemed more violent than anything I'd seen yet. Whoever had decorated the street with pigs' heads must have been pretty pissed off, I thought, killing some innocent pigs to send a message to the cops.

That afternoon, everyone gathered at Darius Court again, even though there were no buses. The pigs' heads were gone, but you could still see FUCK THE POLICE on the street. The neighborhood was still upset about the TPF beating on women and children at the Rabbit Inn. They were all talking about it when we came upon the crowd. The crowds started chanting again: "Here we go Southie, Here we go!" A circle of teens started rocking a police car that had been left in the middle of the street while the cops chased some kid who'd thrown a boulder at them. They rocked the cruiser from side to side, and just when it rocked high enough they tipped it over on its head. The cops chased them too, but they got away through the maze of tunnels and hallways and ended up on a rooftop at Darius Court, where they threw fistfulls of pebbles onto the heads of their pursuers, who by that time had given up all the chasing and were now inspecting their upside-down cruiser.

I ran further up Dorchester Street when I heard the gunshot. There was a commotion at Jolly Donuts. A cop stood at the intersection with his gun pointed in the air, and he fired a second shot. He was trying to disperse a crowd that was dragging a black man from his car. The man ran from the crowd as people threw rocks at him.

More and more angry people ganged up on the black man, who I could see was crying. He was trying to get away, but there was nowhere to go. He ran to a house just outside the project, and tried to climb over a railing. "Kill the nigger!" my neighbor shouted. That was Molly's mother, running to join the commotion. Everyone made fun of Molly at school because they had seen her mother bleeding down the legs of her pants more than once. They said she was so poor she couldn't afford a Kotex pad. But she wasn't as bad off now as the black man, who was clenching his fingers onto the railing of the house before the boys dragged him onto the pavement and beat his skull with baseball bats and hockey sticks. The people living in the house were no help; they booted his fingers off their railing. A photographer flashed his camera at the man from all angles: hands reaching for an escape, baseball bat to the ribs, crying face to the pavement. I remember the man's tears clearing paths in the blood on his face. That's how close I was to him. Scores of police came to the corner at Jolly Donuts and brought out their tear gas and riot shields, and another riot broke out. Kathy and Kevin brought me home and I was sick: sick of the police, sick of busing, sick of being thrilled or scared, and sick of the hate.

The next day it was all over the news. Some pictures were from angles that I could've taken myself if I'd had a camera. Once again I was seeing a replay on the news of what I'd just seen in real life. I was sick of the news too. The newsman said that there were no suspects in the beating that almost killed the man, who was from Haiti and had been on his way through Southie to pick up his wife at a laundromat. I went back to the site where he was beaten. I don't know why I was drawn there—maybe I had to feel the sadness, like at a funeral. I saw an aluminum baseball bat covered in blood and wondered why the cops hadn't taken it in for evidence, fingerprints and all that. *Whose side are they on, anyway?* I thought. They certainly weren't on our side, and now I knew they probably weren't on the Haitian's side either.

Ma was mad about the beating, and I was glad about that, because

I didn't like being the only one around who wanted to talk about it. No one else ever mentioned it again. It never happened. "He probably had no idea what he was driving into," Ma said. She called him a scapegoat, and I knew exactly what that meant even though I'd never heard it before. I'd seen it. He was new to this country and probably didn't even know about South Boston or Old Colony. He mustn't have known that we all hated the communists, Judge Garrity, the rich liberals, the *Globe*, and the cops, who were all to blame for the pain in our lives, and he didn't expect that he'd be the only one my neighbors could get their hands on . . . someone worse off than us, a nigger.

The day after the Haitian man was beaten, the news said that a white man driving through Roxbury had been stoned and beaten unconscious by about two hundred black teenagers roaming the streets, setting fires, and smashing things. They showed the pictures. It looked like Darius Court, except everyone was black. The news reports made it seem like the blacks were getting back at us. The white guy wasn't from Southie, though. No way! No one from Southie would drive through Roxbury; most people I knew had never even been outside the neighborhood, and since busing no one wanted ever to leave again. When I was smaller we used to spend hours at the welfare office in Roxbury, with black and white mothers and kids. Never again!

Nor were we welcome in too many places outside Southie now. But going downtown once in a while was the only way to get away from Mayor White's "rule of three," which made it illegal in Southie for more than two people to stand around on the corners. Kevin and his friends went downtown to scam, so I sometimes followed them. One time they showed me and Danny how to rob the parking meters for bags full of quarters, and we were chased home by a bunch of black kids who knew we were from Southie. We had to run all the way back to the Broadway Bridge, which blacks could never cross over unless they were in a yellow bus. Kevin swore at

Danny for wearing his green jogging suit with a shamrock and SOUTHIE on the back. Kevin's friend Okie showed us how he'd covered up the Southie dot on his wrist, the way he always did when he went into town, pulling his sleeves down past his hands.

Ma wanted us to stay away from the troubles. But as much as we tried, it was all around us. You couldn't help being in the middle of it unless you stayed home all the time. And there was nothing to do at home except set traps for the cockroaches. We were getting used to all the craziness from the busing; now on top of it all, it seemed as if the confusion was spilling into people's homes. Teenagers in the neighborhood had started dropping out of school, especially once the police had gained a firm presence at Southie High. State troopers and the TPF were almost in a competition, it seemed, to flex their muscle on our streets. They did their drills in formation up and down Dorchester Street and around the high school. "Hup, two, three, four," with their boots crashing on the road every day before and after school. People still lined the streets to protest, and Louise Day Hicks, Ray Flynn, and Jimmy Kelly kept the rallies going, but the younger people were losing all interest in school. It seemed that all at once, the girls who would've been juniors and seniors were pregnant. And teenagers spent a good part of their day figuring where they could hang out without being caught and arrested for drinking.

Even though Kevin was in Catholic school, most of his friends were in public school and playing hooky to hang out or go into town to pull scams, like the one with the parking meters. He was doing poorly at St. Augustine's, and the nuns didn't like his sense of humor. He'd get everyone in class laughing by asking the teacher a question that had nothing to do with the long speech she had just given about the Assumption of Our Lady.

One time Sister Veronica threw him out of class, and instead of waiting outside the door, he wandered the corridors pulling pranks on the other classrooms. He came to my third-grade class, knocked on the door, poked his head in, and asked the teacher if she had a spare pencil. Everyone knew my teacher was a pushover. She wasn't a real nun—they called her a lay minister, and she could never control a class. Miss Shea gave him a pencil and he left. A minute later he knocked again while she was mid-sentence in a lesson, and asked her if she had a pencil sharpener. She sighed, and let him use the sharpener on the windowsill. The whole class was silent as he took his time sharpening away and blowing the sawdust off the tip of his new pencil. He finally left. A minute later, he knocked again, interrupting the lesson once more, and asked if Miss Shea had an eraser to go with the pencil. The whole class burst out laughing, and she chased him down the hall. But that was when Kevin did go to school. When Ma found out he was playing hooky, she got so mad, with all the money she was spending to send him to St. Augustine's, that she wanted to give him a beating. He ran too fast for her, though, and slept in an abandoned car in Old Colony for a few nights, till Ma cooled off.

Kathy was getting more involved with boys and dating the toughest guys around, the ones with the criminal faces, as Ma said. She'd turned thirteen, and was thrilled no longer to be one of the "three little kids." She hooked school sometimes, and went into town to shoplift with her friends. She hung out with Linda Coyne and Doreen Cassio. The three of them got arrested one day for climbing up the side of the State House. Kathy had a hammer and chisel in her hand and said they were trying to chip the gold from the dome on top of the building. She said they'd almost made it up to the dome when a state trooper yelled, "Freeze!" She said Doreen Cassio got her into that one. Doreen had started to stay at our house. She was running away from home, and told Ma that her father was digging a big hole in their yard to bury her alive in. She showed us all the bruises from the beatings he'd given her. Ma wanted to call the cops, but Doreen begged her not to. No one in Southie really trusted the cops anymore, so Ma just let her stay at our apartment on the couch. Kathy was always adding runaway girls to our family.

Before he dropped out, Frankie was still enjoying the fights at

Southie High. He had big fists and a hatred for blacks since he'd been beaten and stabbed on his way to Boston Tech in Roxbury. When he left Tech, he entered Southie High set on revenge. So whenever Ma heard the police sirens heading up to the high school, she put on the TV to get the news flashes that always came on when there was another riot. She watched, afraid she would see Frankie being arrested for starting another fight. But at least he was going to school, which was more than many of the other kids in Southie were doing. One day in December when I was home with the flu, the sirens kept passing by for a good half hour. Ma turned on the news and heard that a white South Boston teenager had been critically stabbed at the high school. They didn't know his name. Ma had a crying voice and told me to go outside and find out; she knew there'd be more information out on the streets.

There was hardly anyone outside, but those I did see were running up to the high school, carrying things to fight with. At the high school the streets were so crowded you couldn't move. They were tipping over police cars once again. Just when I'd made it through the crowd, a woman pulled me back by the arm and I fell onto the pavement. She had saved me from being trampled by a police horse. The cops on horses were charging at people, the horses climbing on top of the rioting crowds with their two front legs. I remember looking at the horses and thinking that they didn't look as if they wanted to be doing the stunts their masters were forcing on them, knocking people's heads with their hooves. I found out it wasn't Frankie who was stabbed, but a kid named Michael Faith.

They'd made all the white kids leave the building. So now the black kids were in the high school trapped by the thousands of people that I was standing with. I wanted to get home to tell Ma the news, but now I was stuck. We were surrounded. The police had us trapped, while we all had the blacks trapped. If I left the safety of the crowd, I'd be run over by one of the horses or motorcycles that were surrounding us. And now came the staties, marching in all kinds of crazy formations. You couldn't tell what direction they would turn next, and if you were ever in their way, forget it. The only way out was up, and now that was covered by a helicopter flying in circles above our heads. It kept coming at us to scare us off, then changing direction instead of killing us all. Nothing scared this crowd—the people just gave the helicopter the finger and screamed things into the choppy wind that I couldn't hear. I didn't get home for another two hours, when the riot had simmered down, but all the way home people were still worked up. Teenagers on the corners were doing what they always did at the end of a day of battle: drinking and retelling stories of fights, reenacting blow after blow in slow motion. Michael Faith was in critical condition.

Ma said at this point what's the use in going to school. It certainly wasn't worth the risk of getting killed. Frankie was ready to quit after being kicked out so many times for getting in fights. He'd knocked out one black kid at Southie High and was suspended for ten days. When he'd come back, he'd knocked out another black kid as soon as he walked through the high school doors, and got suspended for twenty days. After twenty days out of school, he'd had no idea what the teacher was going on about at the front of the class. Then yet another racial fight broke out in the classroom, and Frankie'd knocked out one more black kid. That's when they suspended him for thirty days, and Frankie never went back. By the ninth grade he was a dropout, and Ma couldn't afford to send any more kids to Catholic school. I was surprised that Frankie'd ended up a dropout; he was the one who'd always made me sit down after school to recite all of the times tables for him. I knew the times tables before the rest of my class had even started studying them. And besides that, he'd been admitted to Boston Tech in the seventh grade, which meant he was smart, because Tech was an exam school. But that was all before he was stabbed, and long before the buses started to roll.

Mary left school too. She'd recently walked by a black table in English High's cafeteria—black kids sat with blacks, whites with whites—when one of the girls stood in front of her and accused her of trying to have hair like a black girl. Mary had naturally tight curly hair that spread out big and wide on its own. "You wanna look like one of us?!" the black girl said. Mary had already been jumped by a gang of black girls and had had enough. She said back, "What the fuck would I want looking like the ugly bitch that you are?" Then the whole cafeteria erupted into a food fight, which was becoming an everyday occurrence. Mary got jabbed deep with an Afro pick. She never went back to school after that, and Ma didn't blame her—she just got after her to get enrolled in night school at Southie High. Mary started working full time at Jolly Donuts.

Around the same time, Johnnie was getting his cap and gown ready for graduation from Boston Latin School, and I wondered if this would be one of the few family high school graduations I'd ever see. It was.

"Get your coats on," Ma said. "We're gonna pay Coley a visit in the hospital." She was talking to Johnnie, Joe, and Frank, since they could protect her while she gave Coley the beating she intended to. Coley was in the Carney Hospital in Dorchester. He'd had an operation on account of something happening to his pancreas from all the years of drinking. But that was the least of his problems; he'd put Ma in a rage, denying that he was Seamus's father. He wasn't Seamus yet, actually; we didn't even know if it was a boy or a girl that Ma had inside of her. Anyway, off they went to Coley's bedside, Ma four months pregnant, protected by her three muscled bodyguards, determined never to let a man fuck her over again, no victims here.

I waited up, and when they got back I heard them retelling the story to each other, laughing their heads off. They'd been arrested but it was all worth it. "Did you see the son of a bitch shaking in his bed?" Ma laughed. She pulled the curtain around Coley's bed and told his roommate to sit still. "We're only gonna take care of this guy," she said. With the curtain closed, Ma started ripping tubes and shutting off machines. She yanked the two tubes that were going up Coley's nose to drain some kind of fluid out of him. Then she sucker punched him a few times. The boys just watched. She said the other guy in the room was scared shitless when he got a look at Coley, all beat up, pressing some button for the nurse, and screaming something in his Connemara Gaelic. When they ran down the back stairwell of the Carney, they were stopped by two doctors who couldn't restrain them. That's when security was called and they were brought in for questioning. The security guards sided with Ma when she told them about Coley denying his kid. "You shoulda kicked him in the balls too," said one of them.

Ma filed a complaint, bringing Coley up on charges for punching her in the stomach. He never did punch her in the stomach. Ma could beat him in a fight even if he wasn't in a hospital bed. She just wanted to file before he did. Besides, he'd done something far worse than punching her in the stomach—he'd abandoned his own kid that was inside her, a kid with no defenses, except for the wrath of Ma. I liked Coley and felt bad when I pictured him twisted up like a pretzel after Ma got through with him. And since I didn't remember Mac, it was scary to see such fury—as I'd only known in the riots—creep into our home. But my thoughts turned to wondering if my own father had denied me. *If he had, he'd deserve the same thing Coley got, maybe worse,* I thought. *He'd deserve the wrath of the TPF!* To me there was nothing worse than a no-good bastard of a father. But I put those thoughts out of my head, reassuring myself that I had a good father, as Ma had told me. Sure enough, Coley did press charges: assault and battery. And Ma was scheduled to appear in court after the St. Paddy's Day holiday.

St. Patrick's Day 1975 brought more armed camps to our town. The authorities figured that with all the drinking, the Southie people would erupt into antibusing violence once more. There were so many TPF, state troopers, and army types on the sidelines of the parade that we kids could hardly see the step dancers or the posters with the faces of Irish martyrs from the 1916 rebellion. We heard the bagpipes, but whenever any of us climbed a mailbox or lamppost for a better view, some cop on a horse came at us with his club drawn. *The whole thing's ruined,* I thought.

I found a staircase to stand on just as Southie started to let out roars for our saviors from the busing terror: City Councilor Louise Day Hicks, head to toe in the brightest green old lady clothes, followed by her right-hand man, Jimmy Kelly, a gangster from the Mullen gang, looking more like a politician since the busing started; Senator Billy Bulger, comical smirk and green tie, marching straight-shouldered and strong, and bouncing the shelaliegh he gripped, as if he were the conductor and we the orchestra; Representative Ray Flynn, out of breath because of all the jogging he was doing from handshake to handshake, zigzagging Broadway and pointing at each of us as if he knew us personally. He had one of those red faces that looked like it was melting, like the guys who sat on the wino wall on Broadway. Then there was Dapper, who marched down the street, fists clenched and a scowl on his face, as if he was looking for Judge Garrity himself to personally rip his throat out. The parade was turning into an antibusing rally, a political one. I only wanted to see more floats, with shamrocks and the guy dressed up like St. Patrick chasing the snakes out of Ireland.

I had a great time anyway, and whenever I saw Kevin, he had another green plastic bugle or ENGLAND GET OUT OF IRELAND button for me and Danny, stolen from one of the stands. He even gave Kathy a kelly green woolen scally cap, and she wore it tilted sideways, just like her little gangster boyfriends. Kevin also gave her his last STOP FORCED BUSING pin with a shamrock in the middle. When the adults disappeared into the bars that lined Broadway, gangs of kids roamed the streets looking for ways to get in on all the booze that was flowing or the fights that were breaking out with outsiders who'd come to Southie for the parade. I went with my cousin Paul, Nellie's son, to wait for our mothers outside the Car Stop Cafe. Ma was playing the accordion there, and I knew she'd have all kinds of free food in her pocketbook when she came out. I'd have to share it with Paul, though, because Nellie would have none. She was just in there to drink, while Ma was scamming up some cash and food.

As we were waiting, paddy wagons sped right up to the door of the Car Stop. Cops got out with billy clubs. Then more police cars came wailing down the street, a whole line of them stretching two blocks. Then the TPF showed up, jumping out of a big police bus, with their helmets on and shields drawn. They all charged into the Car Stop, which was packed to begin with. I saw through the door that they were strutting slowly through the bar, banging their billy clubs on each table they passed until the whole place was filled with the organized rhythm of thumps. I was terrified and tried to get in, yelling, "Ma!" A cop pushed me out the door onto the pavement, and I could see through the window that someone had shut off all the lights. That's when they started beating everyone senseless. Paul didn't seem too worried—he knew Nellie would be all right some-how, like she always was when she got drunk. But Ma was pregnant, and I thought she'd be dead.

The door opened again and I saw one of the TPF beat into the skull of an old man who was on all fours under a table. I started crying and ran home to find my big brothers. Paul sat in front of the bar waiting for his mother, as if none of it fazed him at all. When I got home, there was Ma climbing the stairs, in her green maternity suit and spike heels. She was holding her head. She said the Gestapo had knocked her on the head but that she was fine. She'd slid out the back door of the bar, down a narrow corridor filled with cases of beer. She said she almost didn't fit through, with her stomach and her accordion. She didn't know what happened to Nellie. "They're gonna kill people down there," she said.

Ma turned her big leather pocketbook upside down and dumped all kinds of corned beef, Irish bread, and potatoes onto the kitchen table. It was all squished between wet napkins that had to be peeled off. She told us she'd been the cause of the riot at the Car Stop, with her accordion. She'd been playing her favorite reel "The Siege of

Ennis," when the owner announced that the bar was closed. He was trying to get rid of one troublemaker who was drunk and starting fights. The owner ordered Ma to stop the music. He said the party was over. Ma stopped, but then the troublemaker ordered her to keep playing. "He was this big fat truck driver," she said, stretching her arms out to show us the width of him. She'd started playing again while he stood over her, clapping his hands to the reels. That's when the owner called the police. "He probably figured one or two cops might come and get rid of the guy," she said. She let out a big sigh and plopped herself onto the couch with her feet up. "Make me a cup of tea," she said. "Jesus Christ, it's good to be home." I put on the kettle. I was glad she was home too, but I didn't tell her that I'd been outside the bar scared that she'd be dead. "That'll teach him not to call the cops in Southie. They destroyed the place." Everyone knew that the cops were the enemy and that you shouldn't call them unless you wanted the Gestapo, marching in with their boots and shields, looking for bones to break.

We didn't see Nellie for a couple more days, not until Ma had to go to court for beating up Coley. When we got to the courthouse, there was Nellie in a lineup of people who were being charged with inciting a riot at the Car Stop Cafe on St. Paddy's Day. She looked like a raccoon, with two black eyes and a big purple nose. And some of her partners in crime in the lineup looked worse than she did for the beatings they took from the cops. "What in the Christ happened to you?" Ma said, covering her mouth in shock at the sight of Nellie. Nellie said the TPF had beaten the shit out of her. The two of them were laughing hysterically. "Well, isn't this a great bit of luck," Ma whispered to her. "When you get done with the arraignment come upstairs to my courtroom—you'll be my prize witness against Coley. I'm gonna say he gave you a beating too."

Nellie loved to play the actress in any real-life drama. She fell right into the victim role. She walked into Ma's courtroom with her head down. The room was packed with people waiting to go before the judge for "drunk and disorderly," wife-beating, writing phony checks, and so on. Everyone stopped to look at Nellie, as she shuffled her feet through the court to sit next to Ma on the front bench. Ma had to keep her own head down to keep the judge from seeing her laugh. Coley looked back at Nellie, and he knew the two of them were up to something. He got so nervous, the piece of paper he held in his hand, some kind of note from a doctor, started to rattle. When Ma got to speak before the judge she said, "Your honor, he punched me in the stomach where you can't see any damage that could've been done, but look at what he did to my cousin who's just off the boat from Ireland looking for a better life." She paused, then yelled, "Two black eyes!" She pointed to Nellie behind her, who now stood up from her seat, a proud witness. Nellie piped up in her Kerry accent, "And a broken nose!"

The clerk who knew Ma told Coley he'd better drop the charges, and he did. Ma agreed to drop her charges too, but that didn't stop Judge Concannon from letting into Coley about the coward that he was, hitting a pregnant woman, and that he should know better, being an Irish immigrant himself, about how hard it is for someone like Nellie to get accustomed to a new land without the likes of him showing off his manhood in America. Later the whole family was in stitches at the table, with Nellie still playing her role. "That'll teach the little man to hit me again!" she said. I think she was starting to convince herself that Coley really had beat her—that's the actress Nellie was. And there was no mention of the TPF at all; we'd forgotten all about them.

The buses were gone for the summer, and we were left with our frustrations and anger, with high school dropouts, alcoholism, and drugs galore. Ours was one of the worst buildings in Old Colony for trying to sleep on the humid nights. Not only were the lights on all night for the cockroaches, but the Duggans were always up late breaking things and beating each other. Moe Duggan, one of the few fathers I ever saw in Old Colony, came home drunk and beat on all six kids, while the mother screamed and tried to tear him off. She put up a pretty good fight most times, and he never seemed to beat her, just the kids. Then there was Molly next door. Her wall was against mine, and it was always banging with her head. She and her mother were always shrieking and chasing each other around the room, and I could never tell who was winning. They were both the same size, about four and a half feet, and everyone called them dwarfs. Al lived across the courtyard from us, and sat up all night drinking at his kitchen window. He'd invite the neighborhood teenagers up to join him, and they'd all get into a screaming fistfight by about four in the morning. He was always in his tank top, boxer shorts, and black socks pulled up to his knees. The mothers sat out on the front stoop until early morning, watching a TV that they'd carried outside. They'd talk about Al, looking up to his window occasionally, waiting for something to happen. On some mornings you'd see people who'd never gone to bed, chasing a good friend of theirs down the street with a baseball bat. "That's what the booze will do to ya," Ma said.

I knew there'd be trouble that hot day in August, when the neighbors all came out to get a good seat on the stoop. I heard the ladies on the stoop talking about how Chickie was pissed because Kevin had broken her window playing stickball. Chickie slammed the steel door to our building behind her. She was drinking. She swayed her skinny hips right past me down a couple of steps. She put her long fingers to the side of her mouth to send a message up to Ma: "Helen MacDonald's a fuckin' douchebaaaag!" she sang. I looked at her with big eyes, in shock. She didn't even take notice of me. She walked further down the front steps, holding onto the railing. "Helen MacDonald's a dickie puller!" she was singing, looking up to our window for a reaction. I ran up to the apartment. Ma was limping over to the parlor window, hands to her back, to help support her stomach. She was eight months pregnant and carrying huge. "What in the Christ!" she said to herself, looking down at Chickie, whose two eyes were magnified and distorted by the thick glasses on her tiny head. Chickie yelled some more swears up to the window. Just then Mary came around the corner into the front courtyard, and Ma told her to wait down there. When Ma got down-stairs, one hand to the railing, the other to her back, she told Mary to cover her in case Chickie's boyfriend jumped in. Chickie was go-ing out with this guy, Jerry. He was like a real father to Chickie's son, my friend Danny. He took Danny and me to see the Red Sox, the only time either one of us had ever been to Fenway Park. I knew he wouldn't touch Ma—he was a nice guy who didn't fit in with the scene under my window.

"Ma," I yelled from the third floor. I didn't want her to get in a fight. I knew Chickie was crazy. I was terrified of her. Ma marched over to Chickie. "Come over here," Ma said with her finger. Chickie walked over to Ma, hands on hips, all attitude, getting closer to Ma's face and saying more things about Ma and dicks. She called Ma a whore. Pow! Ma sucker punched Chickie, knocking her to the ground. Ma couldn't bend over with her stomach and all, so she let Chickie get up and then grabbed her by the hair and slammed her head against the brick wall. Chickie's thick glasses fell to the ground and Ma jumped up and down on them, then twisted and ground her wooden heel into the glass, crushing them to small bits. Ma walked slowly and triumphantly, holding her back, past the ladies on the stoop, who now cleared the way for her, never saying a word. That was that.

I was glad Ma was okay, with her being pregnant and all. I just didn't know what to say to Danny. He was my best friend. Then I thought maybe he'd be glad that his mother got her ass kicked. I figured if anyone thought she'd deserved it, he would, even though he only said good things about her. I sat on the stoop with the ladies. They weren't talking much around me, though. They were proba-bly afraid they'd say the wrong thing, and I'd run up and tell Ma.

Teens were now hanging out on the corners and reenacting Ma's blows in slow motion. I knew they were talking about her because one motioned a round belly with his two hands. When Danny came out all he said was, "Wanna go to the store?" It was as if it never happened. Still, I could feel his embarrassment. But I never found out whether he was embarrassed because his mother had one of the filthiest mouths in Old Colony, or because she got her ass kicked by a pregnant lady.

"This is worse than Mass Mental," Davey laughed. He said he'd be better off staying on the inside, at the hospital. Davey always talked about "the inside" and "the outside," two separate worlds divided by the brick walls of Mass Mental. He'd seemed glad to be free until a stream of speeding police motorcycles almost ran him down while he was doing his bouncy walk across Patterson Way, in deep meditation. I'd cracked up at the window when I'd seen him forced out of his private world long enough to give them the finger. Then he'd bounced a little faster, looking back at them, as if they would've even noticed. They were probably off to some riot or something. Anyway, Davey was serious about it sucking on the outside. "Everyone's nuts," he said. Before deinstitutionalization, he'd only been out on the weekends, when there'd been plenty of drinking, but not so many people running across rooftops or hiding out in alleys, or squadrons of troopers appearing out of nowhere to march right over you, breaking into your concentration. Davey said he couldn't think with all the "espionage" going on in Old Colony. "For Chrissake, I'm a paranoid schizophrenic and look where they dumped me, the KGB looking in our windows while I'm taking a shit!"

Davey started telling jokes that he'd made up. He was getting a kick out of Southie people. He couldn't believe the craziness. "What's the only parade bigger than St. Paddy's Day in Southie?" he'd ask. "The lines going into J.J.'s Liquors on welfare check day!" It seemed he always arrived at his words of wisdom right after a long pacing session. One day after pacing the kitchen floor he asked me what Judge Garrity looked like. I didn't know. "But he's the enemy, everyone in Southie should know what he looks like—they should have WANTED posters up everywhere with his face on them." I laughed. He took on this look he got when he was paranoid. "Hey, that's pretty good!" he said. "They don't want you to know what the enemy looks like, so you can end up killing each other, or yourself, in the frenzy. You become your own worst enemy!"

CHAPTER 5

LOOKING FOR
WHITEY

"ANOTHER ONE TO MAKE YOU A SLAVE." THAT'S WHAT Nana said to Ma, looking at Seamus in the nursery at St. Margaret's Hospital. Ma just laughed at her. She'd never gotten along with her mother—Ma said she was old-fashioned—and there was no sense in trying to relate now. Nana and Grandpa hadn't even known Ma was pregnant until she went into labor. Ma kept it from them, knowing they'd judge her and her baby since she wasn't married to Coley. She just wore big coats and held her big leather pocketbook in front of her stomach whenever she went to their house, among those lace curtain Irish neighbors in West Roxbury. Nana and Grandpa knew about me being illegitimate, but they never mentioned it, since most of their friends from Ireland thought that I'd come from Ma's marriage to Mac—"a bad marriage but a marriage before God nonetheless," as Father Murphy said. I was close to Nana; she was my godmother and had been Patrick's godmother too, so she took a special liking to me. I just had to brush off the bad things she said about Ma, and now I had to ignore her frowning gaze at Seamus. To make things more confusing for Nana and Grandpa's

Irish friends, Ma gave Seamus the last name King, from her short marriage to Bob King, whom they'd barely met. She had to put some name on the birth certificate; she knew welfare would never find Bob King, since he was probably homeless; and even though she'd gotten back together with Coley, we couldn't be sure he'd stick around for too long. Ma was looking out for us again, making sure our welfare check wouldn't be cut.

All I knew was that I was thrilled to come straight home from St. Augustine's every day to see my little brother. I remember how clean and fresh he smelled even when he spit up on my shoulder. I was tired of all the battles, the rock throwing and the protests, and I was excited to be around something so new as Seamus. I just wanted to protect him, to keep him as fresh as the day he was born; and I became aware of how hard that might be when I started to take him out for a push around the front courtyard of Patterson Way, with all the buckled-up concrete catching the carriage wheels.

Ma liked me to take him outside every day after school. She always complained that the air in our apartment was bad for kids, with the smell of cockroach exterminator and the radiators going full blast even on a warm Indian summer afternoon. It seemed as if all the kids in the neighborhood had asthma. I'd walk Seamus in circles, around and around, on the beaten-up cement out front. The women on the stoop followed me with their eyes. I kept count so I could tell Ma how many times I'd pushed him around. "That's twenty-nine times already!" I'd yell up to Ma. "Keep going," she'd say from the window, "the air's good for him." I liked minding Seamus, but everyone wanted to come and look at him and smile in his face. Chickie was friendly to us now, and one time she came up to us, fixing Seamus's blanket in a motherly way, and yelling up to Ma that all Ma's kids looked like movie stars. Then she started talking baby talk. "Hiyaaa, hiyeee sweetie," she sang, in the sweetest softest voice I'd ever heard coming out of her mouth. I started to see how babies did that to people, changed their voices and everything, no matter how mean or tough they seemed right before they'd laid eyes on the baby. Skoochie came by to show me the baby clothes she'd stolen downtown, taking them out of bags and sizing them up against Seamus, lying in his carriage. I sent her up to Ma, and she soon came back downstairs, folding up her empty bags. With Ma's money in her hand, she called over to some teenagers I'd heard were selling pills. I just kept walking in circles, watching the action in the streets. Kids my age would ask if they could push the carriage, and when I let them they'd start running fast right off the curb toward the traffic—for some excitement, I guess. That kind of stuff made me frantic and nearly got me into a few fistfights, but everyone usually backed down from me, since the kids in the neighborhood were still afraid of my big brothers.

The worst thing about minding Seamus was when I'd hear a neighbor down the street calling someone a douchebag or a cunt. I couldn't believe they'd say those words in front of a baby. Of course, they didn't think they were doing it in front of a baby—they were down the street. I half realized that since Seamus was only a few weeks old anyway, it probably didn't matter what he heard; and when they'd come up to the carriage the same people who'd just called someone a douchebag would start talking baby talk to him and tucking in his blanket. But I couldn't help worrying for Seamus, with his fresh clean baby smell and brand-new terry cloth baby suits, in the middle of all this anger and confusion and drug dealing and fighting. I still loved our world of Old Colony, but I wasn't always so sure about that now that I had a little brother to wheel around the broken-up courtyards.

After Seamus was born, the Boston Housing Authority broke down one of our walls for us, adding a second apartment. Only three families in Old Colony had a "breakthrough" apartment. Ma had pulled a few strings with the local politicians she'd met by volunteering for the South Boston Information Center and by playing the accordion at political fundraisers. We were the envy of the neighborhood now, with ten rooms in all, including two kitchens and two bathrooms. We had so much space that Ma had to start collecting furniture from the dumpster to fill up the house. I'd yell out the window to Ma, begging her to stop going through the dumpster, pulling out chairs. I didn't want anyone to see her. My friends all bragged about their expensive living room sets stolen from the backs of trucks. But she'd just play it up, dragging some contraption behind her up three flights of stairs, "Look at this beautiful recliner!" It was really a lawn chair that one of the ladies on the stoop had left outside, expecting it to still be there when she got back. I was always afraid to let friends in the house, because they might find something that they'd thrown in the trash or just left outside.

We had it made now. Most of us had our own bedroom, and I had a feeling we would be in Old Colony forever. Ten fully furnished rooms with wall-to-wall green, blue, and orange shag rugs; free heat, light, and gas; Skoochie's designer-label clothes for a quarter the price; all the excitement right out our front windows—"Scenes better than anything on the TV," Ma said—and the thrill of being on the inside of the exclusive world of Old Colony. We were privileged. And even though I was still a little worried for Seamus, I could convince myself, like everyone else, that we were in a superior kingdom.

No one made us feel better about where we lived than Whitey Bulger. Whitey was the brother of our own Senator Billy Bulger, but on the streets of Southie he was even more powerful than Billy. He was the king of Southie, but not like the bad English kings who oppressed and killed the poor people of Ireland. No way would we put up with that. He had definite rules that we all learned to live by, not because we had to, but because we wanted to. And we had to have someone looking out for us, with the likes of Judge Garrity trying to take away what little we'd gotten for ourselves.

Whatever we had, we were going to keep. Whitey stepped up as our protector. They said he protected us from being overrun with the drugs and gangs we'd heard about in the black neighborhoods, as well as stopping the outsiders who wanted to turn the projects into expensive condominiums. I knew there were drugs and even gangs in my neighborhood, but like everyone else I kept my mouth shut about that one. Whitey and his boys didn't like "rats." And it was all worth it to look the other way as long as Whitey kept the neighborhood as is, and we kept our ten-room apartment for eighty dollars a month. We'd never be able to afford the high rents in other parts of Boston. We might have lost our schools, but we weren't going to let the rich liberals win by doing what Ma said they always do: chase everyone out by bringing in the blacks, and then chasing the blacks out when it's time to build high-rise condominiums. Columbia Point Project was already on its way to being mostly condos for white yuppies with no kids. Whitey Bulger was the only one left to turn to. He was our king, and everyone made like they were connected to him in some way.

I was always looking for Whitey Bulger. I never saw him, but I'd never admit that to my friends. Everyone bragged about how his uncle was tight with him, or his brother had been bailed out of jail by him, or how he'd bought them a new pair of sneakers, or his mother a modern kitchen set. All the neighbors said they went to Whitey when they were in trouble, whether they'd been sent eviction notices from the Boston Housing Authority or the cops were harassing their kid. Whitey was more accessible than the welfare office, the BHA, the courts, or the cops. If your life had been threatened, your mother could always visit Whitey and get him to squash a beef. That is, of course, if your family was playing by the rules of the neighborhood. If you'd received death threats for avoiding the boycotts and sending your kids to school or else for saying the wrong thing to the press, you were on your own.

My own brothers and sisters bragged of their links to Whitey. Frankie came home from sparring at McDonough's Gym with stories of Whitey studying the boxers from the sidelines. Most of the guys Whitey surrounded himself with were boxers. Kevin was always making like Whitey was his father, and that he would grow up to inherit the kingdom. He said Whitey always patted him on the head whenever Kevin would go out of his way to say hi to him.

And Kathy bragged that her boyfriends and their mothers worked for Whitey, selling drugs from the privacy of their modern furnished project apartment, and paying him "rent," in addition to what they paid the BHA. She said she'd be rich someday when her boyfriends got a little older and started making real loot, robbing bank trucks with "the boys," as we called our revered gangsters. I never knew if any of these stories were true, but at the age of nine I was envious of all the teenagers with their connection to so much power. Visible or not, we all had a hero, a powerful champion, in the midst of all the troubles that enemy forces were heaving on us since the busing. Whitey was even more powerful than our elected politicians. They worked for *him*, that's what Ma always said. I wanted to see the face of Whitey Bulger, so that I too could feel that power that everyone else bragged they were so connected to.

No one had his eyes on Whitey more than Kevin. I'm sure he hardly ever saw him, but Kevin always had one up on the other kids in the neighborhood by knowing more about the workings of the Irish Mafia. The conversations on the corners of Southie were changing. From a distance I watched the teenagers who were still reenacting slow motion war stories, but instead of the blow-by-blow punches in the air, they'd started to draw invisible guns, imitating gangsters exchanging slow motion gunfire. And there was Kevin right in the middle of it, claiming to know more about Whitey than anyone.

For a while I was following Kevin to the Boys Club, joining the swim team, playing ping-pong, shooting pool, and basketball. Kevin was winning first place in every league at the club. He left every awards banquet with his arms full of trophies, and a proud face, even prouder than years ago when he'd bring home the spoils from the Irish Field Day or the local bars. But by the time he'd turned twelve, he'd lost interest in the trophies, and instead of following him to the Boys Club I was once again following him around on his trail to make some money.

During the fall of 1975, Kevin had gotten a job as a paperboy for the *Herald American*. He didn't want to work for the *Globe*, because some guys in the neighborhood were hijacking *Globe* trucks and robbing them at gunpoint to protest busing. "I'm liable to get shot," Kevin said; so he went to the *Herald* and carried on about how much he hated the *Globe*. The guys there got a kick out of that one, and hired him on the spot. That year was Phase Two of the plan to desegregate, when more Boston neighborhoods would be dragged into busing terror, so even more regiments of police stood guard over our streets to keep us from sparking a wider rebellion. But the streets were quiet when Kevin and I got up at the crack of dawn to deliver papers with our dog Sarge, and we felt pretty important to see all the troops looking so intimidating just for us.

It was on these long early morning journeys that Kevin told me wild stories about the heroic Whitey Bulger and the Irish Mafia. I'd never heard of the Irish Mafia until recently; I'd always thought the Mafia was Italian. Kevin seemed to know all the details, though. He said that Whitey had been in Alcatraz for robbing banks, but that they'd let him go after he took LSD for the government in some kind of experiments about the drug; that Whitey was part of the Winter Hill gang in Somerville and had taken Southie over from the Mullen gang here. He talked about wild shoot-outs years ago in the very streets we were walking down on our paper route, between the Killeen gang and the Mullen gang, but said that everyone was united now, especially with the busing and all. I couldn't follow his stories about gangs, and shoot-outs and takeovers, and whenever I got confused and asked a question about Whitey or the Mullen gang, or about LSD, Kevin told me to shut my mouth, that I was talking too loud. He told me I had an "Irish whisper." I'd heard Ma say that about people who thought they were telling a secret but couldn't keep their voices down. The Irish made fun of each other for not being able to keep secrets, and for talking too loud when they shouldn't. "Especially with all the bad guys around these days," Kevin added. Then he just went about his business delivering papers, waving hi to the customers, who called him a hard worker, and

walking with his head down past the cops on horses and motorcycles lining the streets for the buses of black kids coming from Roxbury. Before I could ask him in another Irish whisper who the bad
guys were, Kevin jerked his head sideways toward the cops. "Them
are the bad guys," he muttered under his breath. "Well, I already
knew that one," I belted out, "Anyone living in Southie with the
Gestapo everywhere could have told you that."

One day when I didn't go with Kevin on his paper route, he came
home and shouted to Ma that he'd been robbed of all his collection
money. He didn't know what to tell the guys at the *Herald* who were
expecting all the cash. Ma told Kevin just to tell the truth. But Kevin
stopped going to work instead, and when his supervisor called him,
he finally confessed to being robbed on his paper route "by some
big guys that looked like weight lifters.... They put a knife to my
throat." He said he'd told the robbers that they had the wrong
newspaper, that it was the *Globe* they wanted to rob, but that they'd
told him to empty his pockets anyway. He told the supervisor he
wouldn't be coming back to work, that it was just too dangerous
these days. Then he hung up the telephone. Later on he was laughing with Kathy in his bedroom at the very back of the apartment.
She'd brought her friends up to the house to buy some pot from
him. They didn't know that I knew Kevin was selling pot, and when
I walked in on them rolling a joint, they told me to screw. They
weren't letting me in on anything anymore, with my Irish whisper
and all. I listened through the walls, though, and heard Kevin tell
how he'd fooled the guys at the *Herald* into believing he'd been
robbed, and that that was how he could afford to buy a half-pound
of pot and some mescaline to start selling and make some real
money. At the age of twelve, Kevin was now a player in the drug
trade in South Boston. He said he'd have to keep it quiet, though, so
he wouldn't have to pay Whitey Bulger any of the money. He said
that his "connection" paid up to Whitey, so he wasn't really doing
anything wrong.

In the coming weeks, I started answering the door every five or ten minutes. People I had never seen before in my life were knocking and asking for Kevin. "Is Mini Mac there?" It seemed as if the most popular people in the neighborhood got the nicknames, like "Whitey" or "Skoochie." Sometimes the knocks on the door started early in the morning, before any of us had even gotten up with the sound of helicopters and police motorcycles. Ma couldn't believe how popular Kevin was. Kevin would step outside to the hallway for a few minutes, and I'd look through the peephole to see Kevin and some other teenager huddled in a corner. Then Kevin would come back inside, and I would be turning the channels of the TV, as if I was looking for something particular to watch, and minding my own business.

Then adults started knocking, people in their twenties and thirties. Ma thought it was kind of weird, but would only comment on how retarded some of these people were, hanging out with little kids. "They need to get a life," she said. Ma got sick of the knocks and told Kevin he'd better do something about it. That's when we started to see less of Kevin. He started coming and going through his bedroom window. There was a tall oak tree that brushed up against the window, looking as if it would've grown right inside if it hadn't taken an upward turn toward the roof. Kevin kept the upper half of his window open at all times and just climbed in and out from the roof. He could be in that back room all day long, and none of us would know it, except Kathy, who sometimes brought him clients so she could get a free joint for herself. Customers now just went up to the roof, lay face down near the edge, and poked their heads upside-down into Kevin's window, saying *pssst.* My own room was next to Kevin's, and one day Marty McGrail lay down in the wrong spot and poked his head into my window by accident. I was taking a nap and woke up to an upside-down head *psssting* me, and scared Marty away when I yelled for Ma. After that I knew why we weren't getting so many knocks at the door anymore.

* * *

Phase Two of the busing brought Charlestown into the battle. And Charlestown was ready for nothing less than war. Back in the early days of busing, groups had formed with names like ROAR, or Restore Our Alienated Rights. The new group of mothers starting up in Charlestown was called Powder Keg, and their slogan was "Don't Tread on Me." We'd always heard Charlestown was a lot like Southie, with housing projects and people with shamrocks tattooed to their arms. They had an Irish Mafia too, but we always liked to think that our Whitey Bulger was smarter and more powerful. Whitey was so smart he'd convinced us that the addicts we were starting to see more and more weren't really there. Whatever we were seeing, we figured it wasn't half as bad as what the blacks over in Roxbury had. Or Charlestown, for that matter, where the gangsters and the politicians weren't as organized as ours. Whitey kept a low profile during the riots in Southie, but everyone said he had something to do with the South Boston Marshalls, vigilantes who were supposedly passing out guns in Southie, getting everyone ready to protect the town. Kevin said that "the boys" in Charlestown were even crazier than ours, though, and that busing over there would make Southie look like Bethlehem on the first Christmas morning.

During Phase One, Joe had gotten out of being sent to Roxbury by attending the trade school at Charlestown High. The trade school was separate from the regular high school, and attracted kids from all over the city. He said there were blacks in the trade school but that everyone got along because they weren't being brought in on yellow buses yet. They chose to go there. But the peace ended in Charlestown when the buses rolled down the same streets where the Battle of Bunker Hill had been fought two hundred years earlier. The Charlestown kids started chanting the same chants we did in Southie: "Hell No, We Won't Go!" Many of their teenagers got involved in boycotts and sit-ins, but many more ended up lining the streets to give the finger to the buses, to throw Molotov cocktails off project rooftops, and to stick hockey sticks into the spokes of speeding cop motorcycles. They said on the news that one Charlestown gang had filled glass bottles with acid and thrown them at the horses, burning their legs and sending cops crashing to the street. "They got balls over there!" That's what Frankie said when he heard about that one.

Joe had to start being careful hanging around with some of the black friends he'd made the year before. One afternoon he came home shaking. He said he was playing basketball in the high school gym with some black kids, when a group of townies challenged them to a game. The game started off innocently enough, but when Joe's team from the trade school started winning, the townies started calling them niggers and jigaboos, and throwing punches instead of passes. The fight turned into a brawl, with Joe nearly knocking out one townie who'd called him a nigger lover and blindsided him. "That's when the Gestapo came into the school and stopped all the fighting by cracking some heads with their batons," Joe told us. The townies taunted Joe, saying they'd give him a beating after school, along with one of the black kids who'd also gotten the best of them in the fight.

The school officials thought they were helping Joe and the black kid by letting them go home early, before the buses came. But the Charlestown mobs were already lining the streets, and teenagers from the projects were milling around on corners. "I turned around and there were about a hundred townies chasing after us with baseball bats and hockey sticks," Joe told us, with big eyes. He said he ran for his life. "Hey, MacDonald, wait up!" the black kid had yelled, trying to catch up. Joe said he just screamed back to him, "You're on your own," and ran over the bridge out of Charlestown and into downtown Boston.

Joe still looked shaken after he told the story. After that day, he started making friends with some of the townies, and made sure that he joined in some of the boycotts and sit-ins happening over there. He still attended Charlestown High, even though he said it was getting harder and harder not to become "another dropout from Southie." As Ma kept saying, it seemed as if Judge Garrity was using his power to make a whole generation of dropouts and jailbirds in our neighborhood.

"What a vicious son of a bitch," Ma said, looking at the picture of a Southie neighbor from down the road on the front page of the *Herald*. He was aiming the pointed staff of an American flag and charging at a black lawyer in a suit. Ma said she'd just about had it. "Busing is a horror," she said, "but this is no way to fight it. People like that are making us all look bad." She said she was starting to think that some of the politicians in Southie were almost as bad as Judge Garrity himself. She thought they might be stirring things up in the drugged-out minds of people like the teenager in the *Herald*. "And the kids are the ones suffering," she said. "Especially the ones who can't get into the parochial schools with the seats filling up and the tuitions being raised." She said she felt like she was kicked in the stomach every time she heard Jimmy Kelly talking about niggers this and niggers that at the Information Center where she'd been volunteering. She said she couldn't get used to that word, no matter how much she hated the busing. Then there were the South Boston Marshalls, the militant group connected to the Information Center. We all wanted to stop the busing, but sometimes it was confusing. One day you'd be clapping and cheering the inspirational words of Louise Day Hicks and Senator Billy Bulger, and the next day you'd see the blood on the news, black and white people's blood. And here was a black man being beaten with an American flag on the national news. We sat on a legless couch in the Old Colony Project and watched the violent pictures of another bloody protest. Ma said she didn't know where to turn, what to belong to, and neither did I.

We all wanted to belong to something big, and the feeling of being part of the antibusing movement along with the rest of Southie had been the best feeling in the world. But it wasn't feeling so good anymore; we were losing—to the liberals and to the racists. Even Frankie had to find something besides the crowds at Darius Court to be part of. Boxing at McDonough's Gym made Frank a winner. He came home from bouts in a good mood. He said he felt pumped from all the winning. He was proud of his ability in the ring and bragged to us, showing Ma all his moves. Ma showed him some of her moves too. She always said that if she'd been a boy, she would've been a boxer. Coley agreed with her on that one. Frank was feeling good about himself. It got so he could knock out anyone he wanted to in the ring, black or white, when they fought in the statewide bouts.

Ma thanked God that Frank was hanging out at McDonough's Gym every day, away from the buses. The gym was behind the courthouse, and attracted boxers from all over Southie. Many kids went from the courts right into the gym to get away from the trouble in the streets. They were safe there, especially with all the gangsters who watched over them in the boxing ring, cheering the kids on, and sometimes becoming their trainers. Boxing was becoming Southie's prized sport, attracting some of the toughest kids in the neighborhood for bloody but regulated battles. It was better than fighting in the street, where you might get arrested by the bad guys. And it kept Frankie and other kids like him out of Old Colony Project for the day. Frankie said Whitey Bulger joked that someday Frank could be his bodyguard.

The whole country was celebrating America's two hundredth birthday, and the nuns at St. Augustine's kept trying to get us kids to draw American flags and eagles. I was the one in the class who could draw, so the other kids had me draw their pictures. Then they'd scrawl STOP FORCED BUSING with their crayons underneath the bald eagle. One kid even wrote GEORGE WALLACE FOR PRESIDENT underneath the American flag that I'd drawn for him. The Tall Ships were going to be pulling into the harbor right down the street from the Old Colony Project, and the Gestapo were watching over us heavily now, so that we didn't make another bloody scene for all of America to see that we weren't feeling free. But most people in the neighborhood were more excited that George Wallace was planning a trip to South Boston, to run for president and to promise to get the government off our backs.

In Southie all the talk now was about George Wallace, who would end forced busing for sure if he became president of the United States. The South Boston Information Center covered its trucks with his campaign signs, and yelled through their loudspeakers down Patterson Way that everyone should vote for Wallace. He was almost as popular in the neighborhood as Whitey Bulger. At first Ma said she wasn't too sure about Wallace, with all the news reports about him wanting to go back to the days of black people being second-class citizens, and some even said he talked about sending the blacks back to Africa. But eventually she changed her mind and went with Wallace when she realized he was the only one out there who was paying attention to Southie, the only one who'd work to end forced busing forever. The national news focused on us once again, covering Wallace's trip to Southie. And there was Ma one night on TV, with a George Wallace button pinned to her rabbit fur jacket. "Maybe then some of these kids in the streets could go back to school," she said into the news cameras on Broadway.

All the adults were excited about George Wallace's visit. Some of the little kids got excited with the parents, like the boy whose sign I'd help make at St. Augustine's. Some of the older kids went to the fundraiser the local politicians held for Wallace on Broadway, but most of the teenagers couldn't be bothered. The Lithuanian Club was all decked out in the usual banners: STOP FORCED BUSING and STICK TO YOUR GUNS SOUTHIE. Ma brought her guitar and accordion up to the Lith Club and took the stage to do her own antibusing anthems, and she said she never saw Jimmy Kelly so excited as when he finally got to meet George Wallace.

George Wallace spoke against busing, against the government controlling the lives of the little guy, and against the media. That's when I heard the loudest cheers as I listened outside the Lith Club. Everyone loved to hate the media. As I eavesdropped from the sidewalk out on Broadway, it seemed as if we were all feeling a little more power now that George Wallace was speaking up for us. But it didn't last long. In the end, the newspaper reporters said Wallace didn't have a chance, except maybe in places like Southie. And there weren't too many places like Southie. But at least he would win in our neighborhood and maybe bring back the unity we'd felt when the buses first started to roll.

I turned ten the year of the bicentennial. And it was the first time I remember thinking I was depressed. The antibusing movement was disappearing on us kids. It was more of an adult thing now, with all the political events. I was also left out of the teenage wheeling and dealing on the streets, because I was too young. I couldn't hang out with Kevin and Kathy anymore, because they were doing things they didn't want me to know about, with my Irish whisper.

So on the day I turned ten, I decided to call my father. I was home alone minding Seamus, and Ma had told me that she'd seen my father at the Emerald Isle Pub in Dorchester, and that he'd said he'd like to hear from me. I was the one who'd have liked to hear from *him*, but I looked up his mother's number in the telephone book anyway. I knew her name was Gertie Fox, and I knew he lived with her in Dorchester. I finally got up the guts to call, and Gertie answered the phone with a cranky voice. I asked to speak to George. I told her that I was his son Michael and that she was my grandmother, as if we'd all be in for some kind of happy reunion. "He doesn't have a son!" She yelled so loud I had to pull the telephone away from my ear. "Who put you up to this," she said, "your mother? Get your mother on the phone!" I told her my mother wasn't even home, and that I'd just called because it was my birthday—hoping now that I might get some kindness, as mention of birthdays usually did. That's when a man's voice came on the phone. "Michael?" It was the first time I'd ever heard my father's voice. I told him it was my birthday. "Who put you up to this, your mother?" I hung up the phone then, and went back to minding Seamus.

Later in the day, Ma came home with a birthday cake. We celebrated my birthday along with Patrick's, because his was a week later. Kevin's was a week earlier than mine, and ever since we were little we'd celebrated all three birthdays together. But Kevin was thirteen now, and hanging out in the streets too much to be involved in a birthday with me and our dead brother. Ma played "Happy Birthday" on her accordion, and brought all the neighborhood kids in who wanted some free cake.

Nana took me out later that night. I told her all about my telephone call to my other grandmother, my wicked one. She told me I didn't need two grandmothers anyway, and that made me feel better. It was her way of saying that I was *her* grandson. I got along great with Nana—much better than Ma did. It was all right for me to talk about George Fox being my real father, as long as we didn't mention Ma getting pregnant without being married. And I didn't tell Nana that Ma was pregnant again—*and her and Coley still not married*, I thought to myself.

In the eighth grade, the nuns took Kevin out of classes—with all his wisecracks—and put him in the basement with Louie, the janitor, hoping he'd get some interest in a trade while working in the boiler room. But Kevin figured he'd outsmarted the nuns, getting them to send him downstairs where he'd never have to study again. He said Louie liked him so much that every day he'd order Kevin a "spuckie," Southie talk for "submarine sandwich." Whenever Sister Elizabeth came down the stairs in her noisy wooden clogs, Kevin said he'd start looking busy with his head under some pipes, and a wrench in his hand. As soon as she left, he said he'd go back to eating spuckies with his feet up on the table and telling Louie his wild stories about the legendary James Whitey Bulger. "Imagine all the loot he's making!" Kevin said after telling me what he did all day at

St. Augustine's. "Betcha he never went to college." Kevin often made fun of me for carrying so many books home from school.

Every day after school, Kevin and Kathy became part of something bigger than anything the politicians were going on about through their loudspeakers on trucks that came through Old Colony every night: "Attention South Boston Residents! Please attend a meeting at the Gavin School tomorrow night at 7 P.M. sharp. The lives of our children are at stake!" They were talking about the blacks taking over someday and changing our way of life.

Kathy belonged to a group of teenagers that always looked busy out on Patterson Way, walking up and down the streets, going into hallways, darting across rooftops, jumping into strangers' cars, and settling down by nightfall on East 8th Street, at the end of Patterson. Ma called them "the 8th Street gang." Kathy was in the ninth grade at Cardinal Cushing High School, along with most of the other Southie girls who'd fled the busing but were still going to school. But the general feeling in the neighborhood was that school was for suckers. The dropouts were the ones who said that the most, and of course they usually looked as if they were having the most fun, wearing the best clothes, and making the most loot from drugs and petty scams. Ma said Kathy was starting to get into the drugs, but I already knew that. She said she'd heard that the 8th Street gang was getting into angel dust. "That's why they're all as nutty as the day is long," she said. Ma said she didn't like the looks of that Frank McGirk, who led the group and was said to be selling the dust. Kathy's best friends now were Frank McGirk and Julie Meaney, who all of us little kids in the neighborhood were afraid of because she and her mother were supposed to be into witchcraft.

Later in her freshman year at Cardinal Cushing, Kathy wasn't going to school at all. She was fifteen, and sometimes she was staying out until three in the morning. Other times she wouldn't come home at all. One night Ma came home, after walking down East 8th, bringing the groceries from Broadway. "You wouldn't believe that fuckin' place," she said. She looked exhausted from the long walk.

"Mother of God, it's like Las Vegas down there! The street's dark as hell, and everyone's lights are on, with speakers blasting out of the windows." She said that she'd had to weave her way through people staggering around "all dusted out," while others tried to disco dance on streets, sidewalks, and rooftops. She'd walked down East 8th looking for Kathy, who'd been missing for two days, and everyone said they didn't know where she was, if they could talk at all. "For Chrissake, one of them was even dancing with a stop sign that'd come loose from the sidewalk."

Ma told me to go up to East 8th and knock on Mrs. Meaney's door. I'd never seen Julie's mother, and I was scared. Everyone had stories about the strange things she'd done, levitating teenagers, and controlling the minds of her Doberman pinchers with ESP to attack anyone she didn't like on East 8th Street. They said Julie Meaney could do that too, and that one day when the black kids were coming out of Southie High, she'd just looked into the eyes of her Doberman, and that he'd taken the signal and lunged right for a black kid's throat.

When I got up to East 8th, I saw what Ma was talking about. Everyone was having a great time, dancing with whatever objects could hold them up. I saw the one with the stop sign. Like most of the stop signs in Southie, BUSING was spray painted under the word STOP, so it was a STOP BUSING sign. One guy about Ma's age had his two hands stretched out onto the hood of a car while his knees did some bouncy thing to the beat of the Bee Gees. The teenagers were imitating the dances from *Saturday Night Fever* and mouthing the lyrics to "Staying Alive." They were out of breath, and a few beats behind the song: "I've been kicked around since I was born / And now it's alright, it's ok, we'll live to see another day. . . ."

I dodged some of the teens who were beckoning, calling me "little MacDonald." I kept a distance and asked them where Julie Meaney lived. One of them took me to the door and then ran because she said she owed the mother "a fin," Southie talk for five dollars. When I knocked on the door, a voice screamed "Come in," and dogs started barking and throwing themselves against the door. When I heard the wicked voice and the Dobermans I wanted to run with the girl who owed the fin, but then the voice screamed again, "I said come in!" Whoever it was told the dogs to go fuck themselves and they shut right up. I poked my head in the door and saw the dogs lined up, sitting on the couch and staring at me, as if they were waiting for their orders from the witch, whose voice was shouting "Who's that?" from the back room. Mrs. Meaney appeared before me, hunched over, wearing a bathrobe that was too big and long for her bony body, and with long raggedy white hair that looked just like a Halloween witch's wig. I began to sweat; the apartment was hotter than the hottest project apartments I'd been in. I was stunned and just stared at Mrs. Meaney. I believed in witches, too, because Ma and Nellie had talked about a few people in Ireland who they said put curses on people. I don't know what I expected, but I didn't expect Mrs. Meaney to look like a Halloween witch.

She screamed at me then, "Who the fuck are you?" I didn't say anything, and that's when the Dobermans pinned me into a corner, snapping their jaws at my face. I could hear the music blasting and people partying outside on East 8th Street: "Whether you're a brother, or whether you're a mother, you're just stayin' alive, stayin' alive."

"I'm just looking for Kathy MacDonald," I told the Dobermans, and then begged Mrs. Meaney not to let them bite me. She kicked the dogs away—she didn't do the ESP thing—and said she didn't know where Kathy was, but that she "must be out gallivanting with that whore of a daughter of mine." I left the apartment pretty fast, my heart pounding as I raced home past all the people on angel dust singing along: "Life goin' nowhere, somebody help me . . ."

When I got home Kathy was already there, sitting on the floor "dusted out," as they said in Old Colony about the slow motion movements of those who were on the drug. Kathy was wearing short shorts and had her shirt tied above her stomach, her spike heels on the floor next to her. Ma had the scissors pointed at Kathy and was screaming and crying that she was going to cut off all Kathy's long wavy hair. And then she surely wouldn't be out all night sleeping with boys. Ma was afraid Kathy would get pregnant like the other girls in the neighborhood, and figured a bald head might keep guys from liking her. I butted in and reminded Ma that her own mother had done that to her when Ma was just sixteen and hanging out on the corners too much in her leopard dresses. Ma had told me that Nana was jealous of her long red hair and looks, one of the reasons why they'd never got along when she was growing up. She always bragged that she was a rebel back in the fifties. But things were different now, she said, with all the angel dust out on the streets and all the girls getting pregnant. When I tried to stop Ma from cutting Kathy's hair, she told me to mind my own business. "You shouldn't even be listening to this stuff," she said. "Go out and play with the kids your age instead of being all ears."

Ma never did cut Kathy's hair. She asked the older boys to talk to Kathy, and told her she'd better not see her hanging around with Frank McGirk and the 8th Street gang again. But it didn't work; no one could keep Kathy from doing what she wanted to do—her friends were everything. I never did get to tell Ma my wild story about Mrs. Meaney and her long white hair.

"They'll be talking about me all over Ireland," Ma said, as we all pulled up to the church a half hour late for Nana's funeral. Stevie, our youngest brother, was four months old now, and Ma had him and Seamus on her lap. She'd fought with Joe the whole way about his shitboxes breaking down all the time. "Imagine, missing your own mother's funeral." By the time we got into the church in West Roxbury, all the lace curtain types were filing out. We just pretended we'd been there the whole time, and filed out with the rest of them. "Ah, 'twas a great send off, though, wasn't it?" some of our old Irish neighbors from Jamaica Plain were saying to Ma. "It was," Ma said. "She lived a good life." Later on Ma complained about all the people who said Nana went so young. "For Chrissake, she was seventy-three!" Ma said that after losing a baby, anyone would think that seventy-three years was plenty. Ma only seemed sad that so many things weren't understood between the two of them. She'd had a feeling Nana was going to die, though, ever since Nana had dreamt that a man wearing all black came in from the rain and stood in the corner of her bedroom. Nana woke up wondering where the man had gone. She told Leena and Sally that she'd given the man a place to rest for the night up in the attic. When Grandpa told Ma the story on the phone, that's when I heard Ma say, "You know what that means don't you?" Sure enough, two weeks later Nana went to bed, said her nightly Rosary, and never woke up again. "You couldn't ask for a better death," all the lace curtain Irish were saying now, "with the Rosary beads in her hands."

When we went to Grandpa's house after the funeral for the usual food and drink with all the guests, we got kicked out. Grandpa didn't want Seamus and Steven in the house with all the Irish there, who would be asking where they came from. Grandpa and Nana had kept that story away from their friends, for the shame. And here was Ma carrying the two of them into Nana's house, wearing her black miniskirt and fishnet stockings, with no husband and no shame at all. Before I could even eat one of the chicken salad sandwiches that were laid out, it was time to leave. We all piled into Joe's souped-up shitbox and went back to Old Colony, where there were plenty of other kids whose mothers and fathers weren't married.

When Nana died, I was sad. I was the only one in the house who was close to her, even though I had to ignore her frowns when my mother was brought up for discussion. She and Grandpa always made me feel a connection to Ireland and to a world bigger than what I had in Old Colony. I started to feel alone, especially since no one else in the family was talking about Nana's death. Kevin and Kathy had gone their own ways; Frankie was off at the gym; Joe always had his head under the hood of a car; Johnnie was off at Tufts

University—the only one "making it out" as Grandpa said about him—and at eighteen, Mary was now pregnant and moving into Old Harbor Project with Jimmy the Greek. I stayed around the house a lot, minding Seamus and Stevie—and studying Davey.

Davey was walking in circles again out in the front courtyard. I went downstairs to watch him, going in opposite circles with Stevie in the baby carriage. I just stared at Davey when our circles crossed. It broke his concentration a few times, and he jerked his head to look at me, startled, as if I'd interrupted something. "What—are you fuckin' trying to torment me?" he said. When Davey got mean, I'd make it worse, trying to turn it into something funny. I'd tease and "torment" him, hoping to bring him out of the trap he was in. It was August, and every August when his doctor at Mass Mental went away for two weeks' vacation, Davey lost it. When our circles crossed the next time, I aimed right for him with the baby carriage. I'd only wanted to help, but now I felt frustrated and angry at the sickness and suffering taking him over. I needed to attack Davey— to attack whatever demons were overpowering him. That's when he ran down the street, looking back at me as if I was the enemy.

None of us knew Davey when it was August. Normally, he would pace the streets and come up to the women on the stoops, or to the kids on the corners, and tell a joke, getting everyone laughing. They loved him. The little kids all wanted him to do his famous imper- sonation of the Incredible Hulk, right at the moment he transforms into a huge superhero. But in August, Davey's transformations were too scary, and too religious, for anyone to relate to. One time he said he was an ordained priest, and was going to save the "poor souls" of Old Colony Project. He went around in a black shirt, repeating, "The first shall be last and the last shall be first." No one really got that one, I suppose because most of us would not imagine ourselves, ever, as among "the last."

After chasing Davey away, I lugged the carriage, with Steven in it, backwards up the three flights of stairs, one step at a time, as I'd learned to do by now, coming and going every day for my walks in circles. When I burst into the house, I was out of breath and excited to tell Ma what I'd just figured out. "Ma, I think I know what mental illness is!" Ma was lying on the couch, with Seamus asleep on top of her so she could feel that he was still breathing. "Oh, Jesus, Mary, and Joseph!" she said. "Are you at it again? Will you just go out and play or something?" I told her I thought the reason the doctors couldn't figure out what was wrong with Davey or find a cure was because they were focusing too much on his brain, in a physical way. "I think it's his spirit that's sick," I said. "And the spirit is just too much of a mystery for them to figure out." I added that the spirit and the brain are somehow connected, and that the spirit must be located more up there, rather than somewhere in our chests, which was what the nuns at St. Augustine's motioned to when they talked about the soul. "It's just that the spirit is invisible, and the doctors are all confused, focusing on what they can see: the brain." I wasn't really making sense, I thought, but I knew what I was talking about. The brain took things in, analyzing them, "all the shit in the world," as Davey said; but it was the soul that carried the sickness, since the brain had to move on and think about other things. Ma made a face like she couldn't believe what was going through my head. She told me I was smart, and that I should be a psychiatrist when I grow up so that I could help people; but in the meantime she wanted me to go outside and play with the other kids my age, like an eleven-year-old. "And stop being such a goddam worrywart!"

In the spring of 1978, it seemed that busing was all in the past, and disco opened up a whole new era for me and my friends. Everyone was going into downtown Boston now, to hit the clubs and dance to Chic, A Taste of Honey, Chaka Khan, and Taka Boom. The older teenagers snuck into the adult clubs, while we twelve-year-olds were sneaking into Illusions, the new disco for teenagers fourteen and up.

I used Kevin's birth certificate to get in, claiming to be fifteen. Kevin wasn't going anyway. He was too busy making deals to sell his stuff to the older kids, who needed to get high for the adult clubs.

The Southie kids took over Illusions, although there were also Italians from Eastie, townies from Charlestown, who looked just like the Southie kids, and some Puerto Rican kids from the South End and Jamaica Plain. Only one or two black kids came to Illusions. Everyone was getting along that summer, and I felt as if I really belonged somewhere in my own right, away from the streets of Old Colony. Every week, I bought a new pair of bellbottoms with money from the jobs program at ABCD, the antipoverty agency in Boston. At first I was stealing disco clothes to wear, going into a changing room and walking out with a whole new outfit underneath the one I'd come in with. But then, thanks to ABCD, I was able to get an even better thrill by spending my pay on things people like me weren't supposed to be able to afford. Some weeks I would spend a whole check on one pair of pants, getting Ma all worked up over the prices. But I wanted to look good. So did the other kids in my neighborhood, who stole their clothes so they could save the rest of their paycheck for some pills or pot before going out.

I loved whipping out cash in front of store clerks who looked at me as if I didn't belong in the expensive section of Filene's. I got a high from spending money. But I was spending so much money on clothes that I had to start finding ways to make more. Kevin asked me to take his mescaline pills with me to Illusions. I had no interest in using any myself, and he said that was why he could trust me. The tiny red pills went for three dollars a pop, and he gave me a jar with about a hundred inside. I was really popular now. I had the best disco clothes in Southie, better than anything my friends were stealing, and I was winning every dance contest at Illusions. The dance at the time was "the Freak," made popular by Chic's song "Freak Out." I would win fifty dollars every time there was a Freak contest. And now I had the pills that everyone wanted. Kids from all over Boston would seek me out at Illusions to buy the tiny red pills. I felt like a bona fide pimp.

One night, I made the mistake of taking out the jar of pills while I was still on the dance floor, instead of heading off to a corner for the transaction. Danny said a kid from Eastie wanted two, one for him and one for his girl. As I opened up the jar, someone did the Freak right into my elbow and sent about three hundred dollars' worth of tiny red pills flying. When word got out, every Southie kid at Illusions was pretending to help me recover my losses through strobe-lit disco confusion. Some did give me back a few, but later on when we were going home, kids I'd never sold any to were high as a kite. I had to hide out from Kevin for a week. In the end I couldn't believe how important a bunch of tiny red pills could be, making all my friends act differently and cheating me out of the few they'd found on the dance floor, and making my own brother want to kick my ass. By the age of twelve, I was finished with selling drugs.

But booze was okay in my book. Every Friday night before getting on the subway for Illusions, we stood in front of J.J.'s Liquors waiting for a runner. We usually didn't have to wait long before some adult would agree to buy us a couple six packs and a bottle of whiskey. And we didn't even have to wait around the corner for him. It was all out in the open. Usually we gave the runner a couple cans of beer as payment. That's what made it so easy to get someone to go in for us. Then we drank up on the rooftops of Old Colony.

Everyone at Illusions was getting messed up, even inside the club. We all snuck in whatever we didn't finish out on the streets. I was able to smuggle in everyone else's whiskey bottles by tucking them into my sweat socks. The bottles never showed through my pants because I had the biggest bellbottoms. Throughout that summer, the drinking seemed to be getting worse, and some people seemed to be drinking more than others. They were the ones who usually started the riots afterward in Kenmore Square, when mobs of drunk Southie kids would start beating on anyone who came in their path on the way home, especially if there was anything odd about him. I just followed the mob to watch and to pretend to be part of the whole thing. One guy was beaten because he was a "faggot college student." Another guy got it because he was a "rock-and-roll pussy."

Then the kids from different neighborhoods started rioting against each other. There'd always been tension between the Irish kids and the Italian kids at Illusions. Some people said that Irish Southie and Italian Eastie were united against busing, but I could feel the tension if I was the only Irish kid in a bathroom full of Italians from Eastie or Revere, or if there was one Italian kid alone with a group of Southies. It all broke out when two kids, one Italian and the other Irish, got in a fight on the dance floor. Their scuffle triggered an ethnic war that lasted the rest of the summer. Fights between Italians and Irish broke out every Friday night in Kenmore Square. Southie teenagers who hadn't even gone to Illusions before started coming to Kenmore Square to get involved. And anyone in Kenmore Square who wasn't from Southie got it.

That's when I started hearing more people ask, "Where you from?" If they looked Irish, I said Southie. But if they looked Italian, I just ran to the nearest mob of Southie types. One night going home, my Southie mob all jumped onto the Red Line train at Park Street Station and the doors closed before I made it in. Just then about fifty teenagers came down the stairs onto the platform just across from me. They looked Italian and were wearing tight designer jeans and gold chains like the kids in Eastie usually wore. They spotted me across the track and started talking to each other, pointing me out.

"Where you from?" a short fat one yelled across the track, trying to pull up his pants, which were too tight to budge at all. "Who me?" I asked. I was the only one on my side of the track. A few of them laughed and the stout one asked if I wanted to end up on the third rail. Just then I heard my train pulling in, so I yelled "Southie!" across the track. The train stopped and I waited for the doors to open, and watched them all falling over each other to run up the stairs to cross the track and come after me. I knew the doors had to open soon. I waited, and waited, until finally they did open. I made it in just in time. One of the Italians threw a Heineken bottle at the train window and shattered it.

After we pulled out of the station, an older drunk guy who was the only other person on the train got up and asked me, "Where you from?" When I said Southie, he started giving me the handshake and hugging me as if we were long lost brothers. "Those guineas wouldn't try that shit in Southie," he said. "They know we got Whitey over there. And the Italian mob is scared shitless of him. They know he'd shoot 'em in the back as soon as look at 'em."

So now I didn't know what to say if Italians asked where I was from. I'd already learned to say "Jamaica Plain" or "Dorchester" or some other mixed part of the city, never "Southie," to black people. Same thing with anyone who looked kind of intellectual or liberal, like the social worker types when we were applying for jobs through ABCD. But they always found out where we lived by looking up our names in the computer. "Um, the border of Southie and Dorchester," is what I started to say then, so they wouldn't judge me as a racist. There was still no place like home, though, in the safety and security of South Boston.

"Hey, Joe, check it out!" Kevin yelled, rolling down the tinted window in the backseat of Whitey Bulger's car. He waved a large Baggie full of pot in front of Joe, who was working at Adams' Garage outside Old Colony, where Whitey's driver was having some work done on the car. Kevin knew Joe loved pot, and Joe's eyes lit up. Then Whitey slapped the bag from Kevin. "Keep that fuckin' shit down," Joe heard Whitey hiss. Everyone knew Whitey hated drugs—that's probably why he called it "fuckin' shit." He never touched the stuff; he just collected the money that was coming in. And boy was it coming in, by the looks of kids like Kathy, sixteen and walking around with black circles around her eyes. But that was their own fault, for getting into drugs. That's what the ladies on the stoop always said.

They said the big drug dealers were only making money selling the people what the people wanted.

When Joe came home and told me and Mary the story, I ran out of the house to see if I could get a glimpse of Southie's king, or maybe even meet him, since it was my own brother he was chauffeuring around. Fat chance. They were long gone, and who knew when I would see Kevin again, never mind Whitey. Even when Kevin was home, he kept the back room locked and climbed in and out from the roof.

Ma couldn't afford to send Kevin to a Catholic high school. Besides, he'd already wasted Ma's money at St. Augustine's. And forcing anyone to be bused to Roxbury to be the only white kid in the classroom was unthinkable. So Kevin dropped out, like most of his friends in the streets. Ma tried to get Johnnie to talk Kevin into learning a trade, but he laughed at that one. I guess he figured he had it made now, fifteen years old and riding high, in the backseat with the most powerful guy in Southie, James Whitey Bulger.

CHAPTER 6

AUGUST

I ALMOST GOT SHOT LAST NIGHT," JOE LAUGHED, CRAWL-ing out of bed for another Saturday morning of tales from Southie's disco nightlife. Joe had a big head from drinking the night before. He, Mary, and Frankie had been partying at the Lith Club on Broadway, which had become the place to be for Southie's older teenagers. Joe said he was outside the club trying to talk this girl from the suburbs he'd picked up into going home with him, "when all the sudden, this guy with a bloody head ran by." He said the bullets flew past him and the girl, who said she wasn't used to this kind of stuff. When they saw the gunman crouched between two cars, the girl held Joe in front of her as a human shield. "'Fuck this,' I said." Joe said he reversed positions, making his date into his own shield from the bullets. Joe was pissed off that the date didn't work out; she jumped into a cab and said she'd never come back to Southie again.

Joe's stories didn't faze me. I was used to them. Even the times I'd come close to the violence, I still felt comforted by the popular line that Southie was the one place "where everyone looks out for each other." One morning on my way to St. Augustine's, I found three fingers. They were at the bottom of one of the tunnels, the outdoor passages that cut through our buildings from courtyard to courtyard. The one downstairs from us was on a slope, so the pouring rain that morning had formed a lake at the bottom, and there on the edge were the fingers. I remembered hearing some guy screaming the night before, but it sounded normal to me. And even after finding the fingers, I wasn't bothered. It was nothing, really—just another story to tell the kids at school.

We all laughed at Joe, looking for the telephone number the girl had given him before the shoot-out. Frankie said Joe was exaggerating the whole thing, that it wasn't that bad, just another shoot-out among rival gangs from the D Street Project. Davey looked reassured by Frankie's words and joined the laughter after some nervous hesitation. Mary, Joe, and Frankie often had stories about stabbings, with the popular broken bottle or "nigger knife," and occasional gunfire. And before long they'd be making plans once again with their friends for another night out "at the O.K. Corral," as they called it.

Davey sat on the mattress in the parlor and stared at the palms of his hands, crying. He was in agony. I watched him helplessly from across the room, sitting at the old-fashioned school desk that Ma had dragged up from the dumpster. I'd been daydreaming in the stiff wooden seat, imagining the old schoolrooms, like I'd seen on "The Waltons." It was too hot to move; the weatherman had called the day "oppressive." I'd stopped daydreaming when I'd realized Davey was in pain. I couldn't see anything wrong with his hands, so I figured that he was hurting because it was August again. He'd been taking his medication and staying off the Coca-Cola because he said it made him too jumpy. But here he was, falling apart anyway. He asked me if I could see it. "See what?" I asked. "My bleeding fucking wounds," he screamed at me. I squeezed out of the cramped desk ready to run for the front door, because when Davey got like this there was no telling what he'd do. He'd never laid a hand on me, but I was scared to be alone with him when he had "the sickness in his eyes," as Ma called it. Ma said that she could always tell if Davey was getting sick by looking in his eyes. Davey begged me not to leave him by himself now, with the stigmata of Christ and all the blood dripping from his palms. I wanted to tell him that he wasn't bleeding at all, but I knew that would just piss him off.

He got up from the mattress and started pacing the floors with his long strides and a high bounce to every step. Now that we had the breakthrough apartment, he had a long walk to make: from the end of the hallway in one apartment to the far reaches of the second apartment, then back again, over and over. He started singing "Ding dong, the Witch Is Dead" from *The Wizard of Oz;* except he changed the words. "Ding dong, the wicked *stick* is dead," he sang. "Ding dong and merry-o / Sing it high, sing it low," and he made his voice go really high and really low when he sang those words. Davey's T-shirt was wet with all his moving around, and as still as I was, I started sweating too.

"Who's the wicked stick?" I yelled to him from a good distance. I was getting ready to run in case I had asked the wrong question, sending him deeper into the madness. Then he turned around, holding up his two hands, and said, "Who's the wicked stick? Who do you think? Satan, Lucifer, Beelzebub!" As scared as I was, I couldn't stop laughing at that word. I thought he'd made it up, or else was speaking in tongues like in the story he'd told me before about the apostles when they were filled with the Holy Spirit; with Davey I was ready for any kind of mysterious possession. "Beelzebub!" I laughed. "What the fuck is that? You made that up!" I said, trying to lighten things up a little. He told me that Beelzebub is just another name for the Devil. "Beelzebub! That's a good one," I said, laughing hysterically now and plopping myself backwards onto one of the couches. "The Devil has many names," he said, not laughing with me. "And he comes in many forms: like the stick. But," he added, "by the blood of Christ, the stick is dead." He turned around again, marching on his way with "Ding dong, the wicked stick is dead."

I stopped laughing then, and I just prayed to every ancestor I'd ever heard of, and to my brother Patrick, and to the Blessed Mother, to intervene and not let Davey kill himself or anything like that. I'd found myself doing this often. I had to talk to someone about what I witnessed, and I never wanted to scare Ma or the rest of the family whenever they got home, so I just prayed.

Davey had always prided himself in being "a little nutty," since, as he said, none of the people he'd met since moving into Old Colony wanted to "admit to their confusion." It often seemed Davey was working really hard to be well, coming into the house, exhausted after a long day of conversations on the street with people he said were way nuttier than he'd ever been, but who weren't on any medication, not prescribed anyway. He was always jerking his head around toward the sound of commotion in the streets, and saying something that he thought was hilarious or wise about our lives in Old Colony. He was trying really hard to get a kick out of it all. But then in August it wasn't funny anymore; the people in our neighborhood weren't funny he said, no matter how many jokes they told or laughs they had or drinks they took. It was as if he took on all of the suffering he saw around us, suffering that so many in Old Colony tried to ignore with all the partying like there was no tomorrow. They were all "poor souls," especially this time of year, and so was he.

When Ma came home that afternoon, Davey made like everything was normal, closing his hands tightly, as if he was hiding the wounds, and trying not to let Ma look in his eyes. When she looked at him with her own worried eyes, he just jerked his face away from her, heading out into the streets, and I kept him in my prayers.

Ma always looked down on the people who looked through their peepholes and then said they "didn't want to get involved." The

Duggans downstairs were at it again. It was one of those hot summer nights when no one could sleep, so we'd all felt something coming. When Ma heard all the screaming in the hallway, she looked through the peephole and saw Moe Duggan with a knife in his hand, and his thirteen- and sixteen-year-old sons bleeding from their chests, running for the roof to get away. Ma opened the door and pulled Brian and Joey inside, and locked it on Moe.

Brian collapsed onto the floor, and Joey ignored the blood spurting from his own chest to apply pressure to his little brother's wound. Ma called the EMTs. Reenie, the nosy neighbor from next door, came out of her apartment when she saw through her peephole that Moe had left the scene. She said Brian looked cold, and she grabbed Kathy's fur coat to throw on top of him. "Not my fuckin' fur coat!" Kathy screamed, and she knocked Reenie aside and caught the fur coat before it fell onto Brian.

We could see that Brian was turning an ash gray color and heard Ma say that he was dying, as she pressed her own fringed cowboy jacket onto the wound over Brian's heart. Davey came out of one of the back rooms but didn't say a word; he just paced back and forth past Brian and chain-smoked. Then he stopped pacing and looked at Brian and threw his two arms up like he finally knew what to offer. "Hey, Bri, you want a smoke?" When he got no response, he went back to his nervous pacing around the house, glancing at Brian from the corner of his eye whenever he happened to pass by.

Finally, about four EMTs and two cops charged into the apartment and rushed toward Joey, bleeding on the couch. Joey waved them off. "Forget me," he screamed. "Take care of my brother!" One EMT was on the phone with a doctor at the City Hospital, and I listened as he spoke low and said they were losing Brian. Joey panicked and rushed to his brother's side again. But they kept working on Brian and were able to revive him. They put him on life support, and eventually carried him out on a stretcher.

From the window, we watched the crowd that had gathered outside, people stretching their necks to get a good look at Brian going into the ambulance. Reenie was at the center of a circle of women, throwing her arms around and giving her account of the episode. And right in the middle of the crowd was Moe Duggan, stretching his own neck like a nosy neighbor. I knew Reenie wasn't mentioning his role in the stabbing. "Look at that fucker," Ma said, "like he's just a spectator. You wouldn't know that he was the father of two kids who were just stabbed, never mind that he was the one who knifed them."

A week later I began the seventh grade at Boston Latin, and rode the English High bus with Brian, since Latin was just across the street from English. Brian was showing his scars and telling the story to everyone. The last thing he remembered before dying: Davey bouncing around the room, "Hey, Bri, you want a smoke?" People repeated those words for weeks whenever they saw Brian. We all got a kick out of the story. Brian and Joey were both fine, except for the scars, and they never did mention their father's role. Ma never understood why, when she was called to Station 6 as a witness, none of the Duggans wanted to press charges against Moe.

"Solid Gold" blasted from the TV set. I watched the show every Friday night, and played with Seamus and Stevie while Ma got dressed to go play the accordion at the Emerald Isle Pub in Dorchester. I wasn't going out to Illusions anymore, so I was able to babysit when Ma went out to the Irish clubs. Kool and the Gang appeared on the screen, and Ma came out of the bathroom to watch their dance moves, telling me to zip up the back of her sequined minidress. I told her that minidresses were out of style, and that she should wear something longer. That even the younger girls at Illusions were wearing dresses to their knees, maybe with a little slit up the side. "Oh, that's a good idea," and she used her bare hands to rip a slit along the seam of the already too short dress. I hated to see her go out like that, even though all my friends raved about how nice-looking she was for a forty-year-old. Actually she was forty-five, but she got away with lying about her age to everyone, and made me do the same—even on official school documents.

Ma started making another one of her commotions looking for her spike heels and her pocketbook. I turned up the television so I could still hear "Solid Gold" through all Ma's rambling on about Kathy and her thieving friends who might have taken her stuff. I pretended that I was looking for her pocketbook out in the parlor. "Did you find it yet!" she screamed from the bathroom, as if it was a life or death situation. "Let's see . . . Nope, it's not under the cushions. Let me check the closet." Ma was always hiding her pocketbook whenever any company came over from the neighborhood. And when they left, she would've hidden it so well that she couldn't find it herself, and would start screaming that whoever had just left was a known thief, from a long line of thieves who would steal your last dollar as soon as look at you. She was yelling now about Julie Meaney, who'd just left the house with Kathy. "And what shoes did Kathy wear out of the house?" Ma asked, all out of breath now from the excitement. Kathy was always stealing Ma's spike heels for a night out on the town on East 8th Street.

Davey was pacing by the front door, oblivious to Ma's uproar. He was in his own world until the loud thumps came from the metal door, like someone was in trouble again—in a family fight, or else running from the cops. Davey jumped and jerked his head toward the door, staring at it for a minute without responding, like he was imagining the trouble that might come through if he opened it. Then it banged again; it sounded like kicks this time. Davey unlocked the door. It swung open fast and a shotgun came through, pointed right at Davey's head, backing him up against the wall. "Hey, c'mon will ya? Knock it off, huh?" Davey said, as if they were just playing around with him. I grabbed the two little kids to me, and yelled for Ma. About five other armed men in leather jackets and wool hats came charging into the house, covering each other as they checked around corners, guns pointed. One of them aimed at me, Seamus, and Stevie. Then another brought Ma out of the bathroom with her hands up. "My kids!" Ma tried not to cry when she saw the guns pointed at us. There was panic in her voice but she kept control, thinking fast, and trying not to make any false moves. The babies started to cry.

I knew we were all going to die, I just knew it. I could feel my heart beating against Seamus's and Stevie's heads as I covered them.

"I got 'em," one of the guys shouted from Frankie's room. They all rushed in to where Frankie was, except for one who stayed behind to cover us with his gun, telling Davey and Ma to go and sit still on the couch with me and Seamus and Stevie. Davey looked around the room fast, as if he might be planning an escape. Just then we heard fighting and Frankie yelling in the back room. Ma started to plead and cry.

That's when the intruder with the gun pointed at us said he was a cop, and that we were being raided for drugs. He held up his badge; it was upside-down. "Drugs!?" Ma screamed. Davey sat rocking back and forth as he always did, laughing at the cop, or maybe trying to get him to laugh along, and then turning his head away, looking nervously out of the corner of his eye at the gun. The gunman yelled at him, "Hey . . . Stop that! Stop it!" Davey just looked at him again. That's when the guy cocked the trigger and screamed, "I said fuckin' cut it out!" "Cut . . . what . . . out?" Davey asked, looking at the gun as if he wasn't sure he was even allowed to talk, and then looking away from the gun, back at us. The kids were crying, especially Seamus, whose face was covered in tears, looking at Ma. "Stop moving so fast," the guy said. "What are you doing?" "Oh, Davey does that," Ma explained with a smile, like we could all be the best of friends if we connected. "He rocks back and forth. You see, he's mentally ill," she added, looking for some sympathy. "Yeah, schizophrenic!" Davey said proudly.

"Yeah, well, we all got our problems . . . just sit still."

Just then they brought Frankie out, shirtless and sweaty, bent over like the handcuffs were hurting him. I thought he looked like a criminal, which was a real surprise to me. *Frankie's no criminal*, I thought. I guess I would've looked like a criminal too if I was the one being brought out in handcuffs. I realized the ones who had him in handcuffs looked a lot like the gangsters I'd seen around town. "Frank!" Ma screamed. Two guys stood in front of Ma, blocking her from getting closer. Four other guys rushed Frankie headfirst toward the door. "Where are you taking him?" Ma pleaded, her voice shaky, as if she was struggling to stay calm.

"He's goin' to jail, ma'am." Now they were calling her ma'am. They held up the shotgun they'd found in Frankie's room. It was the one that Coley and Ma had got in the D Street Project back when we moved into Old Colony and had to protect ourselves. It had gone missing, and Ma figured someone had stolen it. But Kevin had kept it hidden, under the bed in Frankie's room. "He says he owns the gun, ma'am, but that he can't find his license. Besides that, we found ten hits of acid." I knew then that Kevin had gotten Frankie into trouble again, hiding his stash in Frankie's room. But Frank wasn't about to rat on Kevin. Just then, one of the guys handed the shotgun to the one who was keeping us all under cover like we were Ma Barker and her boys, and they all left. We weren't allowed to follow them. We looked out the window and saw the ladies on the stoop clear the way for Frankie and his captors. They put him into an unmarked car. I still wasn't sure they were really cops; they'd acted more like gangsters. I hated the cops plenty for all the beatings I'd seen them giving out during the busing troubles. And now—*Especially if those bastards are the law*, I said to myself—I could see how some of the kids in the neighborhood could start to feel like criminals whether they were or not; or even why they'd be proud to be outlaws.

The court made a deal with Frankie: he wouldn't be prosecuted if he joined the service. So Frankie went into the Marines. Ma was thrilled to see him get out of Old Colony. Even though he'd stayed out of trouble with his boxing, Ma said it was getting so that trouble would find you easy enough these days.

Everyone missed Frankie. We'd all started to go to his fights, except Ma, who said she couldn't bear to see Frankie get hurt in the ring. Davey missed Frank the most, though; the two of them had gotten close, and like the rest of us Davey felt safe in Old Colony with a brother who could box. When Davey had first been set free from Mass Mental, there were people in Old Colony who didn't know he was one of us—and who thought he seemed odd. But any time he was teased, Frank was the first to his rescue. One time a gang of kids Frankie called "the pretty boys," with their perfect hair and pressed clothes, were making fun of Davey and his bouncy step. "Hey, Frank, some maggots are botherin' me!" Davey shouted up one of the tunnels. Frankie sent Davey back to where the pretty boys were hanging out by the incinerator, and stayed hidden in the tunnel to watch the teasing himself. As soon as it began, he walked up to them saying, "You fuckin' with my brother?" They begged for forgiveness, saying they didn't know Davey was a MacDonald. And off went Frankie, with Davey bouncing behind him and looking back at the pretty boys with a tough-guy stare and clenched fists.

Joe missed Frankie too. He'd just bought his new pimpin' van from our neighbor, Cookie. We'd all envied Cookie in her blue van with ocean paintings on the side, and "The Blue Goose" written on it in sparkly country-western-style letters. Cookie was so big, she had the driver seat pushed so far back that you couldn't see her head when she drove by—she looked all breast and belly. Joe had to get new bucket seats, and he couldn't wait until Frankie got out of the Marines, so they could ride around picking up girls.

The Blue Goose was like an apartment, with a table, sink, and a bed. And Joe stole Ma's curtains to hang in the windows. As soon as Kevin stepped inside, he called it his new pad. Joe never locked his door—he had no need to in Old Colony. So Kevin and his friends Okie, Joey Earner, and Timmy Baldwin practically moved in, playing cards, drinking, and inviting girls over, whenever Joe was home sleeping. One night Davey made a commotion in the street, banging on the side of the Blue Goose and demanding to be let in. Kevin and his friends had girls over and had locked Davey out. "I want some action too," Davey yelled, peeking through the rear windows. That's when Joe went down and kicked everyone out.

The next morning, Joe arrived at his new mechanic job forty minutes outside the city. He turned around and saw Joey Earner crawling out of the bed, scratching his head, and asking, "Where are we, Joe?"

The only one more excited than Joe to see Frankie leave the Marines after three months was Davey. Frankie came home with a bald head and all kinds of military clothes and boots. He was even more obsessed with working out now, jogging five miles a day—sometimes we'd spot him running backwards along the beach, wearing his combat boots. Joe waited until Frankie was ready to party at night, but Davey started to follow Frankie on his runs. Then Frankie got an apartment with Davey in Old Colony. That's when Frankie started getting Davey to focus on his appearance. He taught Davey to shave correctly and more often, got him punching the heavy bag, and doing a hundred push-ups a night. Davey said he was feeling good about himself, said he was going to try to meet a woman. He started wearing Frankie's clothes. But Davey was six-foot-one, three inches taller than Frankie, and sometimes he'd mix Frankie's dress clothes with gym clothes. We suddenly started seeing Davey with his hair slicked back and parted in the middle, wearing a silk disco shirt with Adidas sweatpants that were too tight and too high. But he was walking with a less edgy step, and even if he looked funny, he often had a more relaxed look in his eyes, living with his buddy Frankie.

At the close of the school year in 1979, everyone was thinking about the murder. Francis Stewart had gotten his throat slit by his sister's boyfriend, Charles Fuller—a born-again minister from the neighborhood—as he'd walked alongside Fuller at Houghton's Pond. We all seemed to be able to brush off the stories of gunfire on Broadway, and now and then there'd been vague talk of suicides and overdoses. But that was like background noise, and didn't matter much. We were shocked that a neighbor could be killed so brutally by someone he thought was a friend. No one wanted to say much. Everyone knew you had to be careful what you said, and who you talked to, about things like this. You never knew who was on what side, or who was related in our neighborhood. But despite the worried look in people's eyes when they opened the papers every day to get the update on one of the most brutal murders we'd heard of, the shock only lasted so long. Summer arrived, and soon everything was back to normal for most of us.

"Jesus, I love you," Davey mumbled, pacing past me and the women on the stoop watching the black-and-white TV that someone had carried outside on another hot August night. Then he picked up his pace, and with each "Jesus, I love you," he got louder and louder, until he screamed the words out at the top of his lungs in the middle of Patterson Way: "Jesus, I love you!" People came to their windows, and some even came outside for a better view. The teenagers selling drugs on the corners looked a little nervous. Davey was in the middle of the street now, blocking a few customers from coming down Patterson. Eventually, they just swerved around him, and the teenagers poked their heads into the car windows for a second before the customers sped off again.

Davey disappeared, and then we saw his silhouette pacing the rooftops across the street, bouncing higher than ever, and screaming at the top of his lungs: "Jesus, I love you!" The women on the stoop all looked at me, asking me why he was doing that. I just kept staring at "Happy Days" on the TV set, and started playing with the vertical knob on the set to keep the picture from jumping. "I don't know," I finally answered. "Maybe he thinks Jesus can't hear him." I wished that Frankie would get home. Since he and Davey had moved into the apartment across the street, Frankie was the only one who could make him calm down. I usually made Davey worse with all my questions. Finally Ma came walking up the tunnel with Nellie. The two of them were laughing away at one of Nellie's stories until they heard it: "Jesus, I love you!" from the rooftop. "Nellie, go get him down, will you?" Ma said; then she came over to the women on the stoop, smiling and asking how everyone was doing, to take the attention away from Davey. Nellie walked across the street to yell up to Davey. "Get down here, will you, you son of a bitch, you're tormenting your poor mother!" Then she started screaming as Davey showered her with the small pebbles that covered the rooftop, telling her that she had the Devil in her. Nellie came staggering over to us, laughing, "Well, he's right about that one," she admitted. She pulled out her bottle and took a swig. The women on the stoop all laughed with Ma and Nellie.

Davey's silhouette disappeared. One of the teenagers selling drugs followed him for my mother, and came back to tell us that Davey had gone toward Carson Beach and looked as if he were calming down. It was nine at night now, and we turned our attention away from the TV set to watch the drug traffic, the teenage girls coming out all dressed up for a night of partying, and the arguments and fights breaking out from people's open windows. "Ach, it's gonna be another long hot night, huh?" Nellie said, sitting down on the stoop and taking another swig. "This is a great place. I wish I could get an apartment in Old Colony," she added. "I'm stuck with the niggers over in Dorchester." Nellie was trying to make conversation with the women on the stoop, but they just ignored her since Ma had gone up to the apartment to check on the babies. Nellie was an outsider, and there was no welcome for her, only looks when she took her swigs, as if we'd never seen drinking before in these parts. "Keep her with the niggers," one of the women muttered, staring back again at the jumping picture on the TV set.

* * *

I met up with my friend Danny every day after work at the carpentry job I'd been given that summer through the welfare office. One boiling hot day we went to Carson Beach before it got dark. Davey was there, sitting on the beach wall with his head down. No pacing, no rocking back and forth, and no chain-smoking. I'd never seen Davey look so calm. As if he was letting go of all the battles he'd been waging through his August days, and nights. Only the night before he'd attacked me in the streets, calling me Michael the Dark Angel. When I was a little kid, he'd always told me about Michael the Archangel, who I was named after. But on this night, he'd said that everything had changed, that I'd fallen from the heights, just like Lucifer, who I'd thrown out of heaven, gaining favor with God myself and ruling the heavens. Now it was all over. I was no longer in God's favor; I'd become the Dark Angel, in league with Satan. Danny had been with me when Davey said all that. I was always getting embarrassed by Davey's crazy talk and often tried to make light of it all. I'd called my brother a fool, and he'd quoted something in the Bible that said it was a great sin to call another man a fool, and that I would definitely burn. But now Davey looked peaceful. We called over to him, but he didn't respond; he just kept staring at the sand.

I went home to mind Seamus and Stevie later that afternoon. As usual, Ma called every once in a while to ask about "the babies," as we still called them, and to have me feel Stevie's back while he slept, to make sure he was still breathing. Seamus was three now, and Stevie two, but ever since Patrick, Ma never really trusted that her babies weren't dead when they were just soundly sleeping. "Put down the phone and put your hand on his back to make sure he's breathing," she said. "Come on, will ya, Ma," I said. "Just do it," she said, "I'm not hanging up until you come back and tell me." Stevie was on the couch on his stomach, and I felt his back go up and down a few times before returning to tell Ma. I took my time, because I knew that if I came back to the telephone too soon, she wouldn't believe I'd done it. "All right," she said, "I'll be back later, I'm meeting Nellie up Broadway."

Frankie came up that day, just like every other day, to eat something after boxing at McDonough's Gym. He and Davey never had food in their apartment across the street, and Ma always kept the fridge loaded at our place. He woke Stevie up to tease him and to teach him to box; he said the babies had to learn to fight at an early age. Frankie loved toughening up the little kids. I heard a woman scream outside, but I didn't think anything of it. Just another hot day in August, I figured, and it'll only get worse when the sun goes down. Then it sounded as if someone was breaking down our door, they were banging so hard. Frankie whipped open the door ready for a fight. It was my friend Walter who lived across the street. He was crying. "It's Davey! I don't know what happened! He just came flying off of the roof!" Frankie ran down the stairs, yelling "No! No! No!" over and over again. I wanted to run out that door so badly, but someone had to watch Seamus and Stevie. I paced. I couldn't look out the window. I heard more screams outside. I looked out the window. I didn't want to, but I had to. And there he was, my oldest brother, lying face down on the pavement, his plaid shirt and dungarees soaked with his blood. I felt my heart pumping through my head, my fingers, my feet. I could've fought off an entire army of Davey's demons, but I had to stay in the house with the kids. I saw him moving now, and felt I had to keep looking, to see if there was a chance that he might be all right, as if my watching might help. "Call an ambulance! Someone! Now!" Frankie was screaming. I called 911.

"Emergency, can I help you?"

"It's my brother he's dead—he's dying."

"What happened, honey?"

"I don't know—he fell off the roof—blood"

"Umm—OK. Where are you?"

"Just fuckin' hurry up! Fuckin' hurry!"

"Listen, honey, calm down. Now what's the address?"

"8 Patterson Way in South Boston, Old Colony Project—please!
Oh my fuckin' God."

"What does he look like? What's he wearing?"

"Huh? He's fuckin' covered in blood! Hurry! Please! Please!
Please! Please! Just fuckin' get here!"

"Listen, don't get nasty with me!"

I hung up the telephone—I knew they'd come; they had enough
information. I had to do something else. I still couldn't go outside—
I had to keep the two little kids away from the windows. They knew
something was going on, with all the screams and me crying and
pacing. They kept running to the windows and trying to pull themselves up. There were more screams outside, and the sound of
crowds gathering, and people calling up to their friends to tell them
what happened. Big Lisa from 19 Patterson banged on the door and
walked in asking if I wanted her to mind the kids. I hated big Lisa—
Ma was always trying to bring her over as if she was going to fix the
two of us up. Big Lisa was really big, the fattest girl in the project,
always wearing maternity shirts and pretending she was pregnant.
But I was glad to see her now. I thanked her and threw on my sneakers. She started getting the little kids dressed. I asked her what she
was doing. She said she was going to take them downstairs and mind
them out there. I looked at her like I was hearing things. "No." I
forced a calm voice out of my mouth, "I don't want them to see this."
I wanted to kill her for her stupidity. "Forget it then," she said,
"everyone's outside, the whole neighborhood. I don't want to be
stuck in here." I threw her out.

When I looked out the window again, Davey was standing up,
covered in blood and throwing powerful punches at everyone in his
path. *What's he fighting?* I thought. Frankie restrained him and got
him to calm down. The ambulance hadn't come, and it had been a
good fifteen minutes already. I tried to call 911 again. My hands were
shaking and my fingers kept turning the telephone dial to the wrong
numbers. This made me break down and cry, and Seamus cried too.

Then I went numb, became very calm, and turned the 9, then the 1, then the 1 again.

I got into another fight with the dispatcher. "There are emergencies all over the city," she snapped. "We're doing our best, and there's nothing more I can do."

Just then I heard the sirens. Fire trucks, ambulances, and police cars filled Patterson Way, about twenty-five minutes after I'd first called. I was still numb, not feeling a thing, as I looked out the window. Tears came from my eyes, but it seemed as if they fell on their own. I watched them take Davey into the ambulance, restrained face down on a straight board, as he raged, trying to bust loose from the tight straps around his body. I knew that he wasn't fighting for his life; he was fighting for his death. The crowds of people were now climbing on top of things to get a better look at him.

The ambulance stayed out front for another hour. While they were working on Davey I saw Kathy come down the street, laughing with Tisha Stokes and Doreen. She was high again, looking around to see what all the commotion was. I was hurt to see that her expression didn't change much when she got up to the ambulance to find that it was her brother dying in there. She just hung out front for a while, getting the story retold to her by all the neighbors, who claimed they'd seen the whole thing and gave blow-by-blow accounts, imitating Davey's determined punches in slow motion. She listened to their stories over and over again. Her face didn't change. I don't know what I was looking for in her face, pain I guess. But Kathy looked numb, and I too had already started to feel less and less, like I'd been drained.

I went away from the window, back to the kids. They were hungry and I had to make them some food. I put some leftover macaroni and cheese on the stove. I returned to the window to find that the ambulances had pulled off. Davey was gone from Patterson Way, and I suddenly felt again. I cried out loud.

* * *

Ma came home at about eleven at night with Nellie. The two of them had been at the City Hospital. Ma said the doctors were still working on Davey, but that he was going to be all right. I half believed her, or I wanted to. I stayed up late and snuck to the telephone to call the hospital for patient information. They said Davey was in critical condition. "Is he gonna live?" I asked, and was immediately afraid of the answer. I was relieved when they said that they had no other information except his status: critical. I told Ma, and she yelled at me for being a worrywart. "For Chrissake, go to bed will ya'?" Nellie screamed from the couch, getting comfortable, with only a baby blanket thrown over her torso. "You're keepin' us all up!" Ma reassured me that Davey would be fine; she'd seen him herself and talked to the doctors. She looked as if she believed it, and so I lay down on the other couch opposite Nellie and her snoring all night.

I actually fell asleep after a couple of hours, and when I woke up at about six, I could hear Ma rummaging around the house. I lay still for a while, faking I was asleep, because I didn't want to ask the question I had: "Is he alive?" The door knocked and Ma opened it. It was Johnnie. He was the second oldest to Davey—they were like twins as children, being only ten months apart—but he was more like the oldest in the family since Davey's breakdown. He'd graduated from Tufts and was now in the Navy, but was back in Southie having heard the news. He'd slept over at Frankie and Davey's the night before; Ma didn't know he'd come back. "Oh, John! Hi!" Ma said. I could tell she was forcing a happy voice. Then she let it out, the truth. "Davey . . . died last night," she said in a low voice, and now she sounded defeated. I could tell that her heart broke when she said those words, and so did mine. I let out a long moan, and turned my face into the pillow as if I could stop the pain by stopping my uncontrollable moans. "Motherfucker!" Johnnie screamed, and he punched a dent in the cement wall. Ma said Davey lived for nine hours after his jump, that he'd died of a burst spleen, and had received last rites from a priest. Ma had arranged for the last rites, she told us, and I was mad at her then for not telling me the night before that she knew Davey would die.

Everyone came out of the bedrooms slowly at Johnnie's voice, and when they saw him crying they knew what had happened. Kathy sat silent at the kitchen table. Kevin too came out slowly from the back room and never said a word. Joe had gone out for a walk, Ma said, and Mary came over to join the silence. Frank was nowhere to be seen, and no one wanted to tell him that Dave was dead. He'd taken care of Davey, and had been the closest to him. Nellie staggered up from the couch and went straight for the refrigerator, one half of her hair flattened and the other half standing straight up. She grabbed a whole raw onion, the way she always did when she woke up with a big head, and bit into it like it was a sweet apple. "Poor old Dave," she moaned in low notes that sounded like the beginning of another sad Irish song, crunching away at the raw onion. We all just looked at her, silent, for a few seconds. I started laughing and crying at the same time. Then I wanted to kick her out, as if I was looking for anyone to hate who wasn't feeling the way I was. It seemed so heartless for her to be eating—even if it was a nasty raw onion that only she could enjoy. We'd never see Davey on this earth again, and right then there was no way to understand the meaning of that. It was something I'd never understand for the rest of my life.

The morning of the funeral I watched Ma helplessly, as she tore through closets and bureaus. She was searching for a kerchief to cover her head, since she'd be entering into a Church building and wanted to look respectable for Davey's Mass. In my own lifetime I'd hardly ever seen women covering their heads for Mass, but Ma had been brought up in that tradition, passed down by her church-going mother. And by the looks of her frantically searching through piles of clothes, looking away from us and hiding the tears in her eyes, she seemed to still believe in it.

"This will have to do," Ma said, pulling out a black sparkly tube top and ripping it in half with her bare hands. The limos had arrived. It was almost time to see Davey at Jackie O'Brien's funeral parlor one last time, before the Mass and funeral. Ma bobby-pinned her headpiece on neatly and straightened her shoulders for the rest of us.

"Killed himself? He wouldn't kill himself—he must have been pushed." Grandpa didn't want to accept suicide. None of us did. I too wanted to think Davey had fallen, until I went up to the roof where he'd made the last decision of his life and found broken bottles covered with his blood. I stood on the rooftop looking down at the ground below, his blood on the bottle I gripped, and on the sidewalk. *He really wanted to die,* I thought. I brought the broken glass downstairs to show Ma that he had slit his wrists as well. It was almost a relief to know the truth, to know that he wanted it that bad, that he was in so much pain that he was able to do something that most of us could never go through with, no matter how bad things were. Ma had that crying voice with no tears, and begged me, "Get rid of that thing, please!" I took the glass back up to the roof and threw it as far as I could. Then I found more pieces of glass caked with blood, and I wanted to save some. I put a couple pieces in my pocket. I stayed up on the rooftop, to try to be with Davey in the last moments of his life, when he'd suffered alone. I looked out over the landscape of Old Colony, the maze of red bricks looking like a trap to me now. My neighbors were just starting to stir after a quiet day. The sun was going down, and in the distance the sky turned bright orange and pink and purple. But the people I saw below, moving into another humid summer night of liquor, drug sales, and fights weren't looking up at the sky. They didn't seem as if they wanted to see anything beyond the brick world below. I wondered if Davey on his last evening saw what I was now seeing. I slid myself down against the rooftop stairwell and sat frozen.

I couldn't organize my thoughts. Guilt overtook me. I knew how much he'd been suffering the week before his death, but I'd laughed at him when he'd called me Michael the Dark Angel, and I'd walked away from him when I saw him looking strange and calm at the beach, and I'd done nothing to help him live. And then the anger came: *What kind of asshole would do this to us anyway? Bastard!* I hated Davey for not thinking about Ma, or about Seamus and Stevie having to grow up with a sad family, or about the two seven-year-olds who'd been sitting quietly on the front stoop eating popsicles when Davey's body dropped two feet away from them. *What a fuckin' selfish monster!*

Then I thought about Davey, and his sense of humor, his brilliance, his funny attempts to understand and connect to the bizarre world of Old Colony he'd come to at the height of the busing chaos. I remembered visiting him in Mass Mental, seeing him cry into Ma's lap while she too cried, seeing him attack Ma because he loved us and wanted to be back home with us. Then there was his last Christmas, when he came up to our apartment with a Christmas present for Ma. It was a bottle of Jergens lotion that must have cost less than a dollar. He presented it from behind his back with a little uncertainty in his face, not knowing if it was enough to give. Ma told him it was exactly what she'd wanted for Christmas.

CHAPTER 7

HOLY
WATER

ALL SUMMER LONG WE'D SEEN "WHO SHOT J.R.?" COM-
mercials, billboards, and T-shirts. By that September of 1980,
we couldn't wait to find out who'd pulled the trigger. But I never got
to see the "Dallas" episode everyone was waiting for, because right
before the season premiere came on, Ma got shot by a stray bullet,
while she was standing next to me in our kitchen washing dishes.

Ma was all dressed up to go to the Emerald Isle Pub. She didn't
care who shot J.R. Joe had settled onto the couch to watch "Dallas,"
while Seamus and Stevie played on the floor nearby. We heard two
sharp noises and Joe screamed for everyone to duck. I saw the two
bullet holes in the living room window as I hit the floor. When I
looked up to find Ma, she was crouching in a corner of the kitchen,
holding onto her side. She just said, "I got hit," and looked slightly
bothered, like she'd been hit with a rock, not a bullet. Ma was tough.

Ma lifted her hand from her side and we saw the skin was ripped
off under her armpit. Her white sequined shirt was torn and getting
redder by the second. She told me to grab some toilet paper for her
to stick to the wound, and she crawled fast over to Seamus and Steven, kept them lying low, and dragged them over to a corner of the

house where there were no windows. They were both crying, and we had to keep yelling at them, telling them to stay put. We turned off all the lights. People were hollering throughout the building. We found out later that Frannie O'Malley on the second floor had been struck in the hand, and a six-year-old girl on the first floor had missed getting shot in the head by about three inches. Crowds of women started to gather outside and were pointing in all directions, trying to guess where the gunman had shot from. We stayed upstairs and peeked through the curtain from the corner of the window; we didn't know when the shooting might start again. We wondered who the gunman was, or if it was any of us that he was after. Before long about a hundred people had gathered out front, most of them women in nightgowns and bathrobes. Many of them were laughing and joking about the whole thing. "Fuck this!" I heard one of them say. "Never mind who shot Helen, I gotta get home and find out who shot J.R." She said "Dallas" was coming on in five minutes.

Finally the ambulances came, and by then Ma was joking about the whole thing too. She told the EMTs she was fine, that the bullet didn't lodge in her, and that she wasn't getting into any ambulance unless they were dropping her off at the Emerald Isle where she had to play the accordion and make some money for her kids. She'd already changed into a black shirt, and had more toilet paper stuffed into the side of her bra to sop up the blood. She wouldn't take off her rabbit fur coat to show them the wound. "Sorry, ma'am, you have to get checked. You've been shot," the EMT said. "It's routine procedure." Finally Ma gave in, and climbed into the ambulance, carrying the accordion over her shoulder and waving to the crowds, along with Frannie O'Malley, whose hand was bleeding. All the neighbors waved them off cheering and laughing and went home to the TV. I pulled mattresses into a corner of the house that had no windows, kept all the lights out, and slept there with Seamus and Stevie in case the gunman was still out on Patterson Way.

The next morning Ma told us she'd managed to escape from the back of the ambulance when they'd pulled up to the emergency room, and off she went to the Emerald Isle. In a few days she had to go back to the hospital, because the wound was infected. But she said she'd had a great time that night anyway, playing the accordion and telling some people from Belfast how she'd just survived a shooting.

She wanted to know who had shot her, though, and why. Back at home she followed the straight line from the bullet hole in the window to where a bullet was still lodged in our wall, and extended that path to a spot on the rooftop across the street. "I should've been a detective," she bragged. The cops never even came around to investigate the shooting, but at least Ma was looking into it. A few days later she found out that Packie Keenan had been seen carrying a gun up the stairwell to the same corner of the roof that Ma had pointed to. "That son of a bitch!" she said, and I wondered if all that investigating would have been as easy for the cops. Packie was Kevin's age, about seventeen, and when he heard Ma was looking for him, he sent her a three-page letter of apology, explaining that he was "all fucked up that night" on drugs and "just went crazy shooting the gun off." He said he didn't mean to hit Ma, that he was just trigger-happy with all the coke in him. Ma forgave him, and joked about how she was like Wonder Woman, bouncing bullets off her. But she tried to get Packie to go into a detox. Ma was always trying to get half the neighborhood to go into detox programs those days. Packie promised he would, but he was soon darting around Old Colony again, chewing on the corners of his mouth and staring with wide eyes, like the rest of the kids in the neighborhood who were into cocaine.

Most of my neighbors voted for Ronald Reagan that November, and figured things would be getting better, with the new president getting tough on crime and drugs, tough on the liberals who were always targeting our neighborhood for their experiments, and since he talked about money trickling down to the likes of us in Southie. But the optimism didn't last. In Old Colony in the early eighties it seemed like our whole world was going crazy, and for most of us it really didn't matter who was president. One time Mr. Heaney, three buildings down from us, took his family hostage at gunpoint. I was in the ninth grade at Latin School, and I came home from the library to find all of Patterson Way barricaded by the cops. When I went into my apartment, the whole family was watching live coverage on Channel 5 of what was happening just outside the door. "Mr. Heaney's gone in the head," Ma said. "He lost his job or something." Everyone told me to shut up and sit down to watch the police special forces rescue Mrs. Heaney and her five kids. By morning they'd talked him into laying down his 12-gauge shotgun, and surrendering himself.

Another time I came home to find the paramedics coming out of our building carrying Chickie on a stretcher. My friend Danny was scared. His mother had tried to kill herself, taking a bottle of pills, and we didn't know if she'd live. I was always scared of Chickie, because I never knew what she'd do next. I never wanted to go into Danny's apartment, and I don't think he ever wanted anyone to come in. It's funny, I thought, how the people who seem the meanest, the people we want nothing to do with, might be in the most pain. Like many of the women in the project, Chickie was barely getting by. Who were her husbands, I wondered, Danny and Robbie's fathers? Just like Ma, you wouldn't know that Chickie had many relatives. We never saw any, except for her twin sister, Duckie, who was also living in the project. Now here was Chickie, being brought down the front steps, suspended between life and death, and Danny and little Robbie too were left hanging in the balance, looking to the adults in the gathering crowd for any words of hope. "She's gonna be fine, don't worry," one of the ladies from the stoop said. "Your mother's just not feeling good." But no one could look at Robbie when he asked, "Really? You sure?" with all the anxiety of a nine-year-old who knew that his mother wanted to die.

Chickie was home again in a week, but ambulances were coming down Patterson Way all the time now. My Aunt Theresa in Jamaica Plain had a police radio, and asked me, "What in the hell is going on over there?" She said Patterson Way was coming up on the scanner all night long. I told my aunt that I didn't take any notice, that Old Colony was the greatest. But I did take notice. I started to come in the back door of our building at night, to avoid having to climb over everyone hanging out on the front stoop—I was getting tired of hearing all the comical storytelling about lives falling apart. And at night the neighborhood looked darker to me. Whenever I came home late, I was scared to walk into our pitch-black hallway with all the broken lights. I might turn a corner and get bitten by the rats that were moving in, or someone being chased might mistake me for a cop and shoot me. I had a whole tragic scenario playing in my head whenever I opened the big creaky steel door to our building. A few times I yelled up to the window and had Ma open our apartment door to give me—and the hiding gunman or lurking rat—some light.

Even taxi drivers didn't want to go into my neighborhood anymore. Ever since busing, we couldn't get a black taxi driver to take us to South Boston from downtown. They sped off as soon as they heard where we were going. So we started to make sure we were in the cab first, saying we were going to Dorchester, which was in the same direction, and then making as if we'd changed our mind halfway through the ride and would be jumping out on the edge of Southie. But now even the white cabbies were hesitant about taking us home. One night when I'd said Old Colony, I had to leave my two shoes in the front seat next to the cabby. "That's so you won't screw on me without paying the fare," he told me. We could tell them to take us to Southie, but never to Old Colony Project. I started to say City Point, and from there would walk down the hills to the Lower End. Just before Christmas, a cabby was shot in the head and killed in Old Colony. The next morning people stood on street corners, telling each other that Mrs. Coyne's sixteen-year-old son Mickey did it, after trying to rob the guy for a few bucks. They'd heard the cabby wouldn't give him the money, and Mickey was messed up. They said the guy should've just given him the money.

Mickey wasn't charged with the killing, but he ended up in a federal penitentiary a few years later for other robberies.

The only order I could make in those days was in my complicated schemes for coming and going safely through the project. I was getting pretty good at that, and was even trying to ignore the frequent wails of sirens that had begun to startle me only since Davey's death.

Then the sirens came again for us. I knew right away from the fast knocks, and then kicks, that it was our turn once again. "Kathy went off of the roof," Richie Amoroso yelled when I opened the door. He was out of breath and looked scared, holding onto his head with both hands. I had heard the fire engines going down Patterson Way, but was trying to pay no attention. I didn't know Kathy was lying in a pool of blood down the street. "She crashed onto her head," a woman's voice outside echoed right through me. There was no way I was going to believe this. This couldn't happen twice. Ma came out of the back room, where she'd been keeping to herself since Davey died, retreating whenever she didn't have the energy to be all smiles for the world to see that she was okay after losing her son. She'd heard what Richie had just said at the door, and she held onto a wall, because her knees were buckling under her. Her back arched. Her face looked as if she was being beaten on her back with baseball bats. The house was dark except for the flashing red lights from the fire trucks outside. The little kids came out, asking questions. Stevie, who was five, asked, "Is she gonna die?" Ma straightened up then. She could never let her babies see her fall apart.

Later on, Kathy was in critical condition in the intensive care unit at City Hospital. Ma said she'd be fine. But I didn't believe her— that's what she'd said about Davey the night he died. I don't think any of us slept. When I got out of bed in the morning, I called the hospital for patient information. They said Kathy was on the "danger list." I spoke to a doctor who told me her brain was still bleeding, and that they were working to stop the hemorrhage. I lied and said

I was eighteen so that he'd give me all the details; and he did, but mostly in language I'd never heard before. He talked about contusions and neuro this and neuro that. Mary had come over from her apartment in the Old Harbor Project, and since she was going to nursing school, I handed the phone to her. "She's not feeling anything," Mary told me after hanging up. Kathy was in a coma.

The doctor said Kathy's system was loaded with Valium, speed, and cocaine on the night she fell. Ma went through Kathy's pocketbook that a neighbor found up on the roof, and came across bottles of yellow pills and some coke. The pills were prescribed to Kathy by a doctor who lived up on "Pill Hill," a section toward City Point where quite a few doctors had offices. Ma said she knew people who got phony prescriptions up on Pill Hill, but she was shocked that this doctor would be prescribing to kids since, as she said, he was "as sensible looking as the day is long."

All we knew about Kathy's fall was that she'd been up on the roof with Richie Amoroso, on top of the building where she'd been staying with her new friend, Joanie. The neighbors listening at their windows that night said they'd heard Richie and Kathy fighting over drugs, and that Kathy had accused Richie of stealing her Vals. They said Richie had taken the keys to Kathy's apartment too. And some neighbors said they thought Richie Amoroso pushed Kathy off the roof in the struggle that broke out.

Every day we called the hospital, and it turned into months of hearing the same thing: "Danger list," the voice would say before hanging up on me, as if they were sick of me calling. But I was relieved, after every call, not to be told she was dead. Every day through the winter months of 1981, we woke up to continue our watch. Some nights I couldn't sleep at all, thinking I'd wake up to bad news. No doctor or nurse could tell us whether Kathy would live or die. The nurses said they didn't want to give us too much hope, when she could die at any moment, and I thought they were cold to say such useless words. They did tell us early on, though, that the longer Kathy stayed in a coma, the worse her brain damage; and that it was unlikely she'd ever be the same again.

We all took turns visiting Kathy in the intensive care unit, but it seemed I was there around the clock, in the surgical mask and gloves they made me put on so I wouldn't pass on any germs to her. I should've been at Boston Latin School, but I couldn't sit through class, knowing Kathy might die at any moment. I thought that if I kept talking to Kathy while she was in the coma, it might get her brain working and she'd come back to life. The nurses never asked why I wasn't in school, and every morning Ma saw me leave the house with my huge stack of ancient history and Latin books, not knowing that I was going to the City Hospital. Our telephone was disconnected in those days for not paying the bill, so the school could never call Ma. And I ripped up any mail that would come from Latin. I was relieved that the telephone was out, except that I kept thinking no one would be able to reach us when Kathy died. So whenever I couldn't be at Kathy's bedside, I'd go out to the phone booth at least once an hour to call patient information.

One of our neighbors who was a nurse at City Hospital came by the house every day, to give Ma updates about Kathy and to offer some hope that Kathy would get through this. Karen was always sneaking by Kathy's bedside, checking on her vital statistics even though it wasn't her floor at the City Hospital. Karen said Kathy was a fighter, and that she must really have the will to live, because she was baffling the doctors, overcoming every threat of death that came her way. Karen Young was one of the people in the neighborhood who came and went from Old Colony each day, never getting caught up in the action on the streets. She was always smiling, and some of the younger kids bragged that they knew her whenever they saw her going off to work in her nurse's uniform. One of her brothers, Charlie, hung out with Kevin in the back room. One time I'd walked in on them, weighing white powder on scales and snorting lines. But Karen seemed different. That's why the neighborhood went into a dark and silent state of shock a year later, on the day she was strangled to death by her boyfriend. I remember having seen Karen and her boyfriend the day before her murder, and thinking it might be possible to live a normal life in the Old Colony Project.

I saw all the comings and goings from the room where Kathy lay in a coma. It was like being at a wake, with everyone stopping by with flowers and a card to pay respects over the body. Kathy was listed in "stable condition," but she just lay there with her eyes sealed shut and tubes connecting her to machines. No one knew what to do, the way we never knew what to do around the bodies that we were seeing more and more of those days at Jackie O'Brien's Funeral Parlor. "Should we pray?" "Should we talk to her?" "Can she hear us?"

Early in the day, I was the only one up there. Then Ma would come in the afternoon, and ask me to leave the room so that she could be alone to yell into Kathy's ear and try to wake her up. "Kathy always hated like hell to be woken up in the morning," she laughed. Ma was all smiles when she showed up, like everything was normal. Then, after spending some time alone with Kathy, she looked like she'd been crying, but she still forced a smile when she left to pick up the little kids from nursery school. Ma always told me not to stay too long, and every day she'd say she had "a good feeling" that Kathy would be coming out of the coma.

All the aunts, Ma's four sisters, came in regularly to visit Kathy. My Aunt Mary Kelly would come bursting into Kathy's room to tell her that the hostages in Iran had been freed, or to give other updates, like that Ronald Reagan was doing a great job running the country. But all she got in return was the beeping from the machines that told us Kathy was still alive. My Aunt Leena looked around the room at some of the cards Kathy was receiving and made conversation about Kathy's nice friends. "Ohhh, who's this one from?" she asked about a poem written to Kathy; "my Irish Colleen" it called her. "Oh, just some guy," I said. I didn't have the heart to tell her it was from a convicted bank robber doing time in a federal prison.

Kathy's friends didn't come in much. Most of them were usually too busy getting high on Patterson Way and East 8th Street, the way Kathy would have been if she hadn't crashed onto the sidewalk. Ma said they didn't come around much because they couldn't deal with the pain of seeing Kathy like that. She'd been a beautiful girl, hard to remember now, with half her hair shaved off, infections all over her face, tubes going in and out of her, and the machine that beeped every second. I had a hard time seeing her like this too, I thought, but isn't that what Southie loyalty is all about? Kathy had been such a popular girl, and I wondered why more people didn't seem to care. Some of her friends did come, though, and sometimes I'd walk in to find them blessing themselves or holding Kathy's hands and crying, or talking away and laughing as if she was alive and well.

Timmy Baldwin was one who came in all the time. He wanted to be alone with Kathy, just like Ma. And he always brought flowers. Timmy was known to be a tough kid in Southie—we all knew about his beating someone over the head with a crowbar once when he was high, and about the time he was all messed up and shot a sawed-off shotgun from the project rooftop, yelling, "Look out below!" But I got to see his soft side, like at Kathy's bedside, and remembered the times he'd appeared out of nowhere when I was having a problem with older kids in the neighborhood. "What do you want, a beatin'?" he'd say to them. "Do you know who this is? He's a Mac-Donald!" pointing at me like I was some kind of royalty in the Old Colony Housing Project. I knew the Timmy who was loyal and watching our backs, like you were supposed to do in Southie. When Kathy dated Timmy, I thought they'd get married someday, and I'd have my own personal bodyguard for a brother-in-law. They'd broken up before Kathy went off the roof, but here was Timmy, still loyal to Kathy and to the MacDonald family. Timmy was both tough and loyal, like everything we wanted to believe about Southie.

A few years after Kathy's fall, Timmy was shot twice in the head while sitting in his car in front of the Quiet Man. About a hundred people leaving Triple O's Tavern across the street saw the shooting, but wouldn't rat to the cops. When the judge at the grand jury tried to get Timmy's best friend to tell what he'd seen that night, he just looked at the judge and said, "I'm from Southie. We keep things to ourselves." The word around town was that Mark Estes had killed Timmy. Years later, he would die the same way: shot in front of a crowd spilling out of a pub, none of whom came forward. Everyone said he deserved it for what he'd done to Timmy, but that's what some people had said about Timmy too.

Julie Meaney came in to Kathy's bedside a few times, as high as a kite. I couldn't tell if she was falling apart, shaking like a leaf and crying, for Kathy or for herself. I don't think she knew either, high as she was. In a few years, Julie would walk into the water at Carson Beach and never come out.

Frankie McGirk came in once with Julie. I left the room immediately, because I could feel his badness, and Ma had always said he'd gotten Kathy into the angel dust. Not long after that visit, we heard the screams come down Patterson Way when he was stabbed to death over a drug debt. Everyone said McGirk deserved what he got too. I knew some of my neighbors wanted to downplay how bad it was that someone could lie dead in a project hallway while kids played outside. I remember thinking Frankie McGirk should've been arrested by the cops and put in jail, not given a death sentence from people no holier than he. But that's what some called "street justice" in Southie.

Tommy Dooley came in too, all spiffed up in his cashmere coat, like he had to dress up for Kathy. Tommy was dating Tisha Stokes, who Kathy'd been hanging out with. Ma liked Tommy Dooley, but she didn't like to see Kathy with Tisha or any of the Stokes family. Tisha was heavy into the angel dust and coke, and Ma cringed every time she heard "that voice" squealing up to the window for "Kathy Mac!" When Tommy Dooley came in to see Kathy, he began by cracking jokes with her, but then he would give up like everyone else and just say a prayer over her motionless body. Two years later

Tommy was killed by Tisha's family outside Kelly's Cork and Bull Tavern. Everyone said Joe "Stokesy" Stokes had led his brothers in kicking Tommy and beating him to death with a lead pipe. But when it came time to testify before a grand jury, when Stokesy turned himself in five years later, all the witnesses who'd been at the bar that night couldn't remember a thing. And Stokesy's brother Stippo was married to the niece of Detective Lumsden, the homicide investigator.

Betty LeClair used to come in to see Kathy with her son Eddie. Betty drank a lot, but she was always there for Ma. She wasn't like "the vultures," as Ma called some of the older women who came to Davey's funeral and Kathy's bedside just to see who was grieving properly. Betty had real tears as she talked into Kathy's ear and kissed her forehead, disobeying hospital rules to keep the surgical mask on at all times. Eddie was my age and we had hung out a lot, going to Illusions in the disco days. And he stood now at the foot of Kathy's bed with hands clasped, doing the praying-at-a-wake thing. In a few years, his body too would be lying still like Kathy's, but in a casket at O'Brien's Funeral Parlor. Eddie was run over, murdered some said, at three in the morning outside a crowded bar on Dorchester Street. People kept their mouths shut about that one too.

Kevin came to the hospital with Okie O'Connor. Kevin and Okie were best friends, and it was Okie who made sure the two took time out from their busy day to visit Kathy. Ma always raved about how polite Okie was, carrying her bundles and answering all her questions with a "Yes, Mrs. MacDonald" or a "No, Mrs. MacDonald." Frankie and Kevin said that Okie was a comedian, keeping them laughing all the time. But Frank was worried about Okie's coke use. Still, no one ever imagined he'd be found, two years after I saw him talking to Kathy in her coma, hanging from a rope in his parents' basement, dead by the age of nineteen. Kevin and Frankie broke into Jackie O'Brien's Funeral Parlor in the middle of the night to stay awake by Okie in his casket. Jackie O'Brien was going to press charges to get them to pay for the back door they broke, but Okie's father had no problem with what the kids had done to show their loyalty, and said he would pay for the door himself.

Brian Biladow came all the way to the City Hospital in his wheelchair, with Michael Dizoglio pushing him. When Ma was studying at Suffolk University in the seventies, she'd gotten a social work internship at an alternative school for juvenile delinquents and kids who'd dropped out—mostly since busing began. That's where Ma had met Brian and Michael and a gang of kids from the D Street Project. The teenagers were thrilled that "a Southie lady" was working at the school, rather than "another liberal snob," as they told Ma. They thought Ma was pretty cool in her fringed cowboy coats and spike-heeled go-go boots. They opened up to her, and came by the house to tell her all their problems. Not long after Ma started working at the school, Brian got shot in the spine after getting high and breaking into a neighbor's house for drug money. Ma had made the whole family visit Brian in the hospital, and now here he was, being wheeled into Boston City by Michael Dizoglio, brother to Dizzo, the ice cream man. "Hey, Kathy—how ya doin', hon'," Brian yelled in his nasal voice, like he was wheeling into a party in Old Colony. He brought her some flowers, and jokingly offered her some of the coke he always kept hidden under his ass while he wheeled around the projects, waving to the cops. Michael Dizzo was quiet while Brian did all the socializing in Kathy's room. Some years later Michael was murdered, along with his nephew Stephen Dizzo, in an apartment in the three-decker where they lived in Andrew Square. According to the newspapers, their upstairs neighbor, a seventeen-year-old, shot the two of them with his rifle after Michael had broken down the apartment door in a fight over money. Michael had just gotten out of a detox a few months earlier. His nephew Stephen, a quiet kid getting his high school diploma from Boston High, ran upstairs after hearing the gunfire, and was shot in the head. Stephen's thirteen-year-old sister found them both on the floor.

But then I only knew my own family's pain. First Davey, and now Kathy. We were too closed in on ourselves to know that we were only part of a bigger bloodbath spilling into the streets of the neighborhood we'd thought was heaven on earth. Although we'd seen people like Brian Biladow wheeling around the neighborhood, they seemed more like upbeat survivors than victims of anything. No one took the time to make all the connections. Most of us were too busy picking up the broken pieces of our families. And those who hadn't been hit yet protected themselves by seeing our young dead or wounded as somehow deserving their fate.

Frankie came in to the City Hospital and watched Kathy with anger in his eyes and fists clenched. One time he put a holy medal in her hands and left in tears. That day he walked up to Richie Amoroso on Dorchester Street and gave him a beating that landed Richie in the hospital. Frankie wasn't usually a troublemaker now that he was winning titles in boxing rings all over New England. But he said he was tired of waiting on the cops to investigate Kathy's fall. All the same neighbors who said they'd seen and heard the fight between Kathy and Richie that night, the coldest night of the year, never answered the door when Ma and Frankie showed up with detectives looking for a statement. Ma saw their peepholes go dark, though, from their eyes looking through, so we all knew they were just minding their own business. We knew that minding your own business was the rule in Southie, but it was different for us now that we wanted some answers about Kathy being in a coma. Frankie chose street justice, with no one talking and the cops giving up so easily. But Amoroso was back out on the streets in no time, and people were already starting to ask less often about how Kathy was doing in the hospital.

I started to get to know who Kathy was while she was in the coma. I felt guilty because I knew it was a little late. One day when she went back on the critical list, I was sure she'd finally die. She was only nineteen, and she'd have to be buried in the extra spot we had next to Davey. I went into her bedroom to prepare. Kathy had never wanted me snooping in her room, so I thought I'd probably find drugs or maybe even evidence of witchcraft from her friendship with Julie Meaney. I was looking for any explanation for what had happened to her life. But instead I found out all the things Kathy felt about herself, all the photos and letters she'd saved through her teenage years, all the insecurities of a girl in poems that played up how "K-O-O-L" she was. She'd kept every one of her school pictures, even the ones of her as a chubby fourth grader with hand-me-down clothes, photographs over which she'd scrawled FAT, or else scribbled out the face completely. In her teenage years, Kathy had become thinner, prettier, and she wore sexy stolen designer clothes and put on faces that looked like she was the baddest. "K is for Kool," Kathy wrote in a jingle that spelled out the meaning of the letters of her name. Her other poems were about her friends and how cool her whole crew was. In letters to herself, Kathy wrote about how worried she was about girlfriends like Julie Meaney and Doreen Riordan, and how much she loved Southie. Her doodles on paper said all the stuff we saw written on the walls of the neighborhood: SOUTHIE FOREVER, IRISH POWER, HELL NO WE WON'T GO, RESIST, NEVER, and KATHY # ONE.

Then there was the scrawl WHITEY RULES. I wasn't sure if Kathy was talking about white people being the best, or about Whitey himself, who some said was bringing up the finest cocaine from Florida these days. I already felt myself missing Kathy, but I didn't want to think about that. I gathered up all her secret belongings and got ready for another funeral.

The next day Grandpa met me at the City Hospital. He said he had some holy water from Fatima, where the Blessed Mother was said to have appeared before three children in 1917. He said I'd have to help him throw the water onto Kathy when the nurses weren't looking. Kathy was on the danger list again. Infections were taking over her body, and she had pneumonia—there was no way the nurses would let us dump water on her. But this was holy water I figured, so I went along with him. I was willing to try anything at this point.

The nurses caught Grandpa after he'd managed to pull the jug from out of his baggy trousers and pour it all over Kathy's head, hands, and feet. Grandpa was shaking and in tears, and he told one nurse to go fuck herself when she came in screaming and trying to pull the old-fashioned jug from his hands. More nurses came running in when they heard the fighting. They started to gang up on him, but Grandpa was too strong for them. He kept on reciting the Rosary and telling the nurses in his Irish brogue to shut their fucking mouths. The hospital johnny that they made him wear over his clothes into Kathy's sanitized room was hanging now from his two wrists, and he kept pulling it up over his shoulders, in between throwing more holy water and fighting nurses. The shower cap they'd made him put on over his hair was now barely hanging onto the back of his head. "Kathy, if you can hear me now, move your arm!" Grandpa yelled. And she did. We both looked at each other. After that he just took a deep breath and relaxed. "Now," he said, "are ye right so?" That's what he said when he meant, "Are you ready?" I said I was, and we left the nurses still screaming.

We walked out into the first signs of spring after one of the coldest winters I remember, and the whole way home Grandpa had tears in his eyes, but the brightest smile. He said he had "a good feeling" now that Kathy would be coming out of it. He asked me if I had a good feeling too, and I said I did. But I think I had a good feeling mostly because for the first time in my life I saw how much Grandpa really did care about us, and how much pain he felt for Ma. Even though he could never tell her that.

All winter long, we'd been yelling into Kathy's ears, asking her to move a foot or an arm if she could hear us. Sometimes she twitched, but the day Grandpa threw the holy water on her was the first time she'd clearly heard us, and she'd slowly lifted her limp arm and held it there. The following week, on Easter Sunday morning, Ma got the call. "Kathy woke up!" she screamed, banging on the door to the bedroom where I was sleeping. When we all went in to see Kathy, she was lying there looking at us with her two eyes open, and she smiled. She tried to say "Ma." Her lips said it but she still couldn't talk. It just sounded like air.

Kathy had to start all over again, they told us. The doctors didn't know if she would ever walk again; she had extensive nerve damage that couldn't be repaired. Half her body was almost useless, the right side, which they said was controlled by the left side of her brain, which had hit the sidewalk. When she came home to Old Colony, a crowd had gathered to cheer her arrival out of a handicapped van. Kathy was in a wheelchair. Her mind seemed to be all there, though. She was having speech therapy, and getting a little bit of her voice back. She had chewed off a good bit of her tongue in the coma, so it was hard to make out what she was saying. But she could keep up a conversation and knew who everyone was.

Within a year Kathy took her first steps, at first with a walker, then with a cane. She dragged her right side when she walked. Before long she was dragging her right side around Old Colony, to all of her old haunts. But more and more her walks were up toward Jackie O'Brien's to attend her friends' wakes. More and more often I found myself sitting at the window, noticing how clean-cut all the teenagers in the neighborhood looked, with ties on and wet hair slicked back like Catholic school kids, gathering out on Patterson Way for the three-block journey up Dorchester Street to the funeral parlor. You wouldn't even recognize some of the roughest ones among them. Kathy, Kevin, and Frankie put on their best clothes too. Kathy usually followed at the back of the crowd, with a few others who walked with canes or were wheeled in chairs. It was becoming another one of our Southie traditions, these groups of spiffed-up kids gathering to see their friends in a casket; and Ma found herself wondering which one would be next.

CHAPTER 8

STAND-UP GUY

UNDEFEATED FRANK MACDONALD

Hard hitting Frank MacDonald of South Boston met and defeated a very comparable Jose Miguel from Cranston, Rhode Island. Frank totally devastated his opponent with a series of crippling punches to the body which succeeded in incapacitating Miguel, who was of great courage but unable to fathom Frank's awesome body attack—congratulations Frank, and corner men Paul "Pole Cat" Moore and Tommy "Stove Man" Cronin.

—SOUTH BOSTON TRIBUNE

FRANKIE WAS ONE OF THE FEW YOUNG PEOPLE IN THE neighborhood not being dragged down by drugs and crime in 1980. His boxing career was one of the only things that brought good news to the streets of Old Colony in those days. Frankie was fast becoming a neighborhood hero, not only in Old Colony, but all over Southie. Everyone knew who he was, and he had a nickname now, "Frank the Tank," for his "hard hitting" style that was bringing him championship titles, from Junior Olympics bouts at Free-port Hall in Dorchester to the New England Golden Gloves tournament in Lowell.

Mary and Kathy said all their girlfriends talked about Frankie's looks, and the guys who hadn't yet got caught up in the world of drugs talked about getting a ripped body like Frank's. He was working out seven days a week, running from Old Colony, through the Point, around Castle Island, and back to the project, always in his combat boots from his days in the Marines—and sometimes he ran backwards. Frank was welcome all over Southie. The little kids in the neighborhood would run after him, asking him questions about his bouts and begging him to show how he knocked out his opponents. That's why Frankie was so intent on being what they called "a stand-up guy" in Southie. That's what they called anyone who would never snitch, even if it meant doing a life bid because of it. But in Frankie's case, it just meant he was clean-cut. Sure, he knew all the top gangsters in the neighborhood; anyone with Frankie's status in the Southie boxing world would. But he never got involved in their rackets, stayed away from the dust and coke they were pumping into the streets, and refused to work for Whitey, telling Ma that he never wanted to be "owned."

But still Frankie had "the boys," as we called Whitey's troops, working in his corner as he fought his way through four years of New England Golden Gloves championships, starting out as a two-time middleweight champ in the novice class, and ending up a light heavyweight champ for the whole region in 1982 and 1983. *South Boston Tribune* articles always pointed out the sound advice and leadership "the boys" were giving Frank in the ring:

> Following closely the instructions of trainer Paul "Pole Cat" Moore and manager Tommy Cronin, Frank pursued his opponent most aggressively with a savage body attack which ... wore down O'Han to the point of becoming a bit careless and somewhat frustrated ... at being unable to figure out MacDonald's technique. Frank, once again

following the instructions for his corner, succeeded in landing a barrage of lefts and rights to the jaw and head of his adversary. This will prove to have been a most excellent victory for Frankie in the upcoming bouts he is to have.

In Southie having the gangsters in your corner, in the ring or on the streets, meant that you had the ultimate protection and power. Grandpa didn't believe that, though. He had warnings for all of us, from his own days as a longshoreman on the Southie docks, where he said he'd worked alongside some men who ended up in the Brinks robbery of 1950, "the big one." Grandpa always told us how the rule on the docks was to keep your mouth shut about the rackets you saw. He said many a time the longshoremen were lined up by the cops and asked to step forward and speak about crimes. That's how a waitress from the local diner got killed, after she stepped forward among the silent longshoremen. She was found murdered the next day, her blood scrawled into the letters SNITCH all over her cold-water flat. Grandpa had another rule of his own for the underworld: "Watch out whose hand you shake," he told us. He said there was no such thing as a gangster giving something without wanting more in return. "They'll give you a quarter for a dollar any day," he said. Grandpa had been trying to get closer to us since Kathy's coma and had even bought a condo in City Point. He got a closer look at the neighborhood, and he kept coming around the house cursing "that fuckin' Whitey Bulger, a no-good bum if there ever was one," and wondering if the Bulgers were even Irish at all, with Senate President Billy Bulger's insulting Irish brogue imitations at drunken St. Paddy's Day festivities. "They're a shame to the Irish altogether," he said, "and what respectable Irish person would name their kid William?" he asked. "That would be like a Jew naming a kid Adolf."

We got a kick out of Grandpa's ranting, but Frankie started to avoid him when he came knocking at his door to give more speeches. Frankie had as many admiring eyes on him now as any of the gangsters did, and he didn't have to hijack trucks or sell poison in the streets to get that respect. He knew how to keep himself out of trouble. He was obsessed with the whole role model thing besides. One time Joe cracked open a can of beer while the two of them were walking down the street, and Frankie lashed out at him to "put that fuckin' shit away. There are kids around," he said. Frank called the booze "fuckin' shit," the same thing Whitey had called the pot Kevin was waving out the car window years earlier. But Frank meant it, not because it was illegal to be drinking in public, but because he knew that kids in Old Colony were watching his every move.

Kevin wasn't selling drugs anymore; he'd gotten into the bigger stuff. By the time Kevin was sixteen, he hardly ever slept at our apartment, so I didn't really know what exactly he was into, but I picked up a few clues. He was still very generous, so whatever scores he was making, it seemed the whole project would get some of the spoils. Like the time Kevin knew Ma needed money, and he gave her a few twenties. Ma was glad to get anything she could in those days, as the lines for welfare food seemed to be getting longer. But the guy at "Dirty John's" Sub Shop told Ma her twenty was a fake, counterfeit. He let her use it anyway. "What the hell," he said, "they're all over the neighborhood." Ma played dumb and off she went with her sandwiches, but she cursed Kevin all the way home. Not long after, when Kevin got locked up for driving a stolen car—he wasn't getting caught for the big stuff—Ma got a call from him at Charles Street Jail. I heard Ma tell him, "Jesus Christ, then you better keep your mouth shut." When Ma hung up the phone, she told Frankie that Whitey had sent someone into the jail to visit Kevin, to give him a warning to keep quiet about where he was getting the counterfeit money if it should come up. Whitey knew that any Southie kids arrested for anything were likely to be worked on for information about his operations. And he made sure kids like Kevin, who were in and out of jail, understood that silence was the only way to stay alive in Southie.

After beating his stolen car rap, Kevin was back out on the streets, sharing more winnings with the neighborhood. One night there was a block party on Patterson Way, after Kevin gave out cases of beer and bottles of whiskey and vodka. I knew sometimes Whitey's boys hijacked trucks out on suburban highways, and I figured that was where Kevin had gotten all the booze. All Ma knew was that everyone out front was shitfaced and having a ball, and that we hadn't even seen the delivery man from J.J.'s Liquors making his usual Friday night rounds that hot summer night.

Then there were the clothes. That's when I got in line to get my share of Kevin's generosity. Kevin had what looked like a truckload of Calvin Klein jeans. I picked up four pairs for myself. I ripped the Calvin Klein label off the back pocket, though. Unlike everyone else in the neighborhood, I was going to punk rock clubs, where it wasn't cool to have designer clothes. My punk friends and I were rebelling against the fashion industry. So was Kevin, you could say, but I didn't want to explain to my friends from outside Southie the ideology behind my brother's robbing a truck.

It's when we started seeing the guns that Ma got pissed off. Seamus and Steven were six and seven years old, playing in the abandoned second kitchen in our breakthrough apartment, and found a pistol. When Ma saw the gun they were playing with, she screamed at them to drop it. She told Kevin to keep shit like that out of this house, and he just took his gun and left.

Another time I found a .357 Magnum in the hall closet, underneath a pile of clothes Ma had heaped on the floor. That same night Kevin came to the house after everyone was asleep but me, and started ranting about cops and snitches, and telling me I should do something with my life rather than just going out to see bands at the Rathskeller looking like a nut. He wasn't making a lot of sense. I knew he was high and by the way he paced the floors, I knew it was coke he was on. Then he went into the back hall where the gun was and disappeared into the room where he used to sleep when he was a kid. I heard one shot. I didn't know if Kevin was still alive, and I felt so tired of it all right then that I didn't have the energy to go look. Ma, Kathy, and the little kids never even woke up. Then Kevin came out, looking calmer. He said he felt better and thanked me for talking to him that night, even though I was thinking I'd hardly been able to get a word in. He left the house without the gun. I went into the back room to find the top half of the window open. He'd only fired a shot into the Old Colony sky. When I checked the closet, I felt the gun under the pile of clothes. And it was warm.

"Ma! Can I have fifty cents to go to the Irish Mafia store?" Seamus yelled up to the window, as loud as loud could be. *Jesus, that kid has a worse Irish whisper than I ever did,* I thought. Seamus was talking about the liquor store at the end of Patterson Way that Whitey had taken over, the one that had candy for little kids like Seamus, as well as being the drug headquarters for all of Southie. Whitey didn't live in our part of town. No one was exactly sure where he slept at night. Some people said he had houses all over the South Shore, but that he often came to dinner at his girlfriend Theresa Stanley's house on Silver Street, near City Point. Wherever he lived, I thought it was pretty smart of him to position his liquor and drug business right on the edge of our project, where more and more kids were doing whatever they could to get drug money. Everyone knew that no illegal activity in Southie took place without a stamp of approval from the back rooms of that store, Whitey Bulger's office. George Grogan ran the other office for the boys at another liquor store across the street from the D Street Project. Georgie stood on the corner in front of the store through all seasons, waving to the cops who rode by, and wearing his Notre Dame cap pulled over what Ma called his "killer blue eyes." I always thought it was funny how he stood in front of a red stop sign poster in the store window that said SAY NOPE TO

DOPE. We all knew everything about who was running what, but we didn't yell things like that up to windows on Patterson Way.

The Irish Mafia store was originally owned by one of the Stokes, but the news around town was that Whitey made him sell it to his associates, since Whitey couldn't have all the things he owned in town under his own name, with no job and the feds keeping an eye on him. Everyone said the booze was cheaper before Whitey took the store over. Now all the liquor stores and bars in town were buying their booze from Whitey's hijacking operations. They had to. No one was more powerful than Whitey, not the cops, not the politicians. "They work for him," Ma would repeat. The liquor stores around town were charging way too much money, since they were forced to pay Whitey's high prices. "But what can I do?" asked Ma's friend Al, the one who partied until morning in his apartment next door. "Stop drinking?" Ma let out a howl of laughter at that one.

Frankie got closer to Kevin in those days, to keep an eye on him. Kevin went to all of Frank's bouts, hanging out near the gangsters he knew, who were the biggest boxing fans. Frank did what he could to talk Kevin out of the business he was in, but more often protecting his little brother meant helping him get away from the cops. Kevin was staying at Frankie's when David Reeves, a sixteen-year-old neighbor, yelled up to Frank's window that the cops were planning to raid the apartment. David's uncle, a detective with the Boston Police and I guess a boxing fan as well, had told him to go warn Frankie. Frankie figured there was nothing to raid, so he paid no mind. "Let them," he laughed. When ten plain-clothed agents banged on Frankie's door, he opened it looking groggy and scratching his head, as if the cops had woken him from a deep sleep. They pushed Frank aside and raided the house. They came up with nothing. What they didn't know was that while they were knocking, Kevin was scrambling around the house in all of his hiding places, pulling out shotguns and revolvers. Frankie had no time to fight with Kevin. He could only help him climb out the back window to the rooftop, and pass him the duffel bag full of guns.

Frankie and Kevin got into fights over Kevin's criminal enterprises, which always seemed to get Frankie into the mix. Frankie gave him a beating when he found out that Kevin had used his name again after being arrested, and then skipped bail. In the end, though, they always made up and were the best of friends.

Kevin started to go to the Rathskeller downtown, where Frankie along with some of the other boxers and some of the boys were working as bouncers. They were big and tough looking, and good for keeping the college students and punk rock types in line. Frank's corner man, Pole Cat Moore, worked at the Rat, and introduced Frankie to Ricky Marino, an ex–state trooper, who became Frankie's best friend. Then there was Kevin "Andre the Giant" McDonald, not to be confused with my brother Kevin "Mini Mac" MacDonald. He was a Southie champion too. Ricky and Paul Moore were pretty high up in what the papers in later years would call the "Southie underworld." But Frankie knew his little brother wasn't going to get involved in their plans, no matter how much he wanted to. They were too high up to be bothered with Kevin, who despite his involvement in some of the big stuff was still just a kid to guys like these. They also had a position to maintain, and weren't about to bring someone with Kevin's potential into their rackets.

My brother Joe would go to the Rat too, whenever he was on leave from the Air Force. Joe told Ma it was weird how Frankie's friends pulled each other aside when they were "talking business." We all knew Joe was the tattletale in our family—he told Ma everything—and the boys must have sensed this too. But one night at the Rat, he did overhear Pole Cat Moore telling Ricky that he'd be getting his cocaine directly through Whitey's Colombian connections, rather than going through Ricky. Pole Cat had a job with the Boston Housing Authority, and an apartment with his brother, right next to ours on 8 Patterson Way. Pole Cat never touched the stuff. He was too into his body, coming and going from our building with a gym bag and a clean white towel around his neck. But he was starting to make a killing on the coke, by the looks of the number of kids knocking on his door day and night. Joe said he would know if Frankie was into that stuff, though, and that Frankie had never been involved in Pole Cat's huddled conversations with Ricky at the Rat.

Then I started showing up at the back door of the Rat most nights. Ever since I was fifteen I'd gone there to see bands. Frankie's friends knew who I was, and snuck me downstairs through the piss-puddled hallways, to where the bands played. Frankie snuck me in too, but he didn't know I was there on weeknights, and I told his friends to keep it quiet. I hadn't returned to Latin School since Kathy's coma. They'd tried to make a deal with me that I could be promoted, despite all my absences, if I left Latin and went to Madison Park High School in Roxbury. "Yeah, right," I said, "and be the only white kid in the class."

Latin had been my only escape from the busing, and now I felt guilty for messing it up. I couldn't believe I was a high school dropout. I'd always been the straight-A student Ma bragged about, along with Johnnie, and Davey. For a while I was still pretending to go to school, even after Kathy was out of the coma. I'd wander around Boston all day, freezing at bus stops when I didn't have money for the three-hour-long coffee refills at Mug and Muffin, trying to stay awake after a night at the Rat. Ma eventually found a letter I'd written to myself about my guilt for being a dropout, and she was bullshit that I had pulled one over on her. She confronted me about it and said I'd have to go right to work the next day. She too knew high school in Roxbury wasn't an option. That's when I switched from pretending to go out to school every day to pretending to go out looking for a job. I was still freezing at bus stops, or getting warm at Mug and Muffin; and I still snuck out of the house at night to go to the Rat.

I had my own group of friends at the Rat. While Frankie, Pole Cat, Andre the Giant, and the rest of the gang hung out upstairs, I was down in the basement with misfits from all walks of life. Some were working-class kids, others were suburban white-picket-fence types, and others were rich. "What's a trust fund?" I remember asking. "Ah, man, it's nothing—just 'cause my dad's rich doesn't mean I am. I gotta wait on it. Got a dollar for a beer, dude?" But wherever these people came from, they didn't like it. I'd always preferred black music—soul, then disco, and now hip-hop and rap. The words made more sense to me. But I also liked the energy and rage of punk rock; I just couldn't relate to the lyrics about life in the suburbs, and having strict parents. Then I discovered the original version of punk, from England. I'd never thought about the fact that there were poor and working-class English people who hated the Queen, and her mother, and the whole British establishment. I could get into that. This was a movement of people who didn't fit in where they came from, and they'd made that cool. I could get into that too.

Punk music became an escape for me, but I still had to come back to Old Colony every night. I often hitched a ride with Frankie's friends, the whole way home not knowing what to say to men as powerful as "the boys." Other times I had punk rockers drop me off on the outskirts of Southie, so they wouldn't see that I lived in the project, or accuse me of being a racist for living in my neighborhood. But I was protecting them too; I didn't want them to get bottles thrown at them for being different in Southie.

Even with all our bad luck over the years, Johnnie was a lieutenant in the Navy Seals now, Mary was becoming a nurse so she could save some money and move from her project apartment, and Joe was in the Air Force. They were "getting out." That was what people in Old Colony said in hushed tones when they didn't want anyone to hear them suggesting the neighborhood was a bad environment. And Frankie too was hoping to "get out," making his way, earning honest money, and thinking about becoming a pro boxer.

And then suddenly even Kevin seemed to go straight. He'd been dating a girl named Laura, a rich girl from Wayland who was sometimes dropped off in Old Colony in a limousine. Ma said Laura was "slumming it," hanging out in Old Colony and getting in on Kevin's scams, like the time she helped him claim a back injury by walking ahead of him in a supermarket aisle, pouring liquid detergent for him to slip on. Instead the supermarket had to pay for Kevin's front teeth, which he hadn't planned on losing in the fall. Laura's father was a lawyer in the financial district, "forty-two men under him," Ma said, and her grandfather sat on a fortune from a popular brand of tennis clothes. Her father didn't like Laura dating Kevin, and Kevin said it was because he was from the project, and because he wasn't Jewish. And that was before Laura's father found out Kevin was a criminal by trade. But by then Laura was pregnant, and the two of them were getting married. None of us knew of the wedding. They just got married one day, and when Ma asked about it, Kevin told her only that Whitey Bulger had been his best man.

Kevin was twenty-one and Laura two years younger when their daughter, Katie, was born in the spring of 1984. That's when Kevin's life of crime ended, and the three of them moved into Laura's condo on Newbury Street, an "uppity" section of downtown, as Kevin used to call it. He got used to it, though. Kevin even looked different, when I'd bump into him walking through the Public Garden, carrying his baby girl in one arm and a bag of groceries in the other. He was getting chubby, so I didn't always recognize him before he called over to me. All he talked about was how beautiful his "wittle wittle mosquito" was. I was so stunned I didn't know what to say back to him. But I was glad he was going straight.

But the brightest hope of all now was Frankie, who was a neighborhood star, being looked at by boxing manager Lou Duva, who managed Evander Holyfield. Frankie wasn't sure if he wanted to go pro, though. He talked to Ma about it, just like he talked to her about almost everything. Ma and Frankie were more like best friends than mother and son. We all knew Frankie was Ma's favorite, but no one seemed jealous about that. It was just accepted; "two peas in a pod" is what Ma herself called their relationship. Frankie was solid, a foundation everyone felt anchored to. And Ma loved Frankie for that.

Frankie had gotten a flashy new Lincoln Continental, the size of a boat, from working in the Carpenters Union, working nights at the Rat, and saving his money. He spent any free time he had piling Seamus and Stevie and all their friends into his car—which they called a limo—for ice cream at Frosty Village, or taking Kathy to her physical therapy appointments, or kidnapping me on Dorchester Street on my way out of Southie, to lock me up in his room and make me punch the heavy bag hanging lopsided from his ceiling. And he drove Ma everywhere, taking her slowly down Broadway, waving to admiring kids, and stopping to talk to men-about-town like Pole Cat Moore. "Hey Ma, you wanna go to the graves?" Frankie would offer to take Ma to breakfast, and then to visit Patrick and Davey at the cemetery. They were buried all the way across Boston, at St. Joseph's in West Roxbury, nearly impossible for Ma to get to before Frankie bought his Lincoln.

But Frankie wanted to give even more to Ma—and to Seamus and Stevie, who loved sleeping over at his apartment, and bragging to their friends the next day about how much weight their boxing hero could bench press, or what he ate for breakfast. Frank told Ma about his plans to take the little kids to Disney World, a dream most of us growing up had never even bothered fantasizing about when we saw the ads on TV. One day Frankie took Ma to Mary Kelly's house in the suburbs. Ma loved showing off her greatest joy, her son the champion boxer, handsome, built, and driving a Lincoln Continental. Sitting at the picnic table in our cousins' yard, Frank drifted away from the sisters' conversation, and came back saying, "Hey Ma, wouldn't it be nice to have a place like this some day, once I get some money? A house with a yard?" Ma just brushed the comment off, saying in front of her sister that Old Colony Project was the best place in the world, with the beach nearby, and parks, and plenty of things for the kids to do.

It was driving back from that trip that Frankie told Ma he'd had a dream. They both thought they were psychic, and Ma paid close attention to dreams. Frankie said he'd dreamed of the whole family at the cemetery for another burial. Ma told Frankie then that just a week earlier, a crow had come through our window, and had flown through the house before crashing into Ma's head and flying back out the same window. "I'll tell you, it knocked me for a loop," Ma said. She said she lay down then and slept for hours. The Irish have this thing about birds inside houses; when I was little I couldn't bring in even a picture of one. Once I gave Ma a glass bird to hang on our silver disco Christmas tree, and she threw it into the trash, saying it was bad luck. Ma thought for sure after the big black bird invaded our home, that someone would die, and in the car that day she and Frankie both hoped that it would be Grandpa. "That old bastard has lived a good long life now," Ma said. "Christ, I hope I don't live to be as old as that." They both laughed and drove down Broadway as Frank waved to more admiring eyes.

July 17th was Ma's birthday, which she never wanted us to celebrate because she hated to think she was getting older. She was turning fifty in 1984, but she still told everyone that she was having a hard time turning forty. She put out the TV after watching the eleven o'clock news report of an armored car heist in Medford that had left one dead. The robber was unidentified. He had burned off his fingerprints with acid prior to the robbery, to prevent identification.

The next day Mary came over with Seamus and Steven after keeping them overnight to play with her own two kids. She had already told them the news, and they were both crying. Now Mary had to tell Ma. Ma saw the little kids crying and just looked at Mary. "It's Frankie," Mary said. "He was killed yesterday." Ma collapsed on the floor. Frankie was twenty-four years old.

* * *

The lines went around the block and up the hill, to Jackie O'Brien's Funeral Parlor. Of all Southie's wakes, this was the most people I'd ever seen come to pay respects, and I was proud to be from a neighborhood that cared so much about my brother. But I still wasn't going to believe Frankie was in that casket until I saw him, even though his body had been identified, and even though I'd seen Kevin at the house with baby Katie since the death. At first I was sure that it must have been Kevin who'd been killed robbing the Wells Fargo armored car. Frankie? Robbing a bank truck? Kevin maybe, but not Frank. I didn't want Kevin to have been the one shot down in the afternoon ambush; I just wanted to know the truth. Now I knew Kevin was alive, but I still wanted to see if it was Frankie in the casket. I know Ma was thinking the same thing, and that's why she fell apart when she finally saw her favorite son, the shell of her favorite son, laid out with his huge boxing fists folded and wrapped in Rosary beads. Ma knocked over the people in her way to climb on top of the casket, and she put her arms around Frankie's neck, pulling him up and out of the box. It took Johnnie and four muscled gangsters to tear Ma away from her Frankie. The casket wheeled a few feet, with the strength of Ma's grip. The O'Briens had to send everyone into the other room so that they could reassemble Frank's limbs and straighten out the purple satin robe he was being buried in.

Before the wake, Kevin had run around making the arrangements for Frankie, and everyone agreed that he should be buried in his Golden Gloves championship robe. The rest was the usual for Southie's buried children: Rosary beads, Irish flags, and shamrock trinkets collected from the annual St. Paddy's Day parade. But Frankie's purple robe made him look like royalty. Grandpa didn't get it, though. In a room packed to capacity with people telling stories about Frankie's boxing matches, and reenacting them with slow motion blows to the air, Grandpa walked up to Frankie's body and held his hand. The room got quieter. Grandpa turned around and said to himself, in the loudest of Irish whispers, "That's an awful fuckin' shame! A handsome man like that being buried in an old bathrobe." Ma cracked up laughing then. The whole family did. Later that night Grandpa said to Ma, "I only wish I'd known him better."

All types streamed in to pay their respects: young kids; local priests we'd never seen in the neighborhood before; all of Old Colony; Jimmy Kelly, who was now city councilor of South Boston; teenagers Frank had trained in the ring, like Joey Degrandis and "Little Red" Shea; and the gangsters. Then there were a few suspicious-looking characters, definitely outsiders, who Ma later said introduced themselves as detectives.

It was a good thing we had the breakthrough apartment, with the two joined living rooms, because after the wake the house turned into a full-on disco. It was our Old Colony version of a real Irish wake. "A good send-off" is what they called it that night. People danced in one living room, then went into the other living room where Frank's corner men had laid out mountains of free cocaine, then they went back to the other living room to dance some more. Then the trips back to the coke table got more frequent, and soon some of the neighbors weren't leaving the table at all, and were looking at that cocaine as if the mountain was going to disappear. The house was packed. Ma came out of the back room where she'd been hiding out for a while. She was all smiles but looked a little dizzy. Tommy Cronin said, "Try some—c'mon, Helen, it'll make you feel better." Ma replied, "Well, I'm willing to try anything at this point." Ma did a line and then she was dancing too. Kevin made sure I knew I was welcome to the coke. I'd tried it a few times before, but I didn't like the feeling it gave me of being out of control, desperate for more. And I especially couldn't imagine doing drugs with my family. Ma got me out of it saying, "Mike's never touched drugs, he's too quiet, he thinks too much. I never had to worry about that one," she added. I didn't pass judgment on anyone else taking coke that night, though, and was even willing to let Ma try it if that might numb a pain I couldn't even begin to imagine. I chose to get shitfaced drunk for the heavy weight of sadness I was feeling, sneaking to my stash of whiskey in the back room.

Joe was doing a line and offered the rolled-up hundred-dollar bill to Mrs. O'Connor, Okie's mother. She looked at Joe, then right in front of the boys she said, "That's the shit that killed my son." Mrs. O'Connor had had a couple of years to figure that one out; but we hadn't started to make the connection between Frank's death and the mountains of white powder that Whitey was bringing into the neighborhood from his Colombian connections in Florida.

I don't know how we made it to the funeral in the morning, after about an hour of sleep. My head was pounding as I sat in an aisle next to Frankie's casket. I thought we might have to catch Ma as she walked slowly up to the altar, holding onto any church fixtures she could grab. Ma had written a song that she wanted to read. I knew it was important to her to show she could still "hold her head high" in front of everyone:

> You've broken down my prison walls,
> You've melted the bars,
> You've raised up my soul,
> So that I could see your stars.
> My honky-tonk ways are past
> and now gone,
> And my cold heart now has hope,
> With each dawn. . . .

"That's a shameful poem altogether," Grandpa muttered as Ma continued reading slowly, "some kind of country-and-western song about prison." But we found out later that Grandpa actually kept the poem, scrawled onto wrinkled notebook paper, in his top drawer along with his precious novenas to saints, and letters to him from his own mother from when he'd left Ireland, never to see her again. Although it broke my heart to see our fun-loving hell-raising mother all dressed in black and reading about her dead son, I don't remember much about that funeral. But I do remember that Frankie's casket weighed an awful lot. Frankie was like a rock. My head was pounding, and I couldn't believe that he was really lying there inside the Irish flag-draped box, never again to play with Seamus and Stevie, never again to drive Ma to breakfast or to the cemetery, never again to be seen by any of us.

That night Ma was standing in the kitchen, looking out the back window. She usually looked out the front window, but I figured she probably didn't want to do that now, and see Frankie's empty-looking apartment across the street. *"Frick...ah...frack...n...pfft."* Ma looked fine—she was smiling—but she was talking gibberish. She forced some real words out of her mouth slowly, but said she couldn't feel her left arm. I told her to lie on the couch and I called Mary, who said Ma was probably having a stroke. Ma insisted she was just tired and refused to go to the hospital that night, no matter how much I begged. I was relieved to see her awake later that night. She got up around midnight, flicked on the kitchen light, and started pummeling the ground with her bare hands, killing cockroaches with a vengeance.

The next morning, with the funeral over, and Frankie buried, and the crowds gone, I opened my eyes and looked up from my mattress on the parlor floor to find Ma crying and clawing at the curtains, trying to tear them down to get a better view of Frankie's apartment. We'd always been able to see him in his kitchen window, cooking or shadow boxing, and Ma was looking for him once more. But he wasn't there. His kitchen light bulb was still on, shining dimly onto yellow cement walls and open cabinets. Ma saw that I was awake but just fell to her knees at the window, looking for Frankie, and saying over and over, "He was such a beautiful kid, he was such a beautiful fuckin' kid." Her wailing went right through me. I cried inside, but Ma couldn't hold her pain in any longer. It all spilled out that morning, and I could hardly bear to see it.

* * *

Kevin started coming around the house with Laura and Katie, getting closer to Ma after Frankie died. That's when Ma began to get some of the answers she was desperately looking for about Frankie's death. Kevin blamed himself. "It should've been me," he said. He'd been part of the planning for the job, and then when he went straight, just like Frankie had always wanted him to, he wanted nothing to do with it. But he didn't know how to get out of it. In the end, Kevin was replaced by Frankie, who wanted nothing more than to get the family out of the projects, and saw before him what was supposed to be a simple job. And the more coke Frankie was doing, the more simple the job must have looked, and the more invincible Frankie must have felt. Because Frankie had gotten heavy into coke in the last months of his life. After his death we heard about the all-night parties in his apartment with all the boys around and mountains of cocaine on the tables, and all kinds of plans being laid out for that simple job. Frankie went in on it with his friend Ricky, the former state trooper from the Rat, and some nineteen-year-old named Chico we'd never heard of, from the D Street Project.

The rest of the story Ma got from the detectives who'd started coming around, telling Ma everything while I listened from the back room. Frankie's job was to get the loot, to jump into the Wells Fargo truck while one of the guys put a gun to the back of a security guard, and the other guy sat in the car with shotgun aimed. Frankie got shot by the Wells Fargo driver when he jumped out of the back of the truck, taking a bullet in his upper back. Frankie ran and made it all the way to the getaway car, along with a bag of loot, in the middle of a wild shoot-out. The worst thing for us was that it was a minor wound. Frankie could have lived for hours, and likely survived, if there'd been any attempt to save his life. Even if they'd dumped him off on a highway where he might have been picked up, he could have lived. But of course if he had, there was a chance the bandits and the entire ring would have been caught. Frankie might have talked. So his friends had stuffed his head in trash bags and pushed him under the seat to keep him hidden and quiet, before fleeing with $100,000 to the second getaway car waiting for them. But the real story Ma found out from the coroner: Frankie had a veil of blood in his face and hand marks on his neck. Someone had strangled him.

That's when Ma went after the whole criminal ring. She may have been taking Valium for the pain she was feeling, and walking around in slow motion, but she was determined nonetheless. There was no time for tears. Ma never let me in on her investigations, but I overheard her conversations with Joe, who was driving Ma around in Frankie's Lincoln to track down some of the boys in the streets. But in Southie, it was hard to tell just how extensive any criminal ring was, and who exactly was involved in the various stages of planning and dividing the money. In Southie, for all the clean appearances of the boys who ran the town, nothing was ever what it seemed. Ma walked up to Whitey Bulger, who had nothing but kind words for her, politely calling her Mrs. MacDonald and saying Frankie was "a stand-up guy, God rest his soul." Ma asked him to his face if he'd had anything to do with the Wells Fargo robbery, and he said he hadn't. Whitey's hands were always clean, though. Just like he had nothing to do with all the cocaine flooding the neighborhood, destroying kids like Frankie who had everything going for them except that they lived in the project next to his headquarters with its proud green shamrock painted outside.

Soon after talking to Whitey, Ma was invited by the detectives into a back room of a restaurant in Medford to meet with the FBI. They asked Ma what she knew about this one and that one. Most of them, Ma had never heard of. But when they asked over and over about John Doherty, Ma knew what direction to take her own investigation. She'd been going to hairdressing school, and she carried her sharpest pair of scissors with her into Doherty's house. I'd never heard of John Doherty, but as it turned out, he was the brother of "Lorraine the Lesbian," a neighbor from Jamaica Plain who'd tried to recruit me into the Ku Klux Klan when I was six. Everyone told

Ma that no bank robbery happened from Southie that John Doherty didn't stake out ahead of time, and supply the guns for. "What a strange bastard he is," Ma said to Nellie on the phone. Ma said she thought he might be a pedophile, with all the half-naked teenage boxers running around his house. She said she walked into his den, which was dark except for candles all around and big red velvet couches. Ma pulled out her scissors and politely asked the gangster in his silk smoking jacket if he needed a little trim. Then she motioned across her throat with the scissors, to tell him what she really had in mind. Ma said that in the end Doherty convinced her that he'd had no part in the robbery. He said he'd been cut out of the deal after he'd done all the staking out. "If I was involved, Frankie would've been wearing a bulletproof vest," he said.

Then one night I came out of the back room and found Ma and some detectives peeking out the front window onto Patterson Way from behind the curtains. Ma was pointing out a neighbor who lived across the street with his wife and two children, and who Ma said had another seven kids in Jamaica Plain. Ma said she had information that he was involved in the bank job, supplying the guns after Doherty had been cut out. I never would've suspected the likes of him. He was one of the few fathers in the neighborhood and weighed about three hundred pounds. I'd never seen him get up off the front stoop to go to a job and had always wondered what his scam was. Now I knew. But nothing ever came of Ma's tip-off, and within weeks the whole neighborhood was excited about the new "Clam Shack" the guy opened up on Dorchester Street, purchased with Frankie's blood.

Everyone knew Ma was on a mission. That was why, when the gangsters finally came forward with some money for Frankie's funeral expenses, they avoided dealing with her directly at all. One night Red Shea came by looking for Johnnie, still home on leave from the Seals. I told him Johnnie was at Grandpa's in City Point. Red went there, rang Grandpa's doorbell, and waited for Johnnie out on Kelly's Landing. Grandpa saw what was happening from his window and came downstairs in his long underwear ready to save Johnnie from trouble. Red handed Johnnie ten thousand in cash from the boys, and Johnnie screamed at Grandpa to get the fuck inside. Red took off, and left Johnnie crying at Kelly's Landing with the bundle of blood money in his hand. Johnnie could throw, and he hurled the wad of bills off the landing about twenty-five yards, where it sank into the ocean. The FBI told Ma they'd watched the whole transaction, but that they weren't going to take Johnnie in because he didn't keep the money. The story got around town, and the next day Red and some kids from Old Colony were at Kelly's Landing scouring the ocean floor for all that loot.

After a few weeks Ma had started to look less determined, and her mouth was settling into a permanent downturn. Kathy was able to live independently now, and she'd gotten a subsidized apartment in Manchester, New Hampshire. On the day we took Kathy up to her new home, Ma, Joe, and I sat in Frank's Lincoln in a Dunkin' Donuts parking lot on the way back to Southie. Joe talked about Frankie and told funny stories about the two of them cruising for girls in the pimpin' Lincoln Continental whenever Joe was on leave from the service. Ma just listened with downturned mouth and stared straight ahead at the rain on the windshield. It was a blow to see someone the likes of Ma look at us and say, "I don't think I'll ever be able to smile again."

"I miss that kid so fuckin' much," Kevin told Ma, looking out our front window at Frankie's old apartment. Kevin didn't have Laura and Katie with him. He was starting to come back to the neighborhood to hang out with all the people he and Frank had in common, sharing stories about Frankie in the ring, while drinking and doing lines. Kevin said Whitey wanted to open a bar and have him run the place. Ma told him to get out of Southie. But Kevin kept coming around, and whenever he came up the house he'd start crying about Frankie, especially when he was high.

That September I got out of Southie for a month to stay with friends in Los Angeles. But I couldn't relax. I kept calling home to find out if everyone was alive. Ma told me everything was fine and to stop being such a worrywart.

But then I called my Aunt Leena, and she told me Kevin was all over the papers, that he'd gotten involved in a jewelry store heist with his friend Flabbo from D Street Project, and that the jewelry store owner had been shot and was paralyzed. She said the Stardust Jewelry Store in Framingham was surrounded, but that Kevin got away from the police even after getting shot in the leg. The papers said Kevin ran into a suburban neighborhood and pretended to be a jogger. He rang a couple's bell and said he was really thirsty and needed a glass of water. They gave him water, and then Kevin called a taxi back to Boston. Kevin ran on the taxi driver after jumping out at Newbury Street, where Laura and Katie were. Then he went to hide out at Mary's apartment in Old Harbor Project. The couple and the taxi driver called the cops—they'd seen Kevin's bloody leg— and the paper said the police knew exactly who it was because they knew Kevin had moved to Newbury Street, and they'd been keeping an eye on him to find out more about the Wells Fargo robbery. That night, police special forces had Mary's apartment surrounded, and when Kevin told Mary he would surrender, Mary's husband Jimmy opened the door to five shotguns pointed at his nose. He later said he never came so close to shitting himself as that night.

When I got home from L.A., the detectives were in the parlor again with Ma. They wanted Ma to help them get Kevin to talk about who else was involved in Frankie's hold-up, and about the whole organization in Southie. They told her they had a videotape of Kevin and Flabbo robbing the store. They said the tape showed Flabbo shooting the owner after the man locked them in the store and pressed the button to alert the police. They said it also showed Kevin attacking Flabbo, trying to stop the shooting. From what I'd always heard, Kevin believed in the "nobody gets hurt" rule. The detectives said it was simple: If Kevin talked, they'd show the tape in court and Kevin would get a light sentence; if he didn't talk, no one would ever see or hear of the tape again.

A few months later my Aunt Leena was visiting with me and Ma. Ma showed Leena the black dress she'd just bought at the thrift shop. "Jesus, that's an awful depressing-looking color," Leena said. In absolute defeat, Ma replied that she'd need it for Kevin's funeral. Leena panicked and Ma explained that she'd had a dream, more like a vision she said, of Kevin hanging. She was just accepting that he was next. I walked into my bedroom and locked the door. I begged and pleaded on my knees, to God, to every saint I'd ever seen hanging on Grandpa and Nana's walls, to everyone in my family who was dead: to Davey, Frankie, and Patrick, to Nana who'd always been so close to me. I begged for Kevin's life. I knew Ma's premonition was real by the look on her face, and I didn't like her resignation, even though she'd suffered enough to rip every shred of hope from the strongest heart. I prayed that somehow Ma wouldn't have to suffer more, that Kevin would be filled with a white light, and be changed, that he'd be able to return to Laura and Katie. I remember feeling only the December winds whipping through my bedroom window, sending my tears onto the cement walls around me.

When Christmas came, I was looking at the cards we'd received, mostly religious ones with notes of sympathy for the loss of Frankie. One of the religious cards was from Kevin at Bridgewater State Hospital. I hadn't known Kevin was at the prison for the criminally insane. When he was younger he'd fake like he was crazy whenever he was arrested, to beat the rap, and sometimes he'd be sent there for observation. But now he was there, I had to assume, for real. And I hadn't known Kevin was so spiritual, with all his talk about God and hope and about his heart being changed. "Ma didn't tell you?" Mary said to me. She told me that Kevin had tried to hang himself in jail, but that the sheet broke and he'd crashed to the floor. "He said he was filled with a white light or some crazy shit, and he hasn't been the same since." They transferred him to Bridgewater because of the suicide attempt. She showed me the letters to Ma they'd found in his cell after he tried to kill himself.

Ma, I guess this is the end of the line for me. I am about to end my life in a few minutes. I miss Frankie so much. It hurts so much. That kid was everything to me we had so much fun together. I had a dream last night that me and him were riding around together picking up girls. He was so funny then I woke up and started crying and shaking just like I'm doing right now. I want to be with him and Okie. I love them both. Make sure Laura lets you see my wittle wittle moskito.

Ma don't go blaming yourself or nothing. Thinking you were a bad mother or some shit like that. You were the best mother anyone could have ever had you were so much fun. I never wanted to be a criminal it just came so easy and nothing else ever came my way. Tell Joey Earner he can have my clothes. Tell Mr and Mrs O'Conner that I will slap Okie for them when I see him.

Ma I hope there's no such a thing as hell, but all I know is if there is it cant be anything worse than what I'm feeling right now. Tell the kids not to cry. Love Kevin.

But now in his Christmas card, Kevin was talking about coming to terms with Frankie's death, and with his own life. Maybe there was hope. There was a rumor on the streets, though, passed around by Flabbo's family, that Kevin was a snitch. People knew Kevin had been getting worked by detectives, and they figured he might talk, about everything, all the way up to Whitey's organization. And everyone knew that Kevin knew a lot.

So in spite of everything hopeful in that Christmas card, in March Kevin was found hanging from a bed sheet at Bridgewater. He was dead. The detectives who'd become friendly with Ma told her that the last person to visit Kevin, according to the sign-in book, was Detective Walter Kirby, known to be a good friend to the boys

and to Whitey himself. They thought it was very unusual that anyone would be let in to visit at eleven-thirty at night. Kevin was
found hanging in the bathroom outside his cell not long after
midnight.

I was staying with an artist friend in New York City when Kevin
was found. I'd been trying to reach Ma, only to get a busy signal.
The operator told me she couldn't break through because the telephone was off the hook. I knew then that someone was dead. I had
no doubts because I wasn't panicking. I accepted the fact almost
calmly. I walked all the way to 42nd Street to get on the bus back to
Boston, and as I entered the Port Authority a homeless man stood in
my path, shook his finger at me, and laughed, " 'Til we meet again!"
Those were the very words Ma had always put in gold letters on
a bright green ribbon across the caskets of the children she'd seen
lowered into the ground.

When I got back to our apartment, it was three in the morning,
and I burst through the door to find out who had died. All the lights
were out and everyone was in bed. I was looking for sympathy cards
in the dark room, and I saw the silhouette of a card standing upright
on top of the TV. I turned on the lights and was pissed that someone
had turned them off in the first place, letting the cockroaches take
over. They were running in all directions now to get away from the
light. I grabbed the card: "Happy St. Patrick's Day." But under it
was the *Boston Herald* with a picture of Ma and Seamus with sad
faces and the headline: "Mom Loses Third Son to Violent Death."

"Who's dead? Who's fucking dead!" I went screaming through
the house and into Ma's bedroom. "What are you talking about?"
Ma said. "Go to bed, for Chrissake, you're waking up the little kids."
Steven wasn't in the *Herald* picture, so I thought it might be him.
But because Ma was saying "the little kids," I knew it wasn't. "No
one died; get some sleep for yourself." Ma sounded almost believ-
able, not as if she'd just lost a third son to a violent death. I told her
I'd seen the *Herald* headline. Then she gave in and told me, "It's
Kevin," and her voice broke when she added, "You better get a good

night sleep—we have a lot of work to do in the morning." She spoke from the darkness of her room, and her voice became a muffled cry as she buried her face into the mattress.

I went to bed numb. I wasn't going to feel this one. We'd buried Frankie only eight months earlier, and I never wanted to feel again. I chased away any memories of Kevin that popped up, of us taking baths together as toddlers, of him stealing prizes for me at the Irish Field Day, of him beating up anyone who ever messed with me, and of our walks through Southie on his first paper route. I stayed awake all night, and I remember wondering without feeling how many times tragedy could pound Ma's already shattered heart.

CHAPTER 9

EXILE

"HEY MIKE, YOU GOT FIFTY CENTS SO I CAN GO TO THE Irish Mafia store?" I heard Seamus's voice from inside the dumpster I was about to toss the trash into. He popped his head up and laughed. Stevie was in there too, along with his best friend, Tommy Viens. They said they were playing cops and robbers and were hiding out from the bad guys. "And who are the . . . ? Never mind," I said. We'd all talked about how the little kids had been able to "bounce back" from the tragedy they'd lived through. Seamus was nine and Stevie eight, and here they were, having the time of their lives, making their own fun in the same courtyards and dumpsters where I'd followed Kevin around as a kid. I gave Seamus and Stevie three dollars, one for Tommy, but I told them they couldn't go to the Irish Mafia store, or to the Clam Shack, and then I knocked off a few other stores that I knew had connections to what *I* had started to identify as "the bad guys." My list didn't leave them many places to go, and in the end they just tramped off to Whitey's headquarters anyway.

We didn't feel the same about our neighborhood now that the kids were dead. Ma said she wanted nothing more than to get the hell out. But there was nowhere to go. Ma was getting $250 a month from welfare, less than a month's rent in apartments outside the projects. She was going to hairdressing school, hoping to get a job; but the people in the neighborhood who had jobs, usually at factories and plants that bordered the neighborhood, were losing them. This was while downtown cafes and wine bistros continued to pack in the crowds of yuppies who were taking over traditional working-class neighborhoods like Charlestown and the North End. With the rents outside the projects going up, we knew Southie was next.

Ma worked hard just to keep herself busy after the kids were buried. She said she had no time to sit around feeling sorry for herself, thinking about them. She said they were in a better place, better off than the rest of us. Ma went to hairdressing school every morning, and spent the afternoons cutting hair at the local homeless shelter, even though she always found head lice walking on her scissors afterward. Ma loved being around the homeless. She said it kept her going, listening to all their stories and sending them off "looking like a million bucks." She said when she got through with them they looked like Johnny Cash, Conway Twitty, or one of her other favorite country stars. But when Ma started to hang out with the young gay men from hairdressing school, and going to gay clubs, she updated, and sent the homeless off looking more like Cindy Lauper. Then she started volunteering nights at AIDS wards, giving complete makeovers—hair, makeup, nails—and playing her accordion between stories that kept everyone in stitches—stories about her husbands, her boyfriends, and courtroom scenes with Nellie. Ma said she wanted to help the dying patients prepare to "cross over to the other side," and she figured some makeup and a few laughs were as good as the Rosary any day.

Ma was going mad with the makeovers, though. One time my Aunt Sally cried looking into the mirror after Ma got through with her head. She'd been given what Ma was calling "the windswept look," and the helmet of orange hair plastered to Sally's forehead and chubby cheeks looked like a cyclone frozen over. Ma told her she looked like Liza Minelli, and Sally said she wanted nothing to do with Liza Minelli. Ma had plucked off Sally's bushy eyebrows with the tweezers, and her chin whiskers too, which was really why Sally was crying. "Oh, shut up!" Ma snapped at her younger sister. "Dan'll be thanking me now that I got rid of your beard."

That night we heard a gunshot on Patterson Way and Sally made me walk her to the train station, saying anything was better than spending one more minute with Ma, and her cutting and plucking.

Ma was just doing whatever she could to keep her mind off what she was feeling. But the hearses kept rolling down Dorchester Street, where in better days we'd watched the St. Paddy's Day parade and the antibusing motorcades. And every time it was another Southie mother's turn to see her child off at Jackie O'Brien's, it brought Ma right back to reality. She started going to all the wakes, even if she didn't know the family, and in about a year she counted that she'd been to thirty-two, all dead from suicide, drugs, or crime. Ma started hanging out with other women whose sons or daughters had died, and she started cutting some of their hair too—until they learned to make sure they went to the hairdresser's on a regular basis so Ma wouldn't have them walking down Broadway in one of those new-fangled cosmopolitan hairdos she was bringing to Southie from the gay clubs.

Then Ma got into the holy water, after Grandpa took her on a trip to Fatima where the Blessed Mother had appeared to the three children. Holy water and haircuts. Ma was on a mission. To give whatever she was able to give. She was always pulling something out of her pocketbook, whether a piece of toast for the guys on the wino wall, or a rock for someone who needed strength. Besides the scissors and jug of holy water, Ma's pocketbook was full of rocks that she had brought back from Fatima. "Oh ... thanks. What's this for?" I asked Ma, trying to sound grateful as she handed me a three-pound rock. She told me that when Grandpa and the other pilgrims to Fatima had crawled on their knees to the next holy site, she'd run back to the well where the Blessed Mother had appeared and chiseled out a few stones. "Get down on your knees for Our Lady, you damn fool," Grandpa told her when she returned. "Like hell I would," Ma told me. "You should have seen the face on my father, like he was wearing the crown of thorns himself." Ma was inspired by her own relationship with the Blessed Mother, saying she needed the rocks for some of the mothers burying their kids in Southie. Most people actually treasured their rocks, and some told me that they kept them in their pocketbooks always, to remind them of Helen and all her strength.

I was worried about Ma in those days, with her running out to gay clubs and blessing the mothers of Old Colony with holy water, but everyone else saw her as an inspiration, just to have gotten up in the morning and put her spike heels on the right feet. The mothers who'd lost one kid didn't know how she could do it, having lost four. And Ma was even smiling again, as much as she could make herself do. She said she had no other choice, except suicide, and she couldn't do that, with Seamus and Stevie and all these other people to look after.

Ma got me to go back to school. She said I was sleeping my life away, and I was. She started making calls, setting up appointments for me to get my GED, and then to take the SATs. She knew how to work the financial aid applications to get the most money for school, even with the cutbacks in education grants. I didn't know the point of it all, but it felt good to score high on the SATs despite having dropped out of high school. And before long, I was getting up early mornings for the two-mile walk from our apartment to the University of Massachusetts. Being busy like Ma helped me to forget about the kids being dead, sometimes.

Now Ma had only Seamus and Stevie to worry about. She didn't want them bused across town, and she couldn't afford to keep Stevie as well as Seamus at St. Augustine's. Ma called the Boston School Department and tried to find out where Stevie would be assigned for first grade. It all depended on your address. "If I lived at 8 Patterson Way, would my son be able to go to the Perkins School across the street?" Ma said the woman on the phone understood what she was getting at. She said she was from Roxbury and wanted to send her own kid to school near home. The woman told Ma that if she did live at 8 Patterson Way, her son would be bused, but that if she happened to live at 9 Patterson Way, he could go to the Perkins. Ma hung up the phone and called back, saying she lived at 9 Patterson Way, even though there was no such address. Later that morning, Ma whispered to the mailman that she'd be getting mail sent to 9 Patterson, and to tell the other guys at the post office just to get it to her and to not ask any questions. The mailman was happy to help. "Hey, I gotta try that for my kid," he said.

"Just keep going, and hold your head high!" Ma told her new friend Theresa Dooley as they walked past the gossipers who'd left their stoops in the project to stroll down Broadway. Ma barged her way into Theresa's life after she heard that her fifteen-year-old son had hung himself in his bedroom. "Two kids! That's like a double murder, and these dirty bastard politicians keep saying there are no problems in Southie?" Ma knew that Tony Dooley's suicide had everything to do with the murder of his big brother Tommy—who he'd idolized—in front of Kelly's Cork and Bull. Ma went over to the Old Harbor Project on the feast day of the Mother of Sorrows and asked neighbors where Mrs. Dooley lived. She walked into her house, telling her to get dressed and to come for a walk up Broadway. Ma knew that people liked to whisper when the two of them walked by. Some would stare into their eyes looking for the grief. But Ma said she wouldn't satisfy them. "If they want to talk, they should talk about what the hell is happening in this neighborhood before it's their turn next!" One woman actually told Ma she didn't want to get too close to her or Theresa, that the bad luck might rub off on her. Within a month the same woman nonetheless ended up burying her own son, dead from an overdose. That's when she found out that in Southie it had little to do with luck.

Ma was still trying to uncover details of Frankie's and Kevin's deaths, but no one seemed to have them. Theresa was still pursuing Tommy's killers, but the homicide cops had long since given up on witnesses, and the Stokes family still laughed at her whenever she walked into the Irish Mafia store, before Whitey took it over from them. "The Devil has no conscience," Ma said. They both had it in them to fight, two daughters of Irish immigrant workers who'd raised children on their own in tough housing projects, scraping up money to try to keep them in school and off the streets, against the plans of liberals who knew better and a drug lord who knew best. But there was even less mothers like them could do now, in the face of an extensive criminal drug ring reaching far into the offices of local politicians and the ranks of the police department. Theresa, always more of a churchgoer than Ma, had never imagined the corruption Ma was starting to talk about. She was dealt another blow when Ma told her that Tommy Dooley's case probably wouldn't have a shot, since his killer's family was married into the family of Detective Lumsden. In later years, Lumsden would be investigated for allegedly receiving thousands of dollars to protect gambling rackets associated with Whitey.

People in Southie didn't trust the police, except for the ones they were related to, since the beatings and the cover-ups of those beatings we'd witnessed during busing. For many kids my age, hate for the cops was a good enough reason to be an outlaw. But Ma's opinion of cops only solidified after her kids were dead and she decided to snitch about the drugs in town. "If you're going to drop a dime," her friend Snooka warned her, "you better do it from a phone booth, and whatever you do, don't give a name!" Snooka knew what she was talking about. Her own son was a drug dealer in D Street Project, and one time when she tried to snitch on him, calling the drug unit of the police department, she got a knock on her door the next day from Whitey's underlings, who gave her a warning. "Don't you know who's taking those calls at the drug unit?" she asked Ma, as if she was the only one who didn't. "Patsy Magee, that's who!"

"Don't you know who's taking those calls at the drug unit?" Ma was asking me the same question as if now I was the idiot who should know more about what goes on in Southie's underworld. "And who the fuck is Patsy Magee?" I asked her. I didn't know much about Southie crime, and didn't want to know either. I was just wishing I could sweep my whole family up and take them out of this death trap. Ma told me that Patsy Magee was a sister to Kevin Magee, one of Whitey's top lieutenants. "He's the fat guy Whitey has the liquor store with. Mother of Christ, he can hardly walk with all the fat on him.... Good thing he carries a gun." Ma said she didn't know where to turn, who to trust in the neighborhood. "Let's just get the fuck out," I said. As if it was that easy.

I stayed out of the neighborhood as much as I could, sleeping on friends' couches around the city, and getting up in the morning to go to my classes. I went to New York quite a bit, catching rides there to see bands or go to clubs. But no matter how far I ran, Southie was always on my mind, and I called the house all the time to check up on my family. "Is everyone okay?" was the first thing I'd ask when Ma picked up the phone. "Oh, my aching Jesus," Ma screamed into my ear, "you're driving me up a wall! You'll have to see a psychiatrist or something, with all the calls, day in and day out." But I never believed Ma was telling the truth when she said everyone was okay, so I asked her if she was *sure* everyone was okay, before getting a loud click in my ear.

One time I was in New York staying with friends, sleeping on the floor of an art gallery they owned in the Lower East Side. As grungy as the neighborhood was, I was as removed from the world of Old Colony as I could be, with paintings all around the room—heavenly scenes with angels and comic parodies of New York high society. One night there I had a dream that brought back the sick feeling I'd started to get whenever I walked over the Broadway Bridge, back into Whitey's clean-cut neighborhood. I dreamt I was walking into Old Colony and was approached by some kid crying and begging that I listen to him. "Something terrible is about to happen," he wept. "This shit's gotta stop." I spent the next morning trying to figure out who the kid was. At breakfast I drifted away while my friends were arguing about something artsy and useless to my troubled head. "Johnnie Baldwin!" I said. They all looked at me. "He's just this kid who was in my dream last night. He and three other kids were drinking and driving and crashed into a bus and died four years ago."

I didn't tell them the rest of the story, but I was sure now that it was Johnnie Baldwin who'd come to me in my dream crying and begging me to listen. "I don't want to hear it," I told Johnnie. "This time, I'm not going to know about it, whatever tragedy you're going on about." I told him I just wanted to live my life and ignore all this Southie shit. Johnnie said that it wasn't anything happening to my family, but I didn't believe him, and kept walking while he followed me through the tunnels of Old Colony.

I said goodbye to my friends later that day and caught my ride back to Boston. When I got home it was one in the morning, and I checked on Seamus and Stevie as I always did when I came back home. At six I heard Ma's heels clacking heavily down the hallway toward my room, and she opened my door to throw in piles of clean socks and underwear. "Oh, Mike, you're home," she said. She asked me about New York and started giving me all the latest. "Did you hear the bad news?" she added casually. "Timmy Baldwin was shot and killed two nights ago while you were away. Everyone saw it, but no one's talking." I didn't respond. I froze as I realized that the night before last was the same night Timmy's dead brother had come to me in my dream. "This shit's gotta stop," he said. But how? And what the hell was the point of a dream like that, telling me something terrible was about to happen, when I could do nothing about it?

"South Boston has one of the lowest rates of reported crime in the city, along with Charlestown and East Boston." That's what the paper kept telling us whenever a murder was reported in Southie. *That's because we don't report crime in Southie,* I thought, after reading about Timmy Baldwin's murder on Broadway. "We take care of our own," everyone liked to say. And I'm sure they said the same thing in Charlestown and Eastie, two other neighborhoods where the mob suppressed the truth. Jimmy Kelly assured the world that the shooting was an isolated incident, even though three other men had been shot dead on Broadway in the span of three weeks. Timmy was shot only a few months after they were, and only a few blocks further along the main Southie thoroughfare. "We are certainly not experiencing a crime wave in South Boston," the city councillor told reporters.

It was while reading those articles, and dreaming about the day we'd leave Southie forever, that I got the summons to appear before the grand jury in connection with Timmy's murder. Ma said the whole neighborhood was getting a kick out of that one, and she tried to hold back her own laughter. "Of all people," she said. And then, her voice going serious, "Haven't the cops screwed that case up enough?" After shooting Timmy twice in the head, Mark Estes ran from the crowds outside The Quiet Man pub and carjacked a woman at gunpoint to be his getaway driver. The woman eventually got home to her husband, but the police showed up at her house soon afterward, handcuffed the husband, and told him he was a suspect in the murder of Timmy Baldwin. The guy was locked up for the night while the woman spent hours at the station trying to convince the detectives to let her husband go. When the two were finally let out of the police station in the morning, they saw their car being towed away, taken in for evidence. They got their car back, but were called two weeks later by the cops, who'd forgotten to test the car for fingerprints.

Now they wanted me, of all people. I called homicide, begging them to keep me out of this. "I just come and go in this neighborhood," I said, "ask anyone. They're all laughing at you guys." The detective was quietly listening to me, as if he was taking notes. "The phone's in your name, right?" he asked. Ma had put the phone in my name; her credit with the phone company wasn't good. "Well, there was a threatening call made from your phone to a major witness in this case. Now the witness ain't talking."

I told him the whole neighborhood was coming in and out of our house to use the phone, especially whoever didn't have one. Then I remembered that just a few weeks earlier Packie Keenan had run right in and grabbed the telephone. Then he'd taken it as far as the cord would reach into the other half of the apartment from where I was watching TV, and muttered things into it I couldn't hear. But I didn't tell the detective that. I had finals on the same day they wanted me to come before the grand jury, and I told him I didn't know how to tell my professors I was being called in on a murder investigation. Just then Ma grabbed the phone and told the detective *she* wanted to come, that she knew who'd killed Timmy, and it was her phone anyway, even if it was in my name. Ma was close to the Baldwin family—Joe was going out with Chucka Baldwin and Timmy had always been good to Kathy—and Ma thought she could help them get a little justice.

Later that week, Ma said the detective screamed the bejesus out of her for a good long time ("Twenty-five years, that's how much you'll get for lying to a grand jury! Twenty-five years!"), before marching her in before the jurors. But in the end it was clear Ma only knew what we all knew: the truth from the streets about who killed Timmy. They had no use for her statements before the grand jury, as much as she wanted to lie and say she'd seen the whole thing. Ma went on until they had to stop her about how much she liked Timmy Baldwin, and how he loved her playing the guitar more than the accordion. "I'm a musician you know, and some of the kids used to come around to learn the guitar from me, before they started disappearing with the angel dust and coke." When they brought Ma back to the subject of Timmy, Ma told how when he was just seventeen Timmy had called her from Charles Street Jail to tell her he was a different person altogether on the drugs and that he thought there might be something wrong with him. Ma said she'd told Timmy, "Sure there's something wrong with you, you're an addict." They finally got rid of Ma when she broke her storytelling to ask the court what they were doing about all the drugs in Southie, anyway. The only other person meant to appear before the grand jury that day had got shot in the stomach as a warning. Unlike Ma, he had no stories to tell the jurors.

After Timmy's murder there were more articles about Southie, and for once they weren't about busing and how everyone in Southie was a racist. At first the stories echoed the party line, and quoted only people like the city councillor, working to maintain the myths. The reporters in those days seemed to need to put in a good word about Southie in their articles, referring to the "tight-knit family-oriented neighborhood"—I guess to make up for years of anti-Southie stories since busing. But eventually news stories started to pry into the connection between organized crime in Southie and the violence that left people like Timmy Baldwin dead. One *Boston Globe* reporter named Kevin Cullen made it a point to mention Whitey Bulger when he wrote about Timmy, and he began to write about the "code" in Southie.

Street crime was becoming the main topic of news, along with reports about the poor getting poorer in American cities. Whitey didn't want the kind of media attention that places like Roxbury were getting. People started to say that Whitey didn't like people shooting guns in the neighborhood; that he said shooting a gun was "niggerish." Word around town had always been that Whitey didn't do any shooting himself, except during the 1960s Southie gang wars, when he'd shot and paralyzed a rival gang member. But now, with Whitey's drugs everywhere, and more illegal guns around since busing, and bar fights turning to murder, the deaths were becoming too visible. And reporters had been finding out that, even if Whitey had nothing to do with the actual shooting of Timmy Baldwin—and others like him—he had everything to do with the drugs, guns, and the silence of all the witnesses outside The Quiet Man that night.

That's when the killings slowed. In the late eighties, Whitey made examples of a few shooters in random bar fights. When Killer Kawalski shot someone in the leg at one of the gin mills on Broadway, Whitey tortured him for three hours, holding a gun to his head. "You like shooting off guns, like a nigger, eh?" That's what Whitey said, according to stories on the street. So the gunshots slowed down. People just started to disappear instead. Once in a while you'd hear of a carcass washing up on the beach, or of someone hog-tied in the suburbs. But they would only merit a small news brief, because they were mystery killings, without much of a story to report.

And so most people, at least the ones who hadn't lost their kids yet to the culture of drugs and death, could believe that Whitey really had kept the streets from becoming like Roxbury's. The whole neighborhood seemed to cheer in unison when Whitey forced a crack house in Southie to shut down. But one detective remarked anonymously to a reporter, "If Whitey did force the guy out, it's because the guy wasn't working for him." Whitey continued to keep his hands clean, with all the stories going around about him carrying bundles for old women, and donating generously to the St. Augustine's food pantries for all the struggling families in the projects. "We take care of our own," I heard many a neighbor repeat like a memorized line from the Apostles' Creed. And the Christmas turkey on the table in tough times was the proof of that saying. As the country got deeper into what they were calling a recession, we watched the news footage of growing lines of unemployed people like us. But they were in American towns that weren't lucky enough to have a Whitey Bulger.

Kathy moved back home with us. Her subsidized apartment in New Hampshire had burned down. The couch had caught fire from her cigarette, and Kathy had grabbed her cane, put her coat on, and wandered off to a Dunkin' Donuts on a nearby highway. She drank coffee, smoked cigarettes, and talked to herself at the counter, while the fire engines raced by. The firemen said on the news that they were looking for Kathy in the rubble. But she was fine, at Dunkin' Donuts the whole time. What was clear to us now, though, was that Kathy was starting to lose it. She'd come back so far from the coma, but then no further. She wasn't getting any better with her walking and speech, and she had less company these days—so many of her gang were dead. It seemed that once she realized her life would never be back to the way it was, she gave up, and took off into a world of her own, talking to imaginary friends and going into fits of crying and laughter.

"Mike, have you ever heard of North America?" Kathy took a deep breath with each word, and forced out the sentence with effort from her permanently twisted mouth. I told her with a long sigh, "Kathy, we're in North America." She got a great kick out of that one, laughing away. "Fuck you," she said. "We're in Southie," as if I were trying to pull a fast one on her. Then one day I looked out the window and saw Kathy standing with her cane on the roof ledge above Frankie's window, where Davey had jumped. "Kathy!" She didn't look at me; she just kept staring down at the ground below, as if she was measuring and wondering if it was going to be painful. I ran from the apartment and made it up to the roof across the street, pleading with her but not getting too close. "Mike, do you got any drugs?" She forced the words out slow and calm, taking her deep breaths. I said I did. "Good," she said. She put her cane in front of her and hobbled after me, following me back home. By the time we got there, she'd forgotten why she was following me, and it was a good thing because I had no drugs for her. I never told anyone in my family about Kathy being on the roof, but after that I convinced Ma to get her on medication.

Then Kathy wandered off from Old Colony one day and disappeared for a few months. When Joe came home on leave, he and Ma started visiting the area where Kathy had lived in New Hampshire. They put out pictures of Kathy, and were led to a soup kitchen where she'd been spotted. Some of the homeless people there told Ma Kathy was living in a crack house nearby. And that's where Ma found Kathy, three months pregnant. Kathy was glad to see her, but her boyfriend pulled a gun on Ma, saying she wasn't taking Kathy anywhere. At this point, though, Ma wasn't afraid of anything. She got the gun away from him and beat him with it. Then she carried Kathy on her back down the stairs of the crack house, to where Joe was waiting in the Lincoln.

Ma took custody of Kathy's daughter, after she found Kathy had tried to sell her baby for fifty dollars in Old Colony. The baby's father was Cuban, and Ma named her Fatima Maria, because she thought Maria was a miracle baby, healthy in spite of all the damage Kathy had suffered from her head injury, and from drugs. We were all excited about Maria, a beautiful gift of new life, one sure to keep Ma going. But Kathy only got worse after the birth, making less and less sense. "Mike, she's a cute little girl—where's she from?" I told Kathy that the little girl playing on the floor was her daughter and she practically fell off her kitchen chair laughing. "You're full of shit," she said when she caught her breath again.

It was ten below outside, but the heat blasting from the radiators was enough to kill us all. I opened all the windows and sat on the couch looking out while Mrs. Mercer across the street made trip after trip to throw buckets of hot water onto her ice-covered front stoop. The hot water she was furiously throwing kept freezing over. Mrs. Mercer wouldn't give up, though; I counted her coming and going with the buckets of water fifteen times. Ma said she was on medication for her depression, and was probably just trying to keep herself busy. "She's a very unstable woman, and I think the pills are making her worse."

Then Seamus, Stevie, and Tommy, along with a pack of about twenty other little kids came running up the tunnel, chasing a raccoon that must have taken a wrong turn. They ran after the animal with sticks and bats, and more kids came out of their apartments to join the fun. Then they chased it up to the roof across the street and

EXILE

cornered it at the ledge. Mrs. Mercer's twelve-year-old son, Donnell, stepped out of the pack, hushed up the war chants of the little kids, and crouched down, talking to the raccoon gently, as if he was trying to talk it out of suicide. "C'mon ... here we go ... that's it ... we just want to help you." Donnell inched closer and closer, one crouching step at a time. Then the raccoon jumped off the roof, landed on its feet, and in no time had the pack of kids chanting and chasing him again. The raccoon ran around an abandoned car before heading right toward Mrs. Mercer, who was carrying yet another bucket of hot water to the frozen steps. She dropped the bucket and sat terror-stricken with both feet up on the banister while the hunted animal did a slippery dance next to her on the ice-covered steps, before dashing into the project hallway and through Mrs. Mercer's open door. The little kids followed with their weapons raised for battle, and there was a short silence on the street as they disappeared into the building.

Then screams came from Mrs. Mercer's, and we saw the raccoon jump out of her bathroom window. Some kids climbed out of the first-floor window, while others jumped over the slippery front stoop. Mrs. Mercer's other son, K.J., came outside now with a wet head and a towel wrapped around him. The raccoon and the pack of kids had come through the bathroom while he was taking a shower. And off the whole crowd went down Patterson Way, laughing and chanting in Southie unity, chasing the raccoon out of Old Colony Project for good.

Jesus, this is the greatest place to grow up, I thought, almost convincing myself again. I couldn't control the feelings of joy I got from scenes like that. I was jealous of the little kids, having the time of their lives. But Ma had started to worry about what would happen when the little kids became teenagers, and all that Southie stuff about sticking together would backfire. Seamus and Stevie were already thinking the gangsters were the greatest guys in the world. And all their friends envied them the times a big fancy car pulled up and Seamus and Stevie were handed a twenty-dollar bill, just for

{ 213 }

being Frank the Tank's little brothers. Tommy Cronin was one of the guys handing out the twenties. He knew Seamus and Stevie fought over everything, so he used to rip the bill in half and tell them they had to join forces and tape the bill back together, so they could spend it. A real lesson in sticking together. The only good thing I saw in those twenties the kids taped together with studied precision was that they kept them from stealing from Bell's Market. Stevie and his friend Tommy had been caught there already, and Ma had had to run down to Bell's to get Stevie after the owner had scared the two with threats about the cops and jail. But it wasn't the threats about cops and jail that made Stevie start to ignore dares to steal candy. He later told me he never stole again after seeing Ma break down and cry all the way home from Bell's Market, begging him and making him promise with his right hand across his heart never to do it again. He told me he'd never seen Ma cry before and never wanted to see her cry again.

Stevie and Seamus were worked up, telling us about the gun collection their friend's uncle had showed them. "That's for when the niggers come," he'd told the kids. He'd said he'd been preparing for the race wars since he'd dropped out of Southie High during the busing. "And now they're moving them in."

"There's gonna be a bloodbath," one Southie leader announced on the six o'clock news, as reports came out that Southie was bracing for what was being called "forced housing." The BHA and South Boston's own Mayor Flynn were planning to move minority families into the housing projects of white Southie and Charlestown. The NAACP had sued the BHA for bypassing minorities on the housing waiting list, when there were openings in Charlestown and Southie. Low-income people were usually able to pick their top choices of housing projects to move into. Most whites wouldn't dare go to black sections of the city, and many blacks would never think of coming to Southie, since the last black families had fled Old Colony and D Street during busing. But many new immigrants from

Haiti or Latin America, who'd never heard of Southie and hadn't been in Boston for busing, simply needed an apartment, and had been passed over by BHA officials when an apartment was free in Old Colony.

Mayor Flynn was now promising to integrate the projects on a first-come-first-served basis. To us it felt just like busing: because of past injustices by public officials, BHA applicants would now have no say in where they would live, unless they chose to move into a neighborhood where the majority of residents were of a race other than their own. In that case, they could move to the top of a waiting list of ten thousand families. And how could the new immigrants, who'd never heard of Southie and who desperately needed housing, pass that up?

The battle lines were drawn. Here we go again, I thought. Ma said, "That's it! I'm getting the fuck out. The blacks can have this place." Then she wondered out loud why we were always fighting for the same piece-of-shit schools and cockroach-infested apartments. "Why don't they go after Newton with its beautiful lawns?" she screamed. "I'll join the NAACP, then we'll all get a piece of the pie."

I laughed, imagining Newton seeing the likes of us tinkers coming through carrying everything we own in trash bags, and Ma with the accordion. But beyond that image, I was beginning to find out just how different Southie really was from suburbs like Newton. At school I'd learned that social scientists over the years had dubbed South Boston a "death zone," along with Roxbury, our black counterpart for the failed busing experiment. I had never heard that one before, but I was glad to find out that I wasn't imagining what I'd seen in the streets. Families had been too ashamed to say their kids were dying of anything other than car accidents or freak heart attacks, but the truth was that we had some of the city's highest death rates for suicide, drugs, and alcohol, and through the early eighties had the city's fastest-growing homicide rate. I was relieved reading the statistics. I'd thought I might be going crazy whenever Southie people were appalled by my own death zone stories.

* * *

Police escorts surrounded the moving trucks that came through the project at one in the morning, sneaking the black families into the best place in the world while everyone slept. But the crowds were waiting; it was the end of summer and the neighborhood was always lively until early morning on hot summer nights. And everyone was ripping mad that the black families were being given free rent to be part of what some were calling another experiment on Southie. For some, this was sure to be the most excitement since busing. Something to come together around, another battle to fight, and to lose. Old Colony Task Force leaders and the politicians tried to organize rallies, bringing back the same old chants: "Here We Go Southie, Here We Go." But the chants didn't sound as strong. There'd been drugs in the neighborhood back before the busing, but not nearly as much as we'd seen since then, with so many kids dropping out of school. The neighborhood was more fragmented now. We didn't have the fight in us that we had back in 1974. Ma wasn't the only one who wanted to get the hell out; others were feeling the same way now that the blacks were coming. But most people had nowhere to go.

The first black families had twenty-four-hour police protection at their doors. But much of the time the cops ended up sleeping in their cruisers because there wasn't any action. Ma said the city councilor was going around with his boys, changing the BHA's locks on vacant apartments and moving in homeless white families as squatters. Some people were starting to complain about the newcomer white families too, saying they were "white trash."

Before long busing revival rallies took place in church basements, where residents talked about minorities hanging sheets out the windows to dry, and playing loud music all hours of the night. "For Chrissake, I don't know what country I'm in half the time, between the Haitians hanging their sheets, and the Spanish dancing on top of my head upstairs," a scared older woman shouted from the back row. But we'd always hung sheets out windows, and played loud music. Our leaders played on the fears of elderly folks, stirring up anxieties about things Southie had seen for years before bringing out the big gun in their arsenal of threats: minorities would bring drugs and crime into South Boston.

When the minorities did move in, the little kids in the neighborhood played together fine. Most of the trouble came between teenagers, and in Old Colony we had the most teenagers of all the projects. There had always been fights in Old Colony, long before the first black family arrived. That's life in the projects. But now if a fight broke out between two neighbors with racial differences, the battle lines were drawn, names were called, and the fight was labeled a hate crime.

The Asian families mostly went unnoticed. "Thank God!" I heard one neighbor say when she saw two Asians jumping out of the moving truck backing toward our front stoop. Then she saw about twenty more climbing out of the truck. "For fuck's sake, how will they all fit in that tiny apartment?" Everyone said "the Orientals" were quiet people, though. No one seemed to mind them, despite the occasional dark discussions about people's missing cats and dogs.

No one expected the blacks and Hispanics to last long. These families often demanded transfers back to their neighborhoods once they found out Southie wasn't the clean-cut middle-class neighborhood our politicians had always publicized in the press. "Shit! Those little white motherfuckers are worse than the niggers in Orchard Park!" I heard one black woman on the train telling her friend who was being sent by the BHA to Southie. "I caught this one motherfucker trying to steal my air conditioner right out of my window. I pulled out the biggest blade I had in my kitchen and ran right outside to put it up against his dick. He put it back, but I said, 'fuck this, I'm outta here.'" She went on and on while her friend listened to every word, shaking her head.

There was no way we would've believed integration could work in Southie. Even Nellie, who'd lived with a black man and had a daughter by him, feared Southie opinion. She used to sneak our cousin Lisa in and out of Old Colony in blankets once she realized she wouldn't be able to pass her off as "half Italian." But before long, Ma was inviting our Puerto Rican neighbors into the house to teach them Irish step dancing and to play a few tunes on the accordion. The mothers didn't understand English, so Ma started talking to them louder and stretching the words out. "Aaaaccoooordiiiian," Ma yelled, bringing out the instrument to show what she was talking about. "Muuuusiic." The women looked at Ma with worried faces, either because they didn't understand her or because they thought she was nutty. Then Ma brought out Maria, still sleepy from her nap, and pointed at her, yelling, "Cuuubaaaa!" thinking they might bond over Ma's little girl being Hispanic. But when Ma got the idea that a free haircut might break the ice, and brought out her pair of sharp scissors, they leaned back against the wall looking terrified.

There were also more promising signs that we all might get along. Sometimes black, white, and Hispanic mothers sat on the stoop together, watching out for each other's kids in wading pools on hot summer days. Stevie was excited and proud when he brought home the Alice Casey Award from the Perkins School, an award established after busing to reward kids like Stevie who got along with all races, and the only attempt by liberal leaders that I'd heard of to promote peace since busing.

But any peace that did exist started to crumble when the police dispatched its squads of the Community Disorders Unit. People started talking about the CDU, the cops who dealt with hate crimes, like it was the TPF all over again. All the talk around Old Colony was about how the CDU was targeting Old Colony white kids whenever a fight turned racial. Thirteen-year-olds were being lined up against the walls, frisked, arrested, and given juvenile records for racial assaults they sometimes were involved in, and sometimes weren't. To fit the description "a white youth with a Fightin' Irish baseball cap" was a liability. The resentments built up, the tensions flared, teenagers were criminalized, families were sometimes evicted. And before long no one even wanted to look at, never mind speak to, a neighbor of a different race, for fear of being accused of harassment.

Even Ma stopped her famous hospitality. "Where were my civil rights when my kids' lives were at stake when we first moved in?" she said. Then she laughed, "Jesus, to think, if Chickie had been black I'd probably have been in federal court."

"A trailer park? The Rockies?" I couldn't believe Ma was packing her trash bags to flee Old Colony and move to a trailer park in the mountains of Colorado. "I'm heading for the hills," she laughed. "You can keep the apartment. I had to lie about my welfare benefits being even less than they are and had the rent brought down to $150 a month. I'll send you some food stamps. Johnnie's getting out of the Seals and he'll be staying with you for awhile." Ma said she wanted me to hold on to the apartment in case things didn't work out in the mountains. Seamus was thirteen, Stevie was twelve, and friends their age were being arrested for calling people "niggers" when they got in fights. And Ma was sick of going to wakes. One month in 1989 she was at the confirmation mass for Michael Dizzo, the ice cream man's nephew, and the next month she was seeing him off at Jackie O'Brien's after he and his uncle were shot to death. That was it for Ma. "This fuckin' place is like Sodom and Gomorrah, and if I ever look back may God turn me into a pillar of salt, like that guy's wife in the Bible." Ma had been watching Pat Robertson on the TV and was starting to talk more and more about the end of the world and Armageddon. "There's gonna be a great chastisement, and haven't I had enough chastisement for one lifetime? It'll be safe in the mountains. Lot, that's his name, the guy in the Bible." Ma was half joking and half serious with all her apocalyptic talk.

She didn't tell the little kids they were moving away for good. She thought it would break their hearts to leave what they thought was the best, and the only, place in the world. She told them they were going on a trip and that she'd be joining them. Ma sent the kids along with Kathy, talking to herself, on a plane to Colorado. When

Joe sent money for her airfare, Ma left for Colorado too. She snuck out the back door that day so she wouldn't have to answer all the questions from the ladies on the stoop. She said goodbye to Mrs. Duggan, who she'd always respected, and walked out of Old Colony Project. With Maria in one arm, her accordion over the other shoulder, and two trash bags full of pots, pans, clothes, and religious pictures that had hung on our walls since the day we first moved in, she carted away all that was salvageable from 8 Patterson Way.

She flagged down a cab and made the driver stop off at the wall on Broadway to say goodbye to the homeless guys before taking her to the airport. All Ma had left to give from her trip to Fatima was the scapula around her own neck. She took it off and put it around the neck of one of the guys. Then she went back to the cab and pulled out her crumpled picture of the Divine Mercy and gave it to another man who looked like he wanted something too. Ma held his hand and told him that the picture of the risen Christ had got her through every single morning since the kids died. Ma told them all she'd never see them again, and they all waved goodbye to her cab, calling her "Mother Helen." The cab drove Ma away from Southie and on to the airport.

Early one morning in August 1990, law enforcement agencies woke up some of the town's top businessmen in the cocaine trade. Fifty-two in all were taken from their homes and charged in a criminal conspiracy in South Boston. Stories abounded that day about shotguns to the face and the surprised look of groggy gangsters waking up to squadrons of armed agents in their bedrooms and relatives being taken away by "the bad guys." The televised news reports showed many of my handcuffed neighbors filing into police trucks with T-shirts pulled over their heads, many wearing flip flops and gym shorts on the hazy August morning. "There's Pole Cat Moore! They got Tommy Cronin, and Eddie McGlaughlin! Andre! Little Red Shea!" I was telling Ma on the phone from Colorado everything

I was seeing on TV. We both felt bad about the arrest of Joey Earner, who was like a MacDonald to us.

I watched the replays of news reports all day. That line of neighbors filing into police trucks was a who's who of the Southie drug world. Police said their biggest catches were Tommy Cronin, who used to hand out twenties to my little brothers; Red Shea, who they said was making coke runs down to the Colombian connections in Florida; and Paul Moore, who worked for the BHA. They panned shots of 8 Patterson Way, where Paul Moore ran his business. Then there were the little guys, like Joey Earner, who'd been used by the boys since childhood. I kept watching, wondering which one was Whitey Bulger, who I'd still never laid eyes on. But as I later found out, Whitey wasn't arrested in the roundup at all.

That elusive Whitey Bulger! What a mystery! Always staying out of trouble and keeping his hands clean. Some newspaper articles commented on Whitey's absence among the suckers who got caught, another chapter in the saga of the gangster genius, an Irish leprechaun playing tricks on the most powerful law enforcement agencies federal, state, and local government could muster. It seemed as if every law enforcement agency in town was at the bust: guys wearing jackets that said DEA, ATF, BPD, and even some state troopers were there to help usher Whitey's boys into the trucks with caged windows. Every kind of cop under the sun—except for the FBI.

Then the rumors started, reaching into every crevice in South Boston, from City Point down to the buckled concrete of the Lower End. And the whole neighborhood tried to shield itself from the ugly truth. Which one among us wanted to believe that the man who'd epitomized the Southie code, who'd mouthed the familiar words about loyalty that we desperately wanted to be true, would turn out to be the biggest snitch of all. Kevin Cullen at the *Globe* had been working on stories since 1988 suggesting that Whitey Bulger was one of the FBI's most prized informants, that he'd helped lock up the Italian mob across town, even as he killed our own families with his drugs and his violence and his Southie code. As much as I'd hated Whitey for what I'd seen happening to my neighborhood, it was nothing compared to the rage I felt when I realized that agents of the U.S. government had turned a blind eye while we were slaughtered.

Most of my neighbors continued to grapple with the revelations about Whitey. One Boston Police detective said anonymously that he believed there was more cocaine in Southie, per capita, than in any other neighborhood in the city. "For years the Bulger organization has told the people of South Boston they were keeping drugs out of their community," a DEA agent said. "The people of South Boston have been had." But none of that was news to me, or to all the others who'd seen their families decimated. What was news to me was that the FBI had sponsored the parade of caskets that passed through the streets of Southie.

I'd thought Ma was losing it sometimes with all her talk of conspiracies, and now I thought I might be going crazy. I began to wonder for the first time what my brothers might've looked like if they'd been given the chance to grow into manhood. But then the memory of all that blood overwhelmed me, and I simply gave up trying to picture the kids getting older. I got angry, angrier than I'd ever known I could be.

The people of South Boston *have* been had, I thought. But not simply by a local gangster. He had a little help—from one of the most powerful agencies in American government.

CHAPTER 10

JUSTICE

I
T WAS JUST ME NOW AT 8 PATTERSON WAY, AMONG THE
abandoned wreckage of mattresses, collapsing bureaus, and a
generation's worth of kids' clothes—whatever Ma hadn't been able
to fit into her bags—piled in a heap on top of Coley's wooden couch
that looked like a coffin. It was spooky coming home now to the ten-
room apartment, which had once seemed too small for the excitement coming and going through those heavy steel doors. The doors
squeaked whenever I opened them, and I tried to remember when
that had started or if I'd just never noticed the sound before.

Every time I came up those stairs on a Friday night after passing
by the parties on front stoops, I knew for sure my family would be
there, all together again in the apartment. Ma, all dressed up to go to
the Emerald Isle, would be bent over the washer doing her last load
of laundry, holding the hose in place to keep the machine from rat-
tling like thunder. Seamus and Stevie would be watching "World
Wrestling Federation" and practicing Hulk Hogan moves on each
other. Davey would be pacing the floors and smoking cigarettes.
Mary and Jimmy and their two kids might be over with Chinese
food for everyone. Joe would be waiting for Frankie to finish de-

vouring every last bit of protein in the house, before the two headed out to meet girls. Kevin wouldn't be there, but there'd at least be a story going around about his latest exploits. Johnnie would be calling in from some undisclosed location with the Navy Seals. And Kathy would be all dolled up and sneaking out the front door, as sure-footed and determined as she once had been. But the door creaked shut, and the screams, sirens, and laughter from the street overwhelmed my memories. I wasn't home. I knew I never would be again.

I started sleeping at friends' houses all over Boston, coming back every day just for a change of clothes. I came and went fast, so that I wouldn't have time to sit and wonder what had happened to the family that had once surrounded me. I kept all the windows shut, and the air in the apartment was so thick and heavy that I felt I was swimming through ghosts. I changed my clothes and fled out the door every day.

Johnnie took the apartment after leaving the Seals. Never did I think I'd see the day he'd have anything to do with the Old Colony Project. He was the one who'd "gotten out." He'd never spent much time in the project before. He was always at Latin School, playing football in the afternoons, and studying at the library at night. He'd gone right from Latin to Tufts University, and then straight into the Navy to become a lieutenant. The only time Johnnie came home was when he was on leave for a funeral, taking his position as a pall-bearer, investigating the details of the kids' deaths, and leaving dents with his fist in our concrete walls when nothing seemed to make any sense. But now Johnnie was back. He found the cleanest mattress in the rubble of someone's old bedroom, and made a spot for himself in a corner of the parlor.

Johnnie was immediately welcomed back into Southie, especially by Frankie's old gang. He knew a lot of them from his own days at McDonough's Gym. He started working as a bouncer at some of the gin mills and drug dens on Broadway, owned and run by gangsters and boxers. Johnnie and I hardly crossed paths in Southie. I wanted nothing to do with the town, and he was getting more into it. One night, though, I was starving and came to Southie to borrow ten dollars from Johnnie. I went to find him where he was working at Connolly's Cafe, Eddie McGlaughlin's hole-in-the-wall bar on Broadway. It was all boarded-up looking, except for the window with a blinking Budweiser sign between some dirty country-kitchen curtains. Word around town was that Eddie had defrauded Tim Connolly out of ownership of the bar, now known to be a front for guns and drugs. I walked into the smoky narrow room looking for Johnnie. I passed a woman wheeling a baby carriage through the tavern and bumming spare change, and then by two older men "offering each other out," the way we used to do as little kids in the tunnels of Old Colony. The guy working the front door was leading me through the crowd; he knew me to be a MacDonald. He pulled up a barstool for me, and once again I was surrounded by muscled tough guys recounting Frankie's championship fights. Johnnie was sent for, and when he showed up, the muscle men brought him into the boxing tales too, with a few funny stories thrown in about Kevin being a hell of a con artist. Johnnie's face lit up as he listened to stories about his brothers. *That's what he's doing here, back in Southie,* I thought, and I couldn't blame him after hearing my brothers kept alive like that.

Johnnie had someone give me a twenty from the register behind the bar, and I walked back down Broadway to the train station, passing through the once colorful boulevard that my family had loved, now gone dark and busy with suspicious characters darting in and out of bars, stuffing things into pockets, and looking over their shoulders.

Ma swore she'd never look back. The kids told me they hated Colorado though. They missed their friends. They missed saying they were from Southie, and having it mean something. In their Colorado trailer park they wore the shamrocks, Notre Dame gear, and Southie T-shirts. But it meant nothing. They were in an all-

American world out west, where kids their age took buses for miles to hang out on fake street corners at the indoor shopping malls. There was no front stoop excitement. There wasn't even a front stoop. And Seamus and Stevie commented on how poor everyone in their trailer park looked—as if they'd never met poor people. But when I visited them out there, I saw what they were talking about. These weren't just poor people; they were poor people living on the edge of a godforsaken highway. There was no pretending you were anywhere else, no pretending you weren't poor, and no pride about being from the Federal Heights Trailer Park.

I could tell Ma didn't like Colorado much either, although she talked it up and begged all her old friends from Southie to come out west and move into Federal Heights. "We'll call it the New Colony," she said. She must have promised airfare to about ten different friends, who'd stop me on the street to show me her letters. When I was out there, I could see Ma was trying to find ways to make conversation with the Colorado people. She was thrilled to see this one redheaded guy walking by her tiny kitchen window. "Ohhhh, for Chrissake, are you Irish?" she said to him, opening her window. "Mother of God, he looked at me like I had two heads and he just kept on moving," Ma said in defeat. But she continued to look for any signs of home, pointing out to me the boarded-up highway bar named McIntyre's, and a town alderman named O'Reilly. But the few Irish names were nothing more than names, passed down through generations. In the end, Ma could only point to the green foothills of the Rockies, and say they were more beautiful than Ireland itself. That's when she talked Joe into hauling the trailer to a town called Golden, surrounded by the green foothills.

But Golden still wasn't home. "It's just the people!" Ma decided. "There's no hell-raising to them at all." Ma talked about missing "the craic," as the Irish called a good time. "With the long pusses on them, you'd think they just came from a funeral." Ma said Golden was full of Germans. "That explains it!" she said. Joe bought a house dirt cheap in Golden. It looked like a shack compared to the Swiss-style chalets that surrounded it, with floors that Ma complained made her feel she was walking up and down hills. There was a huge yard, though, for Maria to play in, and a picnic table for Kathy to sit at smoking cigarettes and going at her new hobby of scrawling endless words onto piles of lined paper. Ma didn't want to give up the trailer, so she had Joe plop it into their backyard. The town was up in arms about that one, saying the trailer was an eyesore. They passed an ordinance and made Ma and Joe build a high fence to conceal the trailer.

Ma stopped calling me once her phone was blocked for long distance calls. When I called her, she said Stevie had rung up a big bill calling his friend Tommy Viens in Southie. The two little kids were begging Ma to send them back to Southie that summer to see their friends. Ma swore she'd never look back, but with a place like Southie, it was hard not to. Johnnie was living in the apartment, and she knew I came by each day for a change of clothes, so Ma gave in and sent the kids for a two-week visit. There's no place like Southie. And at the ages of thirteen and fourteen, Stevie and Seamus knew that better than anyone.

It only took a few days of the little kids' visit back home before our world fell in on us again. Mary was working in the operating room at the City Hospital when she was told Tommy Viens was downstairs with a gunshot wound to the head. "I was a nervous wreck," she told me on the phone. "I thought I'd have to dismiss myself from the case." Mary told me all she knew: that Tommy had gotten hold of one of Johnnie's guns. That Stevie had found his best friend, face up under a big swivel bamboo chair. Tommy's eyes were open and blood was streaming from the back of his head. "Stevie's still shaking," she said. "Eighteen cops held him for two and a half hours in the apartment right next to where it happened." The detectives hadn't allowed Johnnie into the house for the interrogation. In the end, they let Stevie leave the apartment to the crowds that had gathered, and to Johnnie. "Oh, one more thing kid," Detective O'Leary said to Stevie, throwing his head up in a quick laugh, "your buddy's Ocean Kai." Ocean Kai was the local Chinese food restaurant, and Stevie didn't know what he meant. "Your friend's dead," O'Leary clarified.

We spent the night and the next day at Mary's. Steven was wearing the same clothes from the day before, and couldn't stop crying. He looked worn out and numb, and kept asking: "When can I go see Mr. and Mrs. Viens?" Seamus was watching cartoons with Mary's two sons when Steven wandered into the kitchen and saw the headline "Cops Say Teen May Have Pulled Trigger on Himself" and the picture of Tommy being brought out on a stretcher, with neighbors covering their mouths in shock. Steven was staring in a daze at Tommy's picture. I grabbed the newspaper and got rid of it. Within the hour Detective O'Leary showed up to take Steven to the homicide unit for more questions.

Johnnie went in the cruiser with Steven. When I arrived at homicide with Mary and Seamus, TV cameras filmed us going in. The homicide detectives were now praising themselves for arresting the alleged "child slayer." Mary's downstairs neighbor, Detective O'Leary's girlfriend and secretary, led us into the detective's office, and there we found Stevie crying in a chair and shaking his head in disbelief at the news O'Leary was telling him, about him being a murderer.

"You want a Pepsi or something kid? Your mouth is gonna get dry." O'Leary looked like he was tired of his job. When the detective left the room, Stevie asked me why his mouth would get dry. I didn't know the answer. He wondered if they'd soon be shining a big bright spotlight on him and interrogating him, like he'd seen in old movies. I felt relieved to be reminded of the innocent child Steven still was through everything he'd seen in life. "How come? . . . How could they think? . . ." Steven started crying too hard now to finish his sentences. He looked at us, trembling all over. O'Leary came back in and let out a big sigh, "Your mouth getting dry yet, kid?"

He explained that people's mouths get dry when they're charged with murder. "He was my best friend," Steven said to O'Leary, hyperventilating between each word. "Ask his mother, she'll tell you!"

"Hey, I would advise you to stay mum until a lawyer shows up," O'Leary said, pointing his finger at my thirteen year-old baby brother about to be formally charged with murder. I wanted so badly to tell O'Leary to fuck himself. Better yet I wanted to grab the broken pipe hanging from the ceiling and beat him to death for what he was doing to my scrawny helpless brother. I wanted to make the pig bleed through every one of his despicable orifices. I'd never felt that way before, but if I could've gotten hold of the gun in O'Leary's holster I would've shot him dead, and gladly gone to prison for it. I helped raise Seamus and Stevie; I changed their diapers and saw their first steps. The hate building up inside me was enough to chase every demon out of hell. But O'Leary had the power of the entire Boston Police Department and the Commonwealth of Massachusetts behind him, and Stevie was just a kid from the projects.

Detective O'Leary was famous in Boston that year. Not for passing out upside-down in stairwells outside his girlfriend's subsidized project apartment—that we knew about after many nights of having to step over his big belly, although it never made it into the papers. But O'Leary, along with Lieutenant Detective Eddie McNeely, was at the center of one of the most racially explosive murder investigations in the history of Boston. Charles Stuart, a suburban white man driving his wife from birthing classes at Brigham and Women's Hospital, called police from his car phone to report that he and his wife had just been shot in the mostly black section of Mission Hill. His pregnant wife had been killed, and he was bleeding from a minor gunshot wound. Stuart said he'd been carjacked by a black man who ran into the Mission Hill Housing Project. In following days, Mayor Flynn and Police Commissioner Mickey Roach dispatched police into the project. That Mrs. Stuart was pregnant might have had something to do with the mayor's promising to leave no stone unturned until the killer was brought to justice. But black ministers, who hadn't seen this kind of attention paid to the neighborhood's black murder victims, were wondering if race also played a part.

Then O'Leary and McNeely found their black scapegoat. They targeted a petty criminal and junkie named Willie Bennett, holding him up to the press as public enemy number one. In the end, though, there was no black carjacker. Charles Stuart jumped to his death from the Tobin Bridge, once the truth started to come out: He'd murdered his own wife, and shot himself to make the hoax more convincing. O'Leary and McNeely's heroic investigation fell apart. Now the newspapers said the witnesses' testimonies against Bennett had been falsified, coerced, and that drugs had been planted on some witnesses to put them at the cops' mercy, so they would sign whatever testimony they had to sign, saying that Bennett had bragged about the murder.

As I sat in O'Leary's dirty office, with piles of disorganized paperwork and posted headlines about this being Boston's worst year ever for homicides that brought few arrests, it all became clear. Steven was just another easy target. His arrest would bring weeks of splashy *Boston Herald* headlines and a feather in the cap of the harassed detective. And Stevie was white, so no one could claim racism with this case.

When Johnnie showed up with a Southie lawyer, Steven was formally charged with murder in the first degree. It was Thursday night and Stevie couldn't be arraigned until morning. He'd have to spend the night locked up. They handcuffed him and took him to Station 6 to await transport to an overnight juvenile lock-up. We walked behind Stevie, and when we all came out of the dilapidated homicide building, the camera crews had the bright lights back on and were about to film Stevie being led to the paddy wagon in cuffs. The police didn't say anything; they just posed with Stevie. "He's fucking thirteen years old!" I yelled. I knew it was illegal to identify juvenile defendants. Stevie had become the city's youngest homicide suspect, fitting into the media's current trend of portraying a generation of child "superpredators." "Steve, don't worry," Seamus yelled to him as he was escorted into the wagon.

When we got to Station 6, Stevie was excited to see us, as if it had been a month instead of a half hour. His voice was a little calmer now, but his hands were still trembling when he wiped his eyes and said something about having bad luck. "Does Ma know yet?" he asked. "She's gonna go crazy." Then he started crying again. He said he hoped the detectives would talk to Mrs. Viens soon, "They'll straighten it out." I didn't have the heart to tell Stevie we'd already seen the Vienses on TV saying they thought he'd killed Tommy, that there was no way their son committed suicide.

Stevie was sitting on top of a table in a small box of a room, wearing his baggy basketball shorts and swinging his skinny legs nervously. We all tried to change the subject a few times, talking about basketball or what lotion Steven might try to get rid of the pimples he was starting to get. But every subject brought Steven right back to stories about Tommy, funny ones about Tommy's pranks in the neighborhood. Like the morning he'd knocked on the door, asked me in the most innocent voice if Stevie was home, and then whipped three eggs at my head while running down the stairs. Tommy always reminded me of Kevin. You had to love him.

Then Seamus interrupted, asking with worried lines in his forehead, "Steve, what happened before you found Tommy shot?" Everything turned serious again, and that's when I asked the question I'd been needing to ask: "How did Tommy know about Johnnie's guns?" Steven and Seamus told me they'd seen Johnnie's Navy Seal duffel bags with the guns in them, and had bragged about them, and that after that kids would go up to the apartment when Johnnie wasn't home, on what they called "gun hunts." Tommy had found the guns, but as far as Seamus and Stevie knew, there was no ammo. Seamus and Stevie still couldn't figure out where the bullet that killed Tommy had come from.

The two began to go over that day for us. Seamus said Tommy had come to the apartment while Steven was still sleeping. Seamus took a shower, and when he came out Tommy was on the telephone. He slammed the phone down saying, "Hey, some cop on the phone said he's gonna come up here and arrest me." Seamus said he didn't believe Tommy. "Let him come, I'll grab one of Johnnie's guns and shoot him," Tommy said, getting more worked up. When the telephone rang again, Seamus picked it up and was told, "If you kids don't stop pranking those adult sex lines, I'll come up there and make you stop." The voice said he was a police officer, and knew they were at John MacDonald's apartment at 8 Patterson Way. Seamus said he apologized, telling the guy that he didn't know Tommy was calling the party lines.

Tommy continued to dance around, talking about how he'd grab one of Johnnie's guns, hide in the second apartment, and shoot the cop when he came through the door. Eventually Seamus left to go to the noon movie, telling Tommy not to touch Johnnie's guns, "or we'll all get our asses kicked."

By then Stevie had come out to watch TV with Tommy. " 'The Price Is Right' was on," Steven told us, excited that he could add something to the story. Stevie said that Tommy told him the whole thing about the cop, and then started calling the party lines over and over, each time getting disconnected. Stevie said he didn't pay much attention, except to laugh when Tommy started swearing at the moderator before she could disconnect him again. Tommy hung up the phone. "You think that cop would come up here?" he asked Steven. But Stevie told us that he was too tired to get into all the excitement about cops and Johnnie's guns.

Steven said Tommy seemed to get bored with "The Price Is Right" and kept carrying on about the cop on the phone. He asked if he could go to the kitchen for a cup of water. Stevie shrugged his shoulders, wondering why Tommy would ask permission in our house. "He walked toward the kitchen, looked at me out of the corner of his eye, then made a sharp turn, jumped on the washing machine, and reached up to the shelf." Stevie said Tommy pulled out the .357 Magnum.

"Put it back!" Stevie screamed as Tommy ran into the second apartment of our breakthrough. But Stevie said everything was quiet; Tommy was hiding. "Johnnie's gonna come home and be pissed!" Stevie yelled into the rooms cluttered with broken-down furniture. But there was no response, not even a movement to give away Tommy's hiding place. Then Stevie told us he gave up, thinking Tommy would come out of hiding if he just ignored him.

"The Price Is Right" ended and the midday news came on. "Let's go out," Stevie said he yelled, shutting off the television. Nothing. Just silence. Then the blast.

"How the fuck did he find the ammo?" Johnnie asked, pounding the wall. Johnnie told us that he'd hidden the ammo separately, in a pouch, under a pile of old shoes in Ma's closet in the other apartment.

Steven said he walked through the narrow passage into the second apartment, and saw only the .357 on the floor. There was no sign of Tommy. He said he grabbed the gun, and that's when he heard the noise underneath the chair tipped over in a corner.

"What noise?" I asked. Steven couldn't talk anymore. He started crying again. "What noise?" I asked again. "He was trying to talk...." Steven could barely get the words out himself. He was hyperventilating again, taking deep breaths and wailing from a hell that I couldn't begin to imagine. He finally told us that he turned the chair over and found Tommy, and all he remembered, he said, was the sound of gurgling, and a moan, like Tommy was trying to say something. The bullet hole was in his head, and a puddle of blood was growing around the two of them. "He was my favorite person, we were like brothers." Then Stevie laughed through his tears as he said, "We were trying to figure out how I could miss the plane back to Colorado. He didn't want me to go back."

I asked straight out if Tommy had ever talked about killing himself. Steven snapped at me, "You didn't know Tommy like I knew him. No one did. He'd never kill himself."

"Then what happened?"

"I don't know."

On the morning of the arraignment, nothing felt real. I'd stayed up all night at Mary's apartment drinking a bottle of whiskey to get back that numb feeling I'd had after Kevin died, and flicking the cable TV channels every time another gun appeared on the screen. But there were guns on every channel, so I turned the TV off and paced the floors drinking, while Seamus, Mary, Jimmy, and their two kids slept. Seamus kept getting up, pretending to go to the bathroom, checking up on me, and asking questions about Stevie. I hid the bottle and sent him back to bed, telling him to stop being such a worrywart. I was worried too though, even though the cops said Stevie would be kept on a suicide watch, "given the circumstances."

It seemed like the sun would never come up as I paced, watching through the window for the faintest hint of dawn. I got dressed for the arraignment. When we all finally went to the Southie courthouse, we were dying to see Stevie again. He was kept in a holding cell downstairs that morning, a dingy cold room with a toilet overflowing with what looked like generations of shit from nervous defendants.

After getting five minutes with Steven, I ran out to the corner store to get a pack of cigarettes and started smoking away as soon as I got them. News reporter types, with a pad and a pen, started hovering around me, staring and wondering who I was in relation to Tommy's death. As I lit up my smoke, the radio on the counter started broadcasting about Boston's youngest murder suspect, my own little brother, "in a case that has shocked city officials." I ran out of the store. It was hot out and a taxi driving by the courthouse was blasting the rest of the story, about how the defendant came from "a troubled family." I felt as if I was outside my own body—

nothing seemed real. On my way into the courthouse, a group of older men sat around reading the *Herald* and talking about the tragedy, and saying how it would make Southie look bad.

Eventually, Stevie was brought up to the courtroom and stood in the defendant's box. The judge arraigned him for murder in the first degree. He pleaded not guilty, and was put on $250,000 bail. That was that.

"Where the fuck are we gonna get $250,000 bail?" I asked out loud. Johnnie *shhh*ed me, explaining that it was $250,000 surety, meaning if you owned a house or anything worth that much, you could put that up. But that it meant $25,000 if we used cash. "Oh," I said. I was relieved for a second. Then I said even louder, "Where the fuck are we gonna get $25,000?"

When we went to the cell after the arraignment, Steven was crying again. "He thinks I did it!" he said, talking about Mr. Viens; he'd seen Tommy's father sitting far away from us in the courtroom. I couldn't answer him. Steven had a bruise on his neck, and explained that he had gotten a beating the night before in the transport van. He said it as if it was nothing, just another part of his bad luck. He said that some older black teenagers had beat him once they found out he was from Southie. "What did the cops do?" Mary asked. Stevie shrugged his shoulders. "They laughed." Stevie himself attempted a laugh now too, but his face was vacant, as if he didn't know how to feel about anything anymore.

The next day's *Boston Herald* said that Stevie was "stoic" in the courtroom, that he'd shown no emotions, or as they put it, "no remorse."

Eddie McGlaughlin had arrived at the courthouse wanting to help out. We all followed him into the office of his new attorney, Al Fallon. Fallon was a fast talker, and my head was already spinning. He told us there was nothing to worry about, that the police had already done so many illegal things in this case that all they'd want now would be to cover their asses before letting Stevie go. "The two-and-a-half-hour interrogation without a lawyer or legal guardian present was illegal," he said, throwing on his coat and rushing us out of his office just when I was getting comfortable enough to ask a question. "But … ," I said. He halted all questions, saying we just had to wait for the results of the gunpowder tests done on Steven's hands the day Tommy died.

Mary, Joe, Johnnie, and I scraped up the $25,000 to bail Steven out, emptying our life savings. We were all relieved to see Stevie walk out of the Department of Youth Services, into whatever freedom he might hold on to, while we hoped for this big mistake to be cleared up.

I made Mary come back into the apartment with me, one last time, to gather up my belongings. The neighbors cleared a path and stared silently as we walked up the front steps. Being in that apartment again was like being in a house on fire. I gathered up what I could, as if I was in the middle of an emergency—and I was. I could feel it all moving in on me. I ran out of my bedroom with two full trash bags to rush Mary out the door. I felt out of breath. "What are you doing?" I asked her, watching her bend over to clean something. "There's brain on the floor," she said calmly, as if she was at work in the OR. That's when my knees went. I fell onto the couch and for some time couldn't move a limb. I could barely get up the strength now to make it out that door. But I did, and it was the last time I ever saw our old home. I swore I'd never come back to Southie again.

I spent the rest of the summer with Seamus and Stevie, hiding out in a cottage on Cape Cod we'd rented from one of Johnnie's new Southie friends. We came back to Boston once in a while for pretrial hearings and visits to Fallon's office; or else to visit Mary, who'd also abandoned Southie once and for all, moving to Quincy. Other than those journeys, we sat in the cottage and talked about the fatal day over and over again, trying to figure out what had happened to Tommy, what was going on in his head when he hid out, and how the gun might have accidentally gone off. Steven wasn't allowed to leave the state, so Ma came to Cape Cod for a few weeks. She talked and talked about her own theories. I felt I was suffocating in the stories. Steven was free, but he wasn't really. None of us were. We were drowning in it. Steven couldn't wait for the gunpowder tests to come back from the FBI in Washington, proving that he hadn't shot the gun.

Finally, in September, the test results came back in Steven's favor. The FBI report was complicated, explaining the properties of "barium" and "antimony," the two chemicals that would show up on Steven's hands in large quantities from the blast of a .357 Magnum. The report said that the blast would've covered his hands in the chemicals, and that, given his age and lack of criminal experience, it was unlikely Steven had fired the gun. Fallon explained that the chemicals were difficult to get off one's hands. He said that even "some of the best criminals" he'd defended didn't get the stuff off.

But the *Herald* report only said the tests were "inconclusive." In the article, the police and the DA's office said that barium and antimony tests were unreliable, and that the department couldn't depend on them. This, even though they'd made such a big deal of the test on the day Tommy died. Even worse, the DA's office said that they had new evidence that would prove "the juvenile's" guilt.

After reading the article, we went into Fallon's office, to find out what this new police evidence was. He closed the door, looked at Stevie, and said, "You know you can tell me anything. No matter what, I have to challenge the state's evidence." He added, "Even if you shot Tommy!" Fallon pulled out an official typewritten police transcript of Steven's call to 911 on the day Tommy died. I scanned the piece of paper and found two lines where it had Steven saying he'd shot Tommy in the head.

In spite of Stevie's reaction—he was crying, saying, "I feel like I'm going crazy, like I'm just losing my mind"—for the first time I thought maybe he had shot Tommy, accidentally. *Maybe he blocked it out,* I thought. On the long journey back to our hideaway on the

Cape, I asked him once again to go over everything that happened the day Tommy died. Stevie just looked at me as if to say, "Not you too!" He said he didn't want to go over it again, that whatever might happen to him, as long as he knew—and Tommy knew—the truth, that was all that mattered.

I should've known better than to trust anything handed down officially, having grown up in Southie. It took two weeks to get the original cassette of Stevie's call to 911 we'd demanded. I went to Fallon's alone, anxious for the truth. It was nightmarish to hear Steven pleading with the dispatcher, seconds after finding Tommy. It brought me back to my own calls for help after Davey had jumped. Stevie was begging them to hurry up. He gave his address a few times to the dispatcher, who asked him to calm down and to speak slower. I listened and listened, waiting for the line, "I shot my friend in the head." But it never came. Nor was there anything that could've been mistaken for those words typed on the transcript that homicide had given us.

Fallon called the DA and asked him if he'd listened to the tape. He said he didn't need to, that he had the transcript. "What, are the cops lying?" he laughed. But he agreed to listen to his copy while Fallon waited on the line. I heard the Assistant DA's voice come through the phone. "Holy shit," he said.

I fled Fallon's office. I wanted to get back to Steven to tell him what I'd heard, and to apologize for questioning him, even for one moment. I sped on the highway back to the Cape. It started to rain. The rain beat down on the car, and my heart felt as if it would explode with hate. I wanted to murder again. I was sure of it. I thought of ten people I would kill. But the amount of suffering I would inflict on them could never match the pain I was feeling for a helpless child railroaded by a cast of demons. Agents of the state, district attorneys, cops and detectives, the police commissioner who ran a department so corrupt it would send children and neighborhoods to hell before admitting a mistake, even the mayor. I pulled over to fantasize about killing every last one of them, and about how to make it worthwhile I'd have to keep from getting caught until I'd gotten them all.

But in the next minute I only wanted to die myself. *The world's nothing but pain. It'll never get better. It's completely useless. Stevie's going to be found guilty of something he didn't do, and how much more suffering and death will that lead to? How soon will Stevie be found hanging in a cell?* I felt the pain of all these thoughts converging on me, and I wanted out. I thought about Tommy, and about the brothers I hadn't had time to cry for, and about my mother, whose suffering was never-ending. The rain poured down so that the windshield wipers couldn't keep up. I was stuck there on the side of the road, and I realized that I could just put the car into drive, and press the gas peddle, and kill myself right then. I couldn't see anything through tears and rain.

I couldn't do it, though. I decided then, that if I ever made it out of this storm, I'd have to spend my life fighting—not only for Stevie, but for everything else that had happened over the years, for the dignity of my family, and for other families like mine. I didn't even have words for what I was promising myself, but something told me that I was making a lifelong commitment. It was justice I wanted, that's all. I wasn't even sure I knew what justice was anymore. But I knew it had to be sweeter than blood.

Steven's case went to trial twice: the "de novo" system in Massachusetts allows defendants to go before a judge for the first trial, and then, if found guilty, to take it to a jury.

For the first trial, Steven had been charged with first-degree murder. The DA worked on a theory that Steven and Tommy had been playing Russian roulette, based on a rumor that two weeks prior to Tommy's death, Stevie had put a bullet in Johnnie's gun, spun the chamber, pointed it at their friend Greg, and pulled the trigger. Greg and Tommy's brother Brian, one of Seamus's best friends, were to take the stand as witnesses. But when questioned under oath, they contradicted the written testimonies that Detective O'Leary had submitted to the court. Similarly, the eight-page memo submitted to the court by the first officer on the scene was undermined by the initial incident report, which said nothing about Russian roulette or a confession from Steven.

When O'Leary took the stand, he denied that holding Steven incommunicado, under questioning without a lawyer or legal guardian, was an interrogation. This, even though Steven testified that when he'd asked to see Johnnie, O'Leary had said to him, "You're going nowhere, kid," obviously meaning he wasn't free to leave. O'Leary said that the questioning wasn't illegal because Steven wasn't a suspect at the time. When questioned about the thirteen-year-old's demeanor on that day, O'Leary said, "He was very calm. He had no remorse." I'd noticed that all of the detectives and officers testifying that day had been huddled in a corner outside the courtroom, going over what they were going to say on the stand. A black detective with a foreign accent stood apart. He clearly wasn't part of the club. When questioned on the stand about Steven's demeanor, this Detective Hensaw said Steven had been hysterical, slumped over in a crouched position, holding his stomach with both arms and crying his eyes out.

The state's experts took turns testifying that the FBI's report on the gunpowder tests wasn't credible, and that the tests weren't an exact science. The police ballistician, Mr. Bogden, showed white cotton sheets that were shot with the same gun at various distances, creating circular patterns of powder burns, or "stippling." He was followed by the state medical examiner, Dr. Feigen, who stared straight ahead as he reported that the stippling pattern created by the gun at a distance of twenty-four inches resembled the stippling pattern on Tommy's face. Then he added that he'd measured Tommy's arm—from armpit to the end of his middle finger—in the autopsy and that it was only eighteen inches long, and that Tommy couldn't have shot himself. When asked if Tommy's hands were ever tested for gunpowder, Feigen said no, and that barium and antimony tests weren't reliable anyway. *Even though they thought the tests were crucial when they tested Steven's hands,* I muttered quietly, struggling to stay in order before the judge.

During a recess, Mary approached Fallon, telling him that it would be impossible for someone Tommy's age, who was five feet eight inches, to have an arm only a foot and a half long, unless the person had some kind of bone disease. "And," she said, "I get all those gunshot victims at the City Hospital, and when they're pronounced dead, their hands are always bagged for the barium and antimony test swabs." She said they must have tested Tommy's hands, but that the results might not have been the results they wanted. Fallon patted her on the back a few times and asked Mary's husband if "the little lady" could cook at all. "You should have married a Greek woman," he laughed, "now they can cook!" Then he patted Mary on the back some more and escorted us all back to our benches.

The evidence, such as it was, was in. Fallon came out of his private meeting with the judge and the DA, and explained that the charges were being reduced to involuntary manslaughter. He said that meant Steven was playing with the gun, "acting in wanton and reckless disregard for another's life." "Like when someone runs a red light and, in the course of breaking the law, runs someone over, even though they never meant to kill anyone," he explained, as if it wasn't so bad after all. Fallon took Steven into a corner alone, trying to encourage him to plead guilty to the new charge, and the next thing I knew Stevie was weeping, "But I didn't do it." Fallon said that Steven would get very little time, and maybe none at all if the judge thought he was finally admitting he did it. But Steven hadn't shot Tommy and he said he wanted to stick to the truth. So we kept fighting.

Grandpa showed up at the courthouse in Southie. He was starting to look a lot older. He came into the courthouse lobby shuffling his feet, with wide blue eyes, bright as ever, and a black leather aviator's hat that was all puffed up on top of his head. He said his heart was very bad, but that he came to the courthouse to warn us. He said he had seen Fallon on the news the night before, and that he couldn't hear a word he was saying about Steven's case, but that he had "an awful criminal face on him." "Where'd you find that blackguard? I suppose some no-good-bum-of-a-gangster led you to him." We all laughed, but he was right, and in walked Eddie McGlaughlin to talk to Fallon about his own case, as he was facing federal drug charges from the Whitey Bulger roundup.

While we awaited the second trial on the new charge, we were able to keep Steven out on bail. He attended school in Worcester, living with Ma's sister Mary. Ma had to go back to Colorado to take care of Maria and Kathy while Joe went off to work every day. Seamus missed Steven terribly, going back to Colorado without him. Steven was discovering that suburban life wasn't that bad after all—it was better than being in the Department of Youth Services and getting beatings from black kids when they found out he was from Southie.

The spring of 1991, Grandpa was dying. Ma had flown back again from Colorado, after hearing that her father kept asking, "Where's Helen," from his deathbed. We all got to see Grandpa one last time in the ICU, and he held Steven's hand the longest, assuring him, "It'll be OK."

Then Ma, knowing that Grandpa had been drifting in and out of consciousness, asked if he'd seen the kids: Patrick, Davey, Frankie, Kevin. Grandpa was hooked up to machines keeping him in his old body. He looked tired and thirsty, but the nurses said he couldn't have water, so Ma kept wetting cloths and pressing them on his trembling lips. Grandpa spoke: "Sure, hasn't Davey been sitting here with me? And your mother, your mother's here." Ma took what Grandpa was saying casually. She'd become used to saying that for her, the line between this world and the next had been blurred. She even joked with Grandpa. "Well, my mother would be bullshit, knowing that you're seeing another woman," Ma said, referring to the female companion Grandpa had befriended in the nursing home. Grandpa laughed.

My cousins, brothers, sisters, and I said goodbye to Grandpa and left the hospital. Ma and her sisters sat up with him for a couple nights. Ma was the only one in his room when he went. She told us that the two of them had said an Act of Contrition together when they knew it was time for him to pass on. Grandpa slipped into a coma state, and the doctors asked Ma if they should try yet another medicine. Ma said, "Let him go."

Grandpa's was the best funeral I'd ever been to. The West Roxbury Church was filled with green and gold carnations, and the choir sang "Danny Boy." Ma's sisters wept bitterly, and Ma scolded them, "What, would you want him to suffer forever?" Ma was elated by the send-off and looked as peaceful as Grandpa in his casket. As I sat in the long procession to the cemetery, I wondered why I was so happy at a funeral. Then I realized it was the first time I'd seen off someone who'd died naturally, from old age.

After the funeral, I went back to our pursuit of justice. I spent days and nights in the library at Suffolk University Law School, reading books on forensic pathology, studying the pictures of stippling patterns on gunshot victims, crying about Tommy, wondering what had happened, and throwing up in the bathrooms. I photocopied the pages that said that stippling tests, especially done on white cotton sheets, which are so different from flesh, were increasingly being discredited as having a twelve-inch range of error. Then I found out that the guy who wrote the book on forensic pathology, Dr. Werner Spitz, was not only one of the foremost forensic experts in America, he was also Dr. Feigen's teacher. But Fallon, who would have been the one to front the money for experts, still said we wouldn't need them to win the coming jury trial. "Piece of cake," he said. I was encouraged to find books that discredited the state's experts, even if only for my own peace of mind and sense of justice. And I was relieved when Mary came back from Southie Savings Bank one day, telling me she'd just bumped into "that black detective." She said he came up to her in the bank and asked how her little brother was doing. He said he felt terrible over the tragedy. "I tell you one thing," he added, "that kid didn't kill anybody!" He shook his head, "He's innocent!"

For the jury trial, the state had gotten rid of the teenage witnesses and the Russian roulette theory. The DA was now calling it "horse-play" that had led to Tommy's death, but he claimed that Steven had pulled the trigger and should be removed from society. Detective Hensaw was now part of the clique. On the stand, he looked down at his hands when he said that when he'd arrived on the scene, Steven was very calm for someone who'd just lost his friend. My heart dropped when I heard him say those words. *They even got to him*, I thought. He'd been the only one I trusted to tell the truth. And you could tell by the way he spoke, slowly, with obvious regret, that he was doing something he didn't want to do. Fallon never brought up the fact that his testimony had completely changed since the first trial.

The state filed in its expert witnesses. We had no experts to do independent test firings with the gun, to challenge the credibility of stippling tests, or to testify to the average arm length of a five-foot-eight teenager. Steven tried to hold up through the whole trial. I kept telling him to have faith in God and in the truth. Ma's friend Mary Scott showed up and gave Steven a rose, a symbol of faith in the divine intervention of St. Theresa, she told him. I gave Steven a small silver cross, one that I'd kept in my pocket the whole time Kathy was in a coma.

Steven took the stand and told the truth, the same truth of every single detail he'd told from day one. Then Fallon threw Tommy's 8 × 10 autopsy photos in front of Steven while he was on the stand. Steven buckled over, wailed in agony, and held onto his stomach. Fallon was asking a barrage of questions about the identity of the person in the photo, who had a bullet hole in his head, and whether it was, in fact, his friend Tommy. I wasn't sure what Fallon was doing. We all cried for Steven. "What's he doing that for? That's wrong to torture a little kid like that!" My Aunt Mary said out loud. Mrs. Viens, too, buckled over at the sight of the photos. The judge called the court to order, and Fallon calmly put the photos away and dramatically requested a recess, speaking in a soft low tone. Fallon explained to us later that he'd wanted to show the jury Steven's gut reaction to the picture of Tommy, without any warning. Steven said he hated Fallon now. "I don't ever want to see those pictures again," he moaned in the marble halls outside the courtroom.

The day we filed into the courtroom for the verdict, a number of court officers followed to keep the peace. Throughout the trial I'd studied each juror. Some guys looked as mean as O'Leary, big fat Irish Americans who kept looking at their watches as if they were wondering when lunch was. My biggest hope was the Haitian woman. *She's black,* I figured, *she knows what the cops are like.* I got nervous whenever I saw her dozing off during the trial, or reading her pocket Bible during recesses—"She's reading the fucking Old Testament, too!" I told my sister. I wanted to rip it from her hands and open it up to the part where Christ is accused by the Pharisees, but we weren't allowed to communicate with the jurors. The lead juror was a black woman too, but I didn't trust her because she looked wealthy and had the sober, oppressive face of a barrister herself.

"And how do you find the defendant?"

"Guilty."

I wanted to do something drastic. I wanted to speak, but I was afraid that the judge would give Steven a harsher sentence if I said the words I wanted to say. I wanted to lash out at every whore representing the government, and every weak sucker on the jury. I wanted to kill again. But I was feeling so weak that I slid from the bench and my knees hit the floor. Johnnie dragged me back up to my seat and told me to stay calm for the judge. Fallon gave his arguments why the judge should be lenient, given the tragic circumstances of the case. It sounded like he was agreeing that Steven had shot Tommy, but that the court should let him go since it was an accident, a double tragedy. The prosecutor called Steven dangerous, and said he should be put away. And the judge determined that he should be sent to the Department of Youth Services. The DYS would be in charge of deciding how long to keep him; it could be a year or until his eighteenth birthday.

The guards led him away. We were allowed down to the basement to see Steven in his cell, before he was transported. We went down the same stairwell that Steven had been taken down five minutes earlier. On the way down, there on a windowsill, I found the crumpled-up rosebud that Steven had been keeping in his pocket, and there also was my cross. I picked them up and put them in my pocket. When we saw Steven, I wanted to ask him why he'd dumped the symbols of faith. But I didn't bother. It was one thing to feel forsaken by the criminal justice system. It was another to feel forsaken by God. I wanted to dump the symbols of faith too, but I couldn't. There was still some fighting left to do.

"My brother, you've got some nerve, strolling in here with no coat on!" Muadi DiBinga was talking about me to an invisible audience, and waiting for my explanation. I had walked to my new job through a blizzard, and I wasn't wearing a coat. Our boss Kathie came out of her office to see what was going on. Then she joined in, harassing me for looking like I wasn't sleeping or eating.

After I'd left Old Colony, I rested a few hours a night on friends' couches around Boston, secretly eating at soup kitchens, and spending my days and nights investigating for Steven's appeal and getting involved in efforts against violence and police abuse, especially in Roxbury, where things had only gotten worse since the Stuart case. At the same time I was trying to finish my studies at UMass, and taking extra courses in juvenile justice. I'd found Citizens for Safety only after many liberal organizations in Boston had shut the door in my face, since my story didn't fit with their upper-middle-class white plans to organize around civil rights issues. While Steven was locked up in the Department of Youth Services, I called every organization in town that talked about violence and the police department's reactionary ways in the black and Latino neighborhoods. One guy listened for fifteen minutes while I told him about the abuses in Steven's case, until I said "South Boston." Then he asked me if Steven was, by chance, a minority who'd moved into South Boston. "Nope." "Well, unless he's a minority or gay, I'm afraid there's not much we can do." That was the end of that conversation.

I finally decided to call just one last place to volunteer. I didn't like the name Citizens for Safety. It sounded wimpy and suburban, and I was looking for a revolution to put all my rage into. But Kathie and Muadi were cool, and I soon figured out the name was a front; they were ready for battle.

Kathie Mainzer had come from a white middle-class background. She said she'd grown up liberal, but blind to the realities of poor people's lives. "I fell from the safety of that high horse," she said. She'd left an alcoholic husband and been forced to raise her child alone on welfare. Kathie found that being on welfare was no picnic, experiencing firsthand the insults and abuses of the welfare bureaucracy. That's when she started fighting, leading welfare rights organizations up the grand steps of the State House. Before long she was executive director of the Coalition for the Homeless, and was eventually asked by a group of civic leaders and activists to run a new citywide organization to deal with the violence that was making headlines every day in Boston. She took the job, and started wearing suits that contrasted sharply with her bright red lipstick and matching hair that looked as if Ma'd gotten hold of her with the scissors.

Muadi DiBinga was from Zaire. "Africa!" she'd add, loud and proud, just in case I needed to brush up on my geography. But she'd grown up in Roxbury, where her family got involved in all aspects of community development in their beleaguered neighborhood. Muadi was pro-black. And she wore her hair in natural twists, and dressed in an urban hip-hop style, with African trinkets that said she was damn proud of where she came from. I thought for sure she'd have resentments toward a white guy from Southie wearing claddagh symbols and lots of green that said *I* was damn proud of where I came from.

But Muadi was one hundred percent behind my cause after hearing the truth about Southie. She asked every day about Steven in DYS. I'd received no welcome from the white liberals running organizations that claimed to champion the cause of people like Muadi. But here was Muadi now, calling me her "brother" and us getting along just fine without them. Muadi called the white liberal organizations "plantations," and said they were dominated by whites who had no clue, "with all these 'house Negroes' running around and fetching their coffee." Muadi was all about black power, which I learned had nothing to do with taking over the housing projects of Southie. I wished that the people from my neighborhood could know someone like Muadi; they'd have been for black power too. They'd love her, I thought. But she was black, and the plantation folks had already divided "us" from "them," as far as I could see.

We were a good team, Kathie, Muadi, and I. We ran around the city, strategizing while riding on buses and pulling together groups in Roxbury for meetings with the police to air complaints from kids who were being detained and harassed and sometimes called "nigger" by cops. Residents spoke out about specific officers they felt were only adding to the violence of the streets. *Just like in Southie,* I thought to myself as we passed on a bus through the dark boulevards of Roxbury's Dudley Square, where I'd always been told never to set foot.

I still hated the cops for what they'd done to my little brother. I was working with many black people now, and even some of the liberal types who ran organizations. But the cops? Never. The strange thing was, whenever I went to meetings with activists from around the city, as much as I related to the black residents, there were still no people from the same place I was. The cops attending those meetings were the closest thing to my Southie neighbors, with shamrocks pinned to their lapels, heavy Boston accents, and stories about growing up tough. I found out that some had become cops because of their experiences with crime and violence. I decided to give them a chance in my own head.

We ended up working with the Boston Police Department when we started to organize a gun buyback program in the city. We had no choice in order to collect turned-in guns legally. The police had already committed themselves to "a new era of community policing," which activists like us had been pushing for. We wanted to make sure their "community policing" was more than just another press conference catch phrase to shut people up after the Stuart case debacle. So we pushed the gun buyback as a way they could prove they meant what they were saying. We held our own press conference, announcing our plans to collect working firearms in exchange for money, amnesty, and anonymity. We knew the cops would jump on board; and they did, once we started getting thousands of dollars in private donations for buying back guns. Eventually, as thousands of guns were handed over, the cops wanted all the credit. We didn't care as long as the deadly weapons were coming in.

"Dudley Square, you're liable to get shot!" Ma screamed over the phone at me when I told her about my new job. "It's not that bad," I told her. "Black people shoot black people, and white people shoot whites," I added. I told her that according to statistics I was safer in Roxbury than I was in Southie or Charlestown. Ma was worried, but she told me proudly that she was an activist now too, in Colorado. Ma had gotten involved in fighting for the handicapped, and was leading a class-action lawsuit against the state on behalf of residents like Kathy, who'd become brain injured before the age of twenty-two, and was labeled "developmentally disabled." Ma had found out that the developmentally disabled had no access to rehabilitation services, except to be thrown into a nursing home, while waiting on a list of eight thousand. The state took only two new clients a year from this list for services. "Now let's see," Ma said in court to Judge Matsch, who presided over the case. "That means Kathy'll be eligible for services when she's four thousand and thirty years old." Ma told me the whole court burst into laughter after she'd done the math on her hands, but the judge wasn't smiling.

Ma was speaking up passionately and leading other mothers in *King vs. Colorado.* She said she felt as if Davey was with her in the struggle—hundreds of mentally disabled people had signed on to the class action suit. She said the Association for Retarded Citizens had presented her with a "My Hero" certificate: "Because of her perseverance, and never taking 'no' for an answer, her daughter and thousands of Coloradans will have services rather than remaining unserved on D.D. waiting lists. Helen King is a model of 'parent power' at its finest."

I too felt as if I brought "the kids" to work with me every day. In Roxbury and Dorchester I met survivors of the bloody streets who were helping us appeal to people to turn in their guns. I saw black mothers telling their stories at rallies, turning their pain into songs of redemption. I started speaking publicly about my own experiences growing up; but only in the black neighborhoods that welcomed my story with open hearts and minds. Never in Southie.

But despite all our keeping busy—Ma in Colorado and me in Boston—the painful truth was that Steven was locked away every night, without the freedom even to go to the toilet unsupervised. Each time I telephoned Ma, it seemed her voice got more and more shrill—she couldn't bear being thousands of miles from her baby. A lawyer had taken on the case for free, but he warned us it would be an uphill battle.

Finally, Steven was sent home to Ma in Colorado, after officials at DYS decided that he'd been "rehabilitated." Some staff members said they didn't even know what he was doing there in the first place. On the day he was released, the DYS psychiatrist apologized to Steven, in front of me and all of his superiors, who sat around the table for Steven's final release. "Even if I do believe you're telling the truth," he said to Steven, having spent hours in one-on-one sessions, talking about Tommy's death and the entire court trauma, "I'm supposed to assume you did shoot your friend. But even if that were the case, I still wouldn't know why the hell you were ever sent to DYS." Tears came to the psychiatrist's angry eyes, and it was obvious that he was breaking the rules here. "For what it's worth, I want to apologize to you for the entire criminal justice system." He went on, talking about all the times he'd heard about kids in affluent suburban towns playing with guns, and accidentally shooting another. "Those kids," he said, "are hardly ever prosecuted. And if they are, they never get put away." In the end, he said, he couldn't help but think that what happened to Steven had everything to do with who he was and where he came from.

There was a long silence around the table. I could tell Steven just couldn't wait to be set free. He looked toward the open window, with a grille breaking up the spring view of trees in bloom. My own anger welled up with the anger of the psychiatrist, who was gripping the table now with both hands. The other case workers gave their testimonies, saying that they would miss Steven, since he got along with everyone and acted as a peacemaker on his floor, easing racial and gang tensions. One woman said she wanted to keep him, and that caught Steven's attention. He laughed when he realized it was only a joke. Finally, they all wished Stevie the best of luck in the appeal process, and off we went.

When Steven walked out those front doors, I felt I too had been let out of the "secure treatment center." I told Steven that we could call off the whole appeal if he wanted to, since it wouldn't make any difference. He wasn't going back to DYS no matter what—his sentence was over. I was relieved, though, when he said he still wanted to prove his innocence. "That was wrong," he said, looking behind and shaking his head with an expression that struggled between anger and disbelief.

In the summer of 1994, two years after Steven's release, I heard the words I'd been waiting for. "We won!" After four years of hell, I collapsed into a chair and wept at what Steven's appellate lawyer was telling me on the telephone. The three judges of the state appeals court overturned my brother's conviction, after calling into question police tactics and Steven's inadequate defense in the face of such abuses of power. Charles Stephenson had taken the appeal pro bono, and the only bad news was that the judges, because of the unusual circumstances of the case, ordered that their finding not be published in law books. The heroic work of our appellate lawyer would never set precedent in Massachusetts Common Law.

As an activist, I'd spent the past three years meeting some of the best people I could ever hope to meet in a lifetime. That was important after years of witnessing so much viciousness and dirty dealing. Like the activists and the mothers of Roxbury and Charlestown, Charles Stephenson helped restore my faith.

At first I wasn't so sure of Stephenson—I had little trust left in me. Although I was relieved Stephenson was from rural western Massachusetts, with no connection to the Boston Police Department, I worried that he wasn't convinced by my ranting about police conspiracies in this case. He seemed to think that it was all a tragic mistake, the result of police incompetence and ineffective counsel.

But Stephenson became increasingly distraught and traumatized the deeper he got into Steven's case, witnessing blatant corruption firsthand. In order to convince the trial judge, June Gonsalves, that the trial she'd presided over was worthy of appellate review, Stephenson said he had to be exact in showing that Steven might have been exonerated had his lawyer done his job. We went before the judge a few times with arguments to get access to the firearm that killed Tommy, so that new ballistics experts could do test firings in the presence of the prosecutor. The judge wasn't budging; no access until Stephenson made the right argument. Stephenson traveled two hours into Boston every time, and the skinny bespectacled man sometimes looked as if he'd keel over from the emotional stress. "I have two young kids, you know," he told me. Stephenson's compassion struck me, and I realized then that this was probably my first exposure to what it meant to be a real father, and how similar it was to the protectiveness I'd only ever seen from mothers.

Finally Stephenson was granted access to the gun. On that day, he called me from a telephone booth, told me the good news, and went for lunch. When he came back to the clerk's office he had a smile on his face and an order from the judge. "That gun's not here, sir," the clerk said, looking up from paperwork. "Says here it was sent to the Boston Police Ballistics Unit. To be destroyed," she added. "This was issued about a half hour ago." That's when Stephenson found out what really had gone on in Steven's case. He sped off to ballistics and saved the gun from destruction with his order from the judge. He later told me that he didn't want to find out who'd issued the order, or to rock the boat, because by then all he wanted was to get through this case and clear Steven's name. And that he did. The new test firings, combined with expert pediatric testimony about the absurdity of Tommy having an eighteen-inch arm, and evidence of questionable police tactics, made three judges unanimously agree to throw out the conviction. Charles Stephenson got nothing out of this case, in spite of what he gave to us. He said he knew Steven was innocent and he wanted nothing more than to undo an injustice— as much as he could. He couldn't give Steven back his friend, but he certainly did help to restore Steven's faith in people.

And for me, discovering there were people like Stephenson—and Steven's DYS psychiatrist—in the world, helped me finally to understand what justice meant.

CHAPTER 11

VIGIL

JAY AND CHRIS KING." "ADAM ENOS." "JOHN FITZPAT-
rick." "James Boyden the Third." "James Boyden the Fourth."
"Bobby Barrett." "Herbie Stone." Shamrocks bedecked the church
altar, and rage came with the tears that fell from Irish eyes. I could
have been in South Boston, but this was Charlestown. I fled out of
the church. I couldn't take any more. It was too close to home.

When I'd read in the *Globe* about mothers in Charlestown speaking up in defiance of the Irish gangsters and the neighborhood code
of silence, I knew I had to meet these people. "Please don't send me
another cold cut platter," Sandy King pleaded with her neighbors in
the article. What she wanted was answers about her two sons' murders in front of silent witnesses, and for the good people of the town
to start speaking up. Most people thought mothers like these
wouldn't live long, with their public attacks of the drug establishment. Instead, complaints came only from the real estate agents,
who'd been making a killing as poor and working-class Charlestown disintegrated and property values boomed in a hot housing
market. "You're giving Charlestown a black eye," said one real estate

agent to Sandy King. I thought, looking at the fierce face of this mother in the articles, that he'd be lucky if she didn't give *him* a black eye.

I'd met the Charlestown mothers while Citizens for Safety was putting together a display at City Hall plaza, posting the faces of people who'd died from gun violence. Most of the victims in the posters were black, but I knew all too well that that wasn't the whole story. I still couldn't get myself to set foot in Southie, never mind talking about violence there. So I went to Charlestown. The mothers volunteered their kids' pictures, at first reluctantly, having trouble trusting, being from a town like mine, always besieged by outsiders with their own agendas. The Charlestown mothers had already joined black mothers across the city in battles with legislators and judges and cops, and when they saw their kids' faces in large posters alongside those of black children, their sisterhood across race felt even more natural. At the exhibit, black and white mothers took turns holding each other up, and sometimes picking each other up off the ground.

The Charlestown women invited me to speak as a "survivor" at their vigil, and that's how I ended up sitting on the church steps, unable to move after seeing all those shamrocks and trinkets, just like the ones I'd buried my own brothers with. But I knew these women like I knew my own mother. They'd kick my ass if I fled the vigil on them. I laughed to myself about that one, still trembling in front of the church. I had to go back inside, I had to speak to the crowd of faces that looked so much like those of my own neighbors, and when I left that place at the end of the day, I knew someday I'd have to move back home—to Southie.

After the Charlestown vigil and my night of wandering through Old Colony among the ghosts of my life, the neighborhood's pull on me was stronger than ever. And after giving a tour of Southie for *U.S. News & World Report,* I was certain about moving back. Steven's case was behind us, and my recent experiences with people who gave yet wanted nothing in return helped redeem my life experiences with those who only take away.

I got an apartment just outside the Old Colony Project, on Southie's West Side. It was summer, and I'd been four years away. I drove past the little kids who ruled the small lanes with their street hockey and their loud cheers of solidarity as they threw water balloons at passing buses. After settling in, I took a walk up toward Broadway, past the curious stares of mothers on lawn chairs, wiping the sweat from their brows and doing anything but minding their own business. When I got to Broadway with its rows of double- and triple-parked cars, I was shocked to be once again in a place where traffic came to a grinding halt to let women with baby carriages cross the street. Tough-looking guys and girls held the door for each other at the corner stores, and I finally admitted to myself that there was no place in the world I'd rather be.

Some things had changed. New people had been buying up and gutting out property in what was becoming the trendy Boston neighborhood of the nineties. Some neighborhood people in coffee shops talked about their property values going up, while others talked about becoming homeless with the new high rents. One day I decided to try one of the new espresso shops that had opened for the yuppies. I waited in line with the "outsiders," resentful of their proud talk about "bringing the neighborhood up." I cringed as they all pronounced the "r" in the sugar that went into their grande-double-shot-skinny-mochaccinos. Bobby Got-a-Quarter wandered in looking like he'd just woken up, head wobbling away, eyes fixed on the breasts of a newcomer. He didn't mean anything by it; he just wanted a quarter. The preppie young woman moved nervously, trying not to look at Bobby. Bobby didn't say anything. He's been asking for quarters for so long he doesn't have to ask anymore. You just give him a quarter; those are the rules. The newcomer didn't know this—she probably just thought he was a slightly horny special needs man.

The uneasiness was broken when a Southie guy stepped out of line and poured some coins into Bobby's hand. "No quarters today, Bob, there's five dimes—you can change 'em in for two quarters if ya want." I felt proud then to be one of the people in line who was from the old Southie, with its loyalty and caring for poor souls like Bobby Got-a-Quarter. The Southie girl behind the counter shook two quarters out of her tip cup and slapped them both onto the counter, proud to abide by a neighborhood obligation to Bobby. "Here ya go, Bob, that's for me and Sheila," she said, pointing behind her to the other young girl making coffee. Bobby never said anything, not even thank you. He didn't have to. This is Southie, and for better or worse some things are understood in the silence.

People in donut shops and on corners seemed to be talking more openly about their problems. Gentrification had added to my neighbors' sense that they were walking on a sinking landfill. Maybe that's why I heard more honest stories of poverty and lack of opportunities for young people, even as one of the biggest development projects in the country was visible from the rooftops of the D Street Housing Project, where black and white teens were still distracted by race, still standing their ground, and still going nowhere. Southie's waterfront, former home to manufacturing and shipping jobs, was set to become "the Seaport District," with plans underway for billions of dollars in development, luxury condos, and jobs that these Boston Public School kids—graduates and dropouts alike—would not be educated for.

Whitey had gone on the lam after the feds, whose collaboration with the gangster had been exposed, finally indicted him for racketeering, drug dealing, and murder. With Whitey out of the way, some people seemed to feel more comfortable talking about the drugs in Southie. But many talked about addiction and social decay as if they were new and wouldn't be happening if Whitey were still around. Walking down Broadway, though, I saw Whitey's legacy everywhere.

"Hey, honey, you got some change for a girl down on her luck?"

I looked over to where she was sitting on the wall, looking as if she were hanging on for dear life. "Debbie!" I said. "You're Debbie Alinardo, right?" I almost didn't recognize her. She'd aged since she'd hung around with Kathy, going to construction school after the two of them got out of a group home. "That's my name, don't wear it out!" she said, stumbling off the wall to approach me. She was drunk. "You don't remember me," I said. "I'm Kathy MacDonald's brother, Mike." "For fuck's sake," she said, "I thought you were some yuppie." She took off her fishing hat with all the badges stuck to it, as if she were paying her respects. Then she looked at me and started to cry. "Kathy MacDonald, I love Kathy MacDonald!" she screamed to all the passersby on Broadway. She made the sign of the cross as if Kathy were dead. Then one of her buddies from the wall, an older guy about twice her age, came stumbling over to ask me for a cigarette. "Fuck off," she said, belting him in the stomach with an upper cut. "That's Kathy MacDonald's brother. I fuckin' love Kathy MacDonald!" she screamed at people all the way across the street. She grabbed me by the shoulders, shaking me and asking, "How's Helen? Helen MacDonald was the best-looking woman on Broadway!" The older guy next to her knew Ma too. "A good woman," he said. "We never went hungry with her pocketbook full of toast." His blurry eyes became clearer with a smile, as he shook his head, looking off into the distance, as if he could see the old days right in front of him. "A saint she was, and with all she went through, to still care about us. . . . Hey, can you help me out with a cigarette?" I gave him one. "Helen MacDonald was a knockout," Debbie added, "the best set of tits on Broadway!"

Debbie was a regular now up at the wall, hanging out with the older guys. She told me that all her friends were either dead or in jail. She'd found some new friends now, but she longed for the old days when her partying was just a normal part of growing up. Now she was thirty-five, looking almost as old as the other guys on the wall, and they were around sixty. She'd been a beautiful girl at one time, wearing the latest flash gear on the corners of Old Colony.

Now she was wearing men's clothes and a fishing hat with veterans' medals and buttons with AA slogans, like one that said EASY DOES IT. I told her I had to go, but she wouldn't let me. She kept hugging me and kissing me and crying over the old days. When she finally released me, she kept waving and screaming the names of my family. "Kathy MacDonald! Joe!" She even screamed the name of Joe's customized van, where she'd slept more than once when she ran away from home: "The Blue Goose!" Then she clenched her fist and threw it up, like a symbol of power or unity, and screamed, "Patterson Way! Fuckin' Patterson Way!"

It felt right being back in Southie, but I started to get depressed. There was still so much sadness around. After a few weeks, I started to bump into other familiar faces, neighbors who'd lost their children, the hidden Southie. And all too often I heard through the grapevine of "shameful" deaths: suicides, overdoses from a new growing heroin epidemic, and occasional murders. But now I knew what I wanted to do. Rather than let it eat at me, or chase me away, as I'd once done, I brought home all the anger, resolve, and organizing I'd learned in Roxbury and Charlestown.

With the help of the Charlestown mothers, we started a group for families of people who'd "died too young." At first the Southie mothers who showed up wouldn't talk about how they'd lost their children, except to say that it was an accident or an illness. But over time, it became clear that most had lost someone to drugs, violence, or suicide. And after hearing from the Charlestown mothers with their keen sense of justice, they were brought to tears, rage, and acknowledgment. More and more families started to come to our weekly meetings. A few had indeed lost loved ones to freak accidents and illnesses, and it was great to see them stay, not afraid to stand in solidarity with the mothers who'd been victimized and silenced by violence and the drug trade. "Blood is blood," as one woman said.

At those meetings, I learned even more how much I loved the real Southie, the good Southie. It all came home to me when one mother, explaining how her son who'd died of AIDS hadn't been allowed a funeral at a local church, and how she'd had to take him to a gay church, brought the lone father in our group close to tears. A tough guy, he'd come because his daughter had been murdered, and he was moved by what he'd heard to talk openly about his deep respect for all life, a rule his daughter had lived by. He held back his tears for the mother's loss as well as his own, demanding a letter-writing campaign to the priests. *That's the real Southie,* I thought.

The group started planning a vigil like the one in Charlestown. The first thing we did was put together a list of names of those we'd remembered dying young. We ended up with a list of 250, most of them victims of the drug trade, crime, or suicide. We published it in the *South Boston Tribune,* alongside the usual articles by the South Boston Information Center, about how our biggest problem was black people bringing drugs into the neighborhood, and the featured City Point weddings, bazaars, and cake sales. We announced that the vigil would be on November 2, All Souls' Day; and with the criticism we expected for a vigil for the likes of drug users, murder victims, bank robbers, and suicides, we were glad we hadn't picked All Saints' Day. But Southie's response was positive, and in the end even mothers who'd lost their children in infancy added their children's names, and stood with the rest of us.

In the summer of 1996, Citizens for Safety was getting ready to organize its fourth annual gun buyback program. One day I was walking by the courthouse on Broadway, reading about Brian Havlin, a neighbor who'd been ambushed in the Old Harbor Project and shot nine times after an argument. As I passed the courthouse, I saw a redheaded woman pacing. I knew that face. She looked like Ma after losing Frankie, with anger and sadness welling up in tears that refused to fall while her daughters stood by her. "Are you Mrs. Havlin?" I asked.

Kathy Havlin started coming to our South Boston Vigil Group meetings along with her three daughters. She was angry about the hypocrisy of our politicians, who'd only sent her their sympathies once they found out how well thought of Brian was and that his murderer was a junkie no one liked anyway. She also vented her fury at the priest who'd come to her project apartment, discovered she was a single mother, and looked around the room asking, "Do you work or anything?" She was working on bringing the murderer to justice and wanted to shut down the bar where the fight had started. She also wanted to do something about guns on the street. Before long she was meeting me at the end of her long work day, showing up on Geneva Ave. in the heart of black Dorchester, to hand out gun buyback fliers with Tina Chery, who'd lost her son Louis to gunfire on that street. Kathy walked up to tough-looking black teens hanging out on corners and pleaded with them to spread the word about the buyback.

By 1996, our buyback program was led by survivors from every neighborhood in Boston. Terri Titcomb, whose son Albie had recently been shot in Charlestown over a fifty-dollar drug debt, led the press conference, her back and shoulders buttressed by outstretched hands of all colors. She asked parents to turn in guns, teenagers to turn in guns, and legislators to make stricter laws on the gun industry.

That buyback, we took in fewer guns, and the Boston Police Department didn't see any reason to continue the project. With their growing emphasis on "zero tolerance" policing and suppression tactics, the cops weren't impressed by our multiracial mumbo jumbo. But as we'd found year after year, the tougher guns were coming in with each successive buyback. I had the buyback hotline in my apartment in Southie, so I knew where the guns were coming from, and they weren't coming from little old widows, as the cops liked to say. I got directly involved in a number of turn-ins, one from a former gang member, another from a thirteen-year-old girl hiding a gun for her boyfriend until he got out of DYS, and one from a murder victim's mother, who'd been hell-bent on revenge until she'd become one of the program's spokespersons.

On the last day of the buyback, I received a call from a priest in Dorchester. A thirteen-year-old had given him a .357 Magnum to turn in. I told him where and how to turn it in, and hung up my last buyback call, having helped to destroy 2,901 guns. And I remembered Tommy Viens, the reason I got involved in the first place.

That year, Ma won the suit in Colorado, setting a precedent to challenge other states that had been getting away with violating the Americans with Disability Act. Kathy was still talking to herself, scrawling the names of her old gang from 8th Street on random pieces of paper and Styrofoam cups, along with the old slogans: RE- SIST, NEVER, and HELL NO WE WON'T GO. But now she was eligible for services, therapy, and day trips with caretakers. Joe, as usual, was working two jobs, and was looking to buy a third house in the Colorado mountains. Maria was entering the second grade and winning swim meets at the local recreation center. Seamus and Stevie were going on to college at the University of Colorado. Johnnie had moved to Maine after all of Frankie's friends had been locked up and he got tired of Southie. Mary was still working in the operating room at the City Hospital, had saved for a house in Quincy, and was raising her third child with Jimmy.

And I was in Southie, watching in the dark as hundreds filed into our vigil at the Gate of Heaven Church. They'd stood in line in defiance of the strong winds and pouring rain, and walked past the bagpipers playing "Amazing Grace." They were children, teenage friends of kids who'd committed suicide, mothers whose kids had been murdered—some as long as fifteen years ago—older men and women with canes, pulling their way up the slippery railing one step at a time with tears and rain streaking their ruddy cheeks. A few black and Latino women got out of taxis they'd taken through the storm, braving the town they'd always been warned not to enter, and being embraced by women like Kathy Havlin and Theresa Dooley. I'd been scared of this day, the day when we'd all do our small part in breaking the silence, by saying names some people wanted us never to mention.

That's how I found myself staring out at a sea of faces, looking for my brothers among the living and the dead. I was looking for the truth about their lives and about their deaths. Like me, everyone at that night's vigil will forever be looking for the truth in Southie, where nothing's what it seems.

Standing at the altar, I at last felt I might be able to reconcile myself with all my memories of confusion, bloodshed, and betrayal. And that I could do it with love. I love my family. And I love Southie.

"These candles burn for my brothers." I stopped and took a deep breath. Then I spoke up. "Davey, Frankie, Kevin, and Patrick . . ."

And for all souls.

ACKNOWLEDGMENTS

I AM DEFINITELY BLESSED TO LIVE IN SOUTH BOSTON, among some of the world's most brilliant, loving, and tough people. Thank you to the overwhelming majority of good people in the town, who, through some of the worst forms of oppression by all sides of the political, social, and criminal spectrum, still believe in the village ideal.

A million and one thanks to my editor, Deanne Urmy, for being the champion archangel of *All Souls*, and for her brilliant and compassionate guidance through every painful and personally redemptive sentence. And to my whole team at Beacon: Helene Atwan, Amy Caldwell, Tom Hallock, and Pam MacColl. Special thanks also to Kathie Mainzer, for acting as my production coach and mentor, urging *All Souls* to life. Thank you to the many friends who have given advice on my manuscript through various stages and encouraged me to keep writing: Margaret Lazarus, who always challenged me to maintain and nurture the voice I'd found, and Renner Wunderlich, Maire Murphy, Judith Gaines, Brian MacQuarrie, Jimmy Tingle, Maureen Dezell, Jeff Lowenstein, Channing Thieme, Jill Cunniff, and Bob Cunniff.

Thanks to Barbara Hindley for being the connection that made *All Souls* possible, and to my agent John Taylor "Ike" Williams for making many more.

I am grateful also to all those who kept me connected to the world, and never let me fall into the pit of writer's isolation. Your good thoughts, support, and company sustained me through what could have been a very lonely process: Reme Del Valle, my cousin Maureen Kelly, Clara and Bill Wainright, Rachael and Madeleine Steczynski, Libby McClaren, Sr. Ann Fox and Barry Hynes, Lew Dabney, the Boston Gun Buyback's founding father, Molly Baldwin and the young people at ROCA Inc., Charlie Rose and Carol Downes, Leo Rull, Jerry Hurley, Paul and Mary Ulrich, Theresa Dooley (a South Boston mother whose presence in my life continues to inspire my work), Sandy King, Elizabeth Bartholomew, Lois Molinari, Pam and Billy Enos, Helen Kearns, Terri and Al Titcomb, Tina Chery, Cathy Tyler, Audrey Smith, Maryann Crayton, Cookie and Tipp Harris, Carol Ann Mehan, Katie Flaherty, the South Boston Vigil Group folks, the Charlestown After Murder Program, Brian Murphy, the Riordans from Castle Island in Kerry, the McShanes from Keady in Armagh, and to the residents of the Garvaghy Road in Portadown.

To all my family: Davey, Johnnie, Joe, Mary, Frankie, Kathy, Kevin, Patrick, Seamus and Steven, and Ma, who talked to me through all the relevant and painful stories, and who every day bears witness to the boundless strength of God's human creation.

I am fortunate to know some incredible young people, my adopted sisters and brothers in Southie who listened to stories or eagerly read *All Souls* at every stage, and whose laughter and tears told me I was doing the right thing: Steven Kozlowski, Billy Coleman, Jimmy Connolly, Justin Downey, Katie Heiskell, Jen McAuliffe, Ronnie Sullivan, John Ulrich, Susan Ulrich, and Tara Van Osdol.

For me, the urgency of this book was emphasized by the town's recent suicides, when hundreds of teenagers attempted suicide, and six young people who saw no other "way out" killed themselves, leaving a void in the lives of friends and neighbors: Kevin Geary, Tommy Mullen, Duane Liotti, Jonathan Curtis, Tommy Deckert, and Kevin Cunningham. You are sorely missed. Thank you to the young people of Southie who will honor their friends' memories by choosing to live.